NAVIGATING
through
DISCRETE MATHEMATICS
in
PREKINDERGARTEN– GRADE 5

Valerie A. DeBellis
Joseph G. Rosenstein
Eric W. Hart
Margaret J. Kenney

Eric W. Hart
Volume Editor

Peggy A. House
Navigations Series Editor

NATIONAL COUNCIL OF
TEACHERS OF MATHEMATICS

Copyright © 2009 by
The National Council of Teachers of Mathematics, Inc.
1906 Association Drive, Reston, VA 20191-1502
(703) 620-9840; (800) 235-7566; www.nctm.org

All rights reserved

Library of Congress Cataloging-in-Publication Data

Navigating through discrete mathematics in prekindergarten through grade 5 / Valerie A. DeBellis ... [et al.].
    p. cm. — (Principles and standards for school mathematics navigations series)
    Includes bibliographical references.
    ISBN 978-0-87353-606-6
1. Mathematics--Study and teaching (Elementary)—Activity programs. I. DeBellis, Valerie A.
QA135.6.N34 2009
372.7—dc22
                                        2008041610

The National Council of Teachers of Mathematics is a public voice of mathematics education, providing vision, leadership, and professional development to support teachers in ensuring equitable mathematics learning of the highest quality for all students.

Permission to photocopy limited material from *Navigating through Discrete Mathematics in Prekindergarten–Grade 5* is granted for educational purposes. On the CD-ROM, the blackline masters may be downloaded and reproduced for classroom distribution; the applets may be used for instructional purposes in one classroom at a time. For permission to photocopy material or use it electronically for all other purposes, please access www.copyright.com or contact the Copyright Clearance Center, Inc. (CCC), 222 Rosewood Drive, Danvers, MA 01923, 978-750-8400. CCC is a not-for-profit organization that provides licenses and registration for a variety of users. Permission does not automatically extend to any items identified as reprinted by permission of other publishers and copyright holders. Such items must be excluded unless separate permissions are obtained. It is the responsibility of the user to identify such materials and obtain the permissions.
    The publications of the National Council of Teachers of Mathematics present a variety of viewpoints. The views expressed or implied in this publication, unless otherwise noted, should not be interpreted as official positions of the Council.

Printed in the United States of America

APR 2 1 2010

NAVIGATIONS **S**ERIES

P**RE**-K—G**RADE** 5

TABLE OF CONTENTS

CONTENTS OF THE CD-ROM

Introduction

Recommendations for Discrete Mathematics, Pre-K–Grade 12

Applets
Bobbie Bear
Graph Creator
Fractal Tool

Blackline Masters and Templates
All blackline titles listed above

Readings from Publications of the National Council of Teachers of Mathematics

Discrete Mathematics in K–2 Classrooms
Valerie A. DeBellis
Discrete Mathematics in the Schools

Graphs, Colors, and Chromatic Numbers
Charles L. Hamberg
NCTM Student Math Notes

Squares on the Geoboard
Bill Kring
NCTM Student Math Notes

Math according to Mooch
Karen L. Kritzer and Claudia M. Pagliaro
Teaching Children Mathematics

Connecting the Dots: Network Problems That Foster Mathematical Reasoning
Jean M. McGivney-Burelle
Teaching Children Mathematics

The Orange Game; Responses to the Counting Squares Problem
Lynae Sakshaug
Teaching Children Mathematics

Do It Again, Sam
Terry Souhrada
NCTM Student Math Notes

Sorting and Patterning in Kindergarten: From Activities to Assessment
    Elizabeth J. Ziemba and Jo Hoffman
    Teaching Children Mathematics

A Bibliography of Print Resources for Discrete Mathematics

About This Book

Navigating through Discrete Mathematics in Prekindergarten–Grade 5 and the companion book for grades 6–12 (Hart et al. 2008) elaborate on the vision of discrete mathematics presented in NCTM's *Principles and Standards for School Mathematics* (NCTM 2000). These books answer an important question: What discrete mathematical content and processes should students understand and be able to use in prekindergarten through twelfth grade? The intended audience is primarily classroom teachers but also includes curriculum coordinators, supervisors, mathematics educators at the college level, and others who are interested in the school mathematics curriculum. An important feature of the books is the inclusion of many rich student activities that are ready for use in the classroom.

Principles and Standards for School Mathematics integrates recommendations for discrete mathematics throughout the Content and Process Standards at all grade levels. In keeping with this integration—and to help navigate through and explain the recommendations—we present specific grade-level guidelines with examples. These guidelines outline a scope and sequence for the study of discrete mathematics in prekindergarten through grade 12, while furnishing a framework for integrating discrete mathematics into a Standards-based curriculum.

The first question for many readers is likely to be a very basic one: What is discrete mathematics? The introduction, which presents an overview of discrete mathematics in prekindergarten through grade 12, answers this question. The chapters of the book then focus on implementing these ideas in prekindergarten through grade 5. *Principles and Standards* recommends that the curriculum include three main discrete mathematics topics: systematic listing and counting, vertex-edge graphs, and iteration and recursion. This volume includes two chapters on each of these topics, one chapter for pre-K–grade 2 and one for grades 3–5.

Each chapter presents a comprehensive set of grade-level recommendations, along with several classroom-ready student activities. Although each recommendation is discussed at least briefly, it is not possible to address all of them fully in the activities or text of the book. Thus, the specific goals for the activities are less comprehensive than the full set of recommendations. References given throughout provide additional information on all recommendations.

Because most teachers of prekindergarten through grade 5 are likely to be unacquainted with the activities in this volume or ways of implementing them, the text offers extensive discussions of how to use the activities in the classroom. Each chapter includes an overview of the activities and a summary of the mathematics that they address. Teachers should familiarize themselves with an entire chapter's activities to understand their development and flow before introducing any activity in the classroom. Working through an activity before reading the discussion or solutions will also prove helpful.

The activity sheets for students appear as reproducible blackline masters in the appendix, along with solutions to the problems. The CD-ROM that accompanies the book includes all blackline masters,

Many of the activities that this book presents for prekindergarten through grade 5 also support core topics suggested for emphasis in NCTM's Curriculum Focal Points for Prekindergarten through Grade 8 Mathematics: A Quest for Coherence *(2006); margin notes highlight examples of links. This publication specifies by grade level essential content and processes that* Principles and Standards for School Mathematics *(NCTM 2000) discusses in depth by grade band.*

Key to Icons

Blackline Master

CD-ROM

Principles and Standards

Three different icons appear in the book, as shown in the key. One signals the activity pages and indicates their locations in the appendix, another points readers to supplementary materials on the CD-ROM that accompanies the book, and a third alerts readers to references to *Principles and Standards for School Mathematics*.

as well as selected readings for the professional development of teachers and special computer applets that complement ideas in the text and activities. Teachers can allow students to use the applets in conjunction with particular activities or apart from them, to extend or deepen understanding.

Margin notes throughout the book highlight teaching tips, additional references, suggestions about related materials on the CD-ROM, and pertinent references to *Principles and Standards for School Mathematics*.

The organization of the companion book, *Navigating through Discrete Mathematics in Grades 6–12,* parallels that of this volume. Although all four authors planned and reviewed drafts of both books, DeBellis and Rosenstein wrote the material for pre-K–grade 5, and Hart and Kenney wrote the material for grades 6–12. Hart also served as organizer and coordinator for the whole project. We wish to thank our reviewers—Jim Sandefur, Peggy House, Jessica Boland, Susan Knowles, and Sherry Trach—who provided many thoughtful and useful comments; our photographer, Colette DeLeo; and the schools that hosted our activities: Montessori Today in Greenville, North Carolina, and W. T. Coole Elementary School in Virginia Beach, Virginia. We also thank the always professional, friendly, and efficient publication staff at NCTM.

NAVIGATIONS **S**ERIES

PRE-K–GRADE 5

NAVIGATING *through* DISCRETE MATHEMATICS

Introduction

"Discrete mathematics should be an integral part of the school mathematics curriculum." (NCTM 2000, p. 31)

The guidelines appear in a concise chart, "Recommendations for Discrete Mathematics, Pre-K–Grade 12," on the CD-ROM.

Discrete mathematics is an important branch of contemporary mathematics that is widely used in business and industry. Elements of discrete mathematics have been around as long as mathematics itself. However, discrete mathematics emerged as a distinct branch of mathematics only in the middle of the twentieth century, when it began expanding rapidly, primarily because of the computer revolution, but also because of the need for mathematical techniques to help plan and implement such monumental logistical projects as landing a man on the moon. Discrete mathematics has grown to be even more important and pervasive today.

Principles and Standards for School Mathematics (NCTM 2000) recommends that discrete mathematics be "an integral part of the school mathematics curriculum" (p. 31). In the area of discrete mathematics, *Principles and Standards* features two major changes from NCTM's 1989 *Curriculum and Evaluation Standards for School Mathematics*, which included a Discrete Mathematics Standard for grades 9–12. First, *Principles and Standards* recommends including discrete mathematics in the curriculum for all grades, from prekindergarten through grade 12. Second, *Principles and Standards* does not include a separate standard for discrete mathematics. Rather, it recommends that the main topics of discrete mathematics be distributed across all the Standards, since "these topics naturally occur throughout the other strands of mathematics" (p. 31).

The goal of this book is to elaborate on the vision of discrete mathematics presented in *Principles and Standards*. In this introduction, we give an overview of discrete mathematics and guidelines for integrating discrete mathematics topics into a curriculum that is based on the NCTM Standards. Because discrete mathematics may be unfamiliar to many readers, we begin by considering a fundamental question: What is discrete mathematics?

What Is Discrete Mathematics?

For further discussion of discrete mathematical modeling and algorithmic problem solving, see Hart (1997, 1998).

Kenney (1991), Maurer (1997), and Rosenstein (2007) offer more answers to the question, What is discrete mathematics? Also see Rosenstein, Franzblau, and Roberts (1997) for a comprehensive view of discrete mathematics (dimacs.rutgers.edu/ Volumes/Vol36.html).

Descriptions of discrete mathematics often list the topics that it includes, such as vertex-edge graphs, systematic counting, and iteration and recursion. Other topics relevant to the school curriculum include matrices, voting methods, fair division, cryptography, coding theory, and game theory. In general, discrete mathematics deals with finite processes and whole-number phenomena. Sometimes described as the mathematical foundation of computer science, discrete mathematics has even broader application, since the social, management, and natural sciences also use it. Discrete mathematics contrasts with continuous mathematics, such as the mathematics underlying most of calculus. However, this association gives the impression that discrete mathematics is only for advanced high school students, although elements of discrete mathematics are actually accessible and important for all students in all grades.

Broad definitions of discrete mathematics identify it as "the mathematics of decision making for finite settings" (NCTM 1990, p. 1) and the mathematics for optimizing finite systems. Common themes in discrete mathematics include the following:

- Discrete mathematical modeling—using discrete mathematical tools such as vertex-edge graphs and recursion to represent and solve problems
- Algorithmic problem solving—designing, using, and analyzing step-by-step procedures to solve problems
- Optimization—finding the best solution

Which Discrete Mathematics Topics Does *Principles and Standards* Include?

Principles and Standards integrates three important topics of discrete mathematics: combinatorics, iteration and recursion, and vertex-edge graphs.

- Combinatorics is the mathematics of systematic listing and counting. It facilitates solving problems such as determining the number of different orders for picking up three friends or counting the number of different computer passwords that are possible with five letters and two numbers.
- Iteration and recursion can be used to represent and solve problems related to sequential step-by-step change, such as the growth of a population or an amount of money from year to year. To iterate

means to repeat, so iteration involves repeating a procedure, process, or rule over and over. Recursion is the method of describing the current step of a process in terms of the previous steps.

- Vertex-edge graphs, like the one pictured in figure 0.1, consist of points (called *vertices*) and line segments or arcs (called *edges*) that connect some of the points. Such graphs provide models for, and lead to solutions of, problems about paths, networks, and relationships among a finite number of elements.

Principles and Standards focuses on integrating discrete mathematics with other areas of the mathematics curriculum. For example, vertex-edge graphs are an important part of geometry. Recursion occurs in all the content strands but is particularly instrumental in algebra. Concepts of systematic listing and counting appear throughout the curriculum. Matrices, which many consider to be part of discrete mathematics, are addressed throughout *Principles and Standards*.

Other discrete mathematics topics that may receive attention in the school curriculum include the mathematics of information processing (such as error-correcting codes and cryptography) and the mathematics of democratic and social decision making (for example, voting methods, apportionment, fair division, and game theory). This book focuses on the three discrete mathematics topics that *Principles and Standards* emphasizes (p. 31): combinatorics, iteration and recursion, and vertex-edge graphs. First, however, let's consider why the school curriculum should include discrete mathematics.

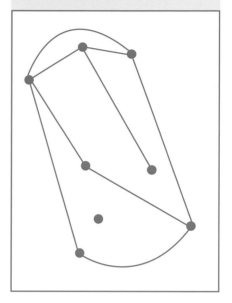

Fig. **0.1.**
A vertex-edge graph

Why Should the School Curriculum Include Discrete Mathematics?

Instructional time is valuable, and the mathematics curriculum has limited space, so educators must make careful choices about what to include in the curriculum. *Principles and Standards* recommends that discrete mathematics be an integral part of the school mathematics curriculum because it is useful, contemporary, and pedagogically powerful, in addition to being a substantial and active field of mathematics.

Discrete Mathematics Is Useful Mathematics

Discrete mathematics has many uses in business, industry, and daily life. Rosenstein, Franzblau, and Roberts (1997) enumerate a variety of applications, asserting that discrete mathematics topics are "used by decision-makers in business and government; by workers in such fields as telecommunications and computing that depend upon information transmission; and by those in many rapidly changing professions involving health care, biology, chemistry, automated manufacturing, transportation, etc. Increasingly, discrete mathematics is the language of a large body of science and underlies decisions that individuals will have to make in their own lives, in their professions, and as citizens" (pp. xiii–xiv).

"As an active branch of contemporary mathematics that is widely used in business and industry, discrete mathematics should be an integral part of the school mathematics curriculum, and these topics naturally occur throughout the other strands of mathematics." NCTM 2000, p. 31)

Discrete Mathematics Is Contemporary Mathematics

Discrete mathematics is a rapidly expanding field of mathematics. It is particularly relevant in today's digital information age. For example, it underlies many aspects of the Internet, from secure encryption of consumers' credit card numbers when they make purchases online to effective compression and decompression of the music, photos, and videos that users download. Moreover, many solved and unsolved problems at the frontiers of discrete mathematics are not only relevant to today's students but also accessible to them. Students can understand the problems and some partial solutions, such as the problem of finding the shortest circuit through a network (the traveling salesman problem) or finding a more secure method for transmitting data between computers. Furthermore, since discrete mathematics has strong links to technology and today's schoolchildren are tomorrow's technological workforce, it is important for their futures, as well as for the future of our nation, that they become more familiar with the topics of discrete mathematics.

Discrete Mathematics Is Pedagogically Powerful

Not only does discrete mathematics include important mathematical content, but it is also a powerful vehicle for teaching and learning mathematical processes and engaging students in doing mathematics. Because discrete mathematics is useful and contemporary, it often motivates and interests students. Discrete mathematics topics can engage and provide success for students who have previously been unsuccessful or alienated from mathematics. Many of these topics are accessible to students in all grades, whether they are engaged in sorting different types of buttons in the early grades, counting different flag patterns in middle school, or using vertex-edge graphs and the critical path method to plan a dance in high school.

Discrete mathematics provides an effective context for developing the skills addressed in the Process Standards.

Furthermore, discrete mathematics is an effective context for addressing NCTM's Process Standards. In working with discrete mathematics, students strengthen their skills in reasoning, proof, problem solving, communication, connections, and representation in many ways. For example, they reason about paths in the visual context of vertex-edge graphs and justify whether certain circuits must exist. They argue about why a recursive formula is better than an explicit formula, or vice versa, in a particular situation. They learn new methods of proof, including proof by mathematical induction. They develop new types of reasoning, such as combinatorial reasoning, which they can use to reason about the number of different possibilities that can arise in counting situations (for example, the number of different pizzas that are possible when they choose two out of five toppings). Students exercise their problem-solving skills when they solve problems in a variety of accessible yet challenging settings. They develop new problem-solving strategies, such as algorithmic problem solving, and new ways of thinking, such as recursive thinking. Students acquire and apply new tools—including recursive formulas and vertex-edge graphs—for representing problems. Thus, students learn important mathematical content and powerful mathematical processes while they study discrete mathematics.

Recent History and Resources

Discrete mathematics surfaced as a curricular issue in the 1980s, when the Mathematical Association of America (MAA) began debating the need for more instruction in discrete mathematics during the first two years of college. This debate culminated in a report released in 1986 (MAA 1986). Although the recommendations of this report were not implemented in full, educators instituted more discrete mathematics courses, which continue to be taught in colleges around the world. In particular, discrete mathematics is now a standard course in collegiate computer science programs and a required course for many mathematics majors.

This discussion about discrete mathematics in college made its way down to the high school level a few years later, when the National Council of Teachers of Mathematics recommended a Discrete Mathematics Standard for grades 9–12 in its seminal Standards publication, *Curriculum and Evaluation Standards for School Mathematics* (NCTM 1989). As a result of these Standards, discrete mathematics expanded rapidly in the school curriculum. The National Science Foundation (NSF) funded teacher-enhancement projects to help implement the Discrete Mathematics Standard.

High schools began offering courses in discrete mathematics, and many states added discrete mathematics to their state frameworks. Discrete mathematics courses play an increasingly important role in the high school curriculum, providing essential mathematics for the technology- and information-intensive twenty-first century, particularly since more students are required to take more mathematics, and the traditional calculus-preparatory high school curriculum does not serve all students well.

Several NSF-funded Standards-based curriculum development projects have integrated discrete mathematics into new high school textbook series. These series include *Core-Plus Mathematics* (Hirsch et al. 2008), *Interactive Mathematics Program* (Alper et al. 2003), *Mathematics: Modeling Our World* (COMAP 1999), and *SIMMS Integrated Mathematics* (SIMMS 2006). In addition, several new textbooks are available for high school courses in discrete mathematics (see COMAP [2006], Crisler and Froelich [2006], and Tannenbaum [2007], for example). Some teacher education textbooks address discrete mathematics, including *Making Math Engaging: Discrete Mathematics for K–8 Teachers* (DeBellis and Rosenstein 2005). Finally, many articles about discrete mathematics and activities for teaching it are available.

Thus far, we have considered what discrete mathematics is, along with some history and resources, and we have described why discrete mathematics should be part of the curriculum. In the remainder of this introduction, we present an overview across the grades of the three main topics: combinatorics (systematic listing and counting), vertex-edge graphs, and iteration and recursion. In developing these topics across the grade levels, we have in mind two important progressions in the prekindergarten–grade 12 curriculum—from concrete to abstract and from informal to more formal reasoning.

The chapters that follow address these topics one at a time, for prekindergarten through grade 2 and grades 3–5 in the present book,

Eric W. Hart and Harold L. Schoen worked on NSF-funded teacher enhancement projects from 1987 to 1994, Margaret J. Kenney's projects extended from 1992 to 1997, the work of Joseph G. Rosenstein and Valerie A. DeBellis began in 1990 and currently continues, and James T. Sandefur's projects extended from 1992 to 1995.

"A Bibliography of Print Resources for Discrete Mathematics" on the accompanying CD-ROM indicates the topics and grade bands covered by the identified resources.

and for grades 6–8 and 9–12 in the companion book, *Navigating through Discrete Mathematics in Grades 6–12* (Hart et al. 2008). In fact, we can use discrete mathematics to reason that since each book includes three topics and two grade bands, each book must include 3×2, or 6, chapters—which brings us to the first topic, systematic listing and counting.

Overview of Systematic Listing and Counting in Prekindergarten–Grade 12

Students at all grade levels should be able to solve counting problems. Examples of appropriate problems at different levels follow:

- In elementary school: "How many different outfits can someone put together with three shirts and two pairs of shorts?"

- In middle school: "How many different four-block towers can a person build with red and blue blocks?"

- In high school: "What is the number of possible computer passwords that use six letters and three digits?"

The common thread in counting problems across grade levels is that students learn to count systematically.

The key to answering such questions is to develop strategies for listing and counting, in a systematic manner, all the ways of completing the task. As students advance through the grade levels, the tasks change—the objects to be counted become abstract as well as concrete, the numbers of objects increase, the representations become more algebraic, and the reasoning becomes more formal, culminating in proof—but the common thread is that the students need to do the counting systematically. If students have enough opportunities to explore counting problems at all grade levels, then these transitions will be smooth, and they will acquire a deep understanding. In addition, knowledge of the counting strategies helps lay the necessary foundation for understanding ideas of probability.

Knowledge of counting strategies helps lay a foundation for understanding ideas of probability.

All the NCTM Standards integrate concepts and methods of systematic listing and counting. In support of this integration, the following recommendations suggest how to develop systematic listing and counting throughout the grades. Many teachers will discover that they have been teaching a number of these topics without recognizing them as topics of discrete mathematics.

Recommendations for Systematic Listing and Counting in Prekindergarten–Grade 12

In prekindergarten–grade 2, all students should—

- sort, organize, and count small numbers of objects;

- informally use the addition principle of counting;

- list all possibilities in counting situations;

- sort, organize, and count objects by using Venn diagrams.

In grades 3–5, all students should—

- represent, analyze, and solve a variety of counting problems by using arrays, systematic lists, tree diagrams, and Venn diagrams;
- use and explain the addition principle of counting;
- informally use the multiplication principle of counting;
- understand and describe relationships among arrays, systematic lists, tree diagrams, and the multiplication principle of counting.

In grades 6–8, all students should—

- represent, analyze, and solve counting problems that do or do not involve ordering and that do or do not involve repetition;
- understand and apply the addition and multiplication principles of counting and represent these principles with algebra, including factorial notation;
- solve counting problems by using Venn diagrams and use algebra to represent the relationships shown by a Venn diagram;
- construct and describe patterns in Pascal's triangle;
- implicitly use the pigeonhole principle and the inclusion-exclusion principle.

In grades 9–12, all students should—

- understand and apply permutations and combinations;
- use reasoning and formulas to solve counting problems in which repetition is or is not allowed and ordering does or does not matter;
- understand, apply, and describe relationships among the binomial theorem, Pascal's triangle, and combinations;
- apply counting methods to probabilistic situations involving equally likely outcomes;
- use combinatorial reasoning to construct proofs as well as solve a variety of problems.

Overview of Vertex-Edge Graphs in Prekindergarten–Grade 12

Another discrete mathematics topic that *Principles and Standards* recommends for study is vertex-edge graphs. Vertex-edge graphs are mathematical models that consist of points (*vertices*), with curves or line segments (*edges*) connecting some of the points (see fig. 0.1 on p. 3). Such diagrams aid in solving problems related to paths, circuits, and networks. For example, vertex-edge graphs can help in optimizing a telecommunications network, planning the most efficient circuit through cities that a salesperson visits, finding an optimal path for plowing snow from city streets, or determining the shortest route for collecting money from neighborhood ATM machines.

More abstractly, vertex-edge graphs may be useful in analyzing situations that involve relationships among a finite number of objects. Vertices represent the objects, and the relationship among the objects is

Vertex-edge graphs aid in solving problems related to paths, circuits, and networks.

shown by edges that connect some vertices. The relationships may be very concrete, such as airline routes that connect cities in the salesman example; or they may be more abstract, as in vertex-edge graphs depicting conflicts or prerequisites. For instance, a vertex-edge graph facilitates scheduling committee meetings without conflicts (where an edge links two committees that cannot meet at the same time because of a shared member) or finding the earliest completion time for a large construction project consisting of many tasks (where directed edges are used to link a task to its prerequisite tasks).

Graph theory is the formal study of vertex-edge graphs. The term *vertex-edge graph* distinguishes these diagrams from other types of graphs, such as graphs of functions or graphs used in data analysis. Nevertheless, a commonly used term is simply *graphs*. In this volume, we employ both terms, as appropriate.

Graph theory is part of discrete mathematics, but it is also part of geometry, since graphs are geometric diagrams that consist of vertices and edges. Graphs share some characteristics with other geometric objects in school mathematics—for example, both polyhedra and graphs have vertices and edges. But in contrast with most of school geometry—which focuses on the size and shape of figures—size, shape, and position are not essential characteristics of vertex-edge graphs. In vertex-edge graphs, it does not really matter whether the graph is large or small or whether the edges are straight or curved. All that really matters are the number of vertices and edges and how the vertices are connected by edges.

The school mathematics curriculum should include several fundamental graph-theory topics. Table 0.1 summarizes these topics. Chapters 3 and 4 furnish more detail and explanation about vertex-edge graphs.

The analysis and representation of all these problems are concrete at the early grades and become more formal and abstract as a student moves upward through the grades. In this volume, chapters 3 and 4 elaborate on specific recommendations for pre-K–grade 2 and grades 3–5, respectively. However, a common set of goals exists for all grades. All students should—

- use vertex-edge graphs to model and solve a variety of problems related to paths, circuits, networks, and relationships among a finite number of objects;

- understand and apply properties of graphs;

- devise, describe, and analyze algorithms to help solve problems related to graphs;

- use graphs to understand and solve optimization problems.

Important themes at all grade levels include mathematical modeling, applications, optimization, and algorithmic problem solving. Mathematical modeling is a multistep process of solving a real-world problem by using mathematics to represent the problem, finding a mathematical solution, translating that solution into the context of the original problem, and finally interpreting and judging the reasonableness of the result. Optimization problems are important throughout mathematics and in many applications. The goal is to find the best solution—for example, the shortest path, the most efficient strategy, the fewest

Vertex-edge graphs are different from both graphs of functions and graphs used in analyzing data.

Size, shape, and position are not essential characteristics of vertex-edge graphs. What matters instead is which vertices are connected by edges.

Table 0.1.
Fundamental Topics in Graph Theory for the School Curriculum

Optimal Paths and Circuits		
Graph Topic	Basic Problem	Sample Application
Euler paths	Find a route through a graph that uses each edge exactly once.	Determine routes for a snowplow.
Hamilton paths	Find a route through a graph that visits each vertex exactly once.	Rank players in a tournament.
Shortest paths	Find a shortest path from here to there.	Measure the degree of influence among people in a group.
Critical paths	Find a longest path or critical path.	Schedule large projects.
Traveling salesman problem (TSP)[1]	Find a circuit through a graph that visits all vertices, that starts and ends at the same location, and that has minimum total weight.	Determine the least-expensive circuit through cities that a sales representative visits.

Optimal Spanning Networks		
Graph Topic	Basic Problem	Sample Application
Minimum spanning trees	Find a network within a graph that joins all vertices, has no circuits, and has minimum total weight.	Create an optimal computer or road network.

Optimal Graph Coloring		
Graph Topic	Basic Problem	Sample Application
Vertex coloring	Assign different colors to adjacent vertices, and use the minimum number of colors.	Avoid conflicts—for example, in meeting schedules or in chemical storage.

[1]When this problem was formulated, there were very few female sales representatives, so the historic name for the problem is the *traveling salesman problem*. We will often call the problem the *TSP*.

conflicts, or the earliest completion time. Algorithmic problem solving is the process of devising, using, and analyzing algorithms—step-by-step procedures—for solving problems.

When teaching these vertex-edge graph topics and themes, don't become bogged down in formal definitions and algorithms. Use the visual nature of graphs to make this material engaging, accessible, and fun. In fact, if you present vertex-edge graphs in this lively manner, many students who have previously experienced difficulty or apathy in mathematics may discover that the study of graphs is refreshing and interesting, and they may experience success in learning this topic, thereby gaining confidence about digging into other topics.

The following recommendations suggest how to develop the topic of vertex-edge graphs throughout the grades in a manner that is consistent with *Principles and Standards for School Mathematics*.

Many students who have previously experienced difficulty or apathy in mathematics may discover that the study of graphs is refreshing and interesting and may experience success in learning this topic.

Recommendations for Vertex-Edge Graphs in Prekindergarten–Grade 12

In prekindergarten–grade 2, all students should—

- build and explore vertex-edge graphs by using concrete materials;
- explore simple properties of graphs, such as the numbers of vertices and edges, neighboring vertices and the degree of a vertex, and whole-number weights on edges;
- use graphs to solve problems related to paths, circuits, and networks in concrete settings;
- color simple pictures by using the minimum number of colors;
- follow and create simple sets of directions related to building and using graphs;
- concretely explore the notion of the shortest path between two vertices.

In grades 3–5, all students should—

- draw vertex-edge graphs to represent concrete situations;
- investigate simple properties of graphs, such as vertex degrees and edge weights, and explore ways to manipulate two graphs physically to determine whether they are the "same";
- use graphs to solve problems related to paths, circuits, and networks in concrete and abstract settings;
- color maps and color the vertices of a graph by using the minimum number of colors as an introduction to the general problem of avoiding conflicts;
- follow, devise, and describe step-by-step procedures related to working with graphs;
- analyze graph-related problems to find the "best" solution.

In grades 6–8, all students should—

- represent concrete and abstract situations by using vertex-edge graphs and represent vertex-edge graphs with adjacency matrices;
- describe and apply properties of graphs, such as vertex degrees, edge weights, directed edges, and isomorphism (whether two graphs are the "same");
- use graphs to solve problems related to paths, circuits, and networks in real-world and abstract settings, including explicit use of Euler paths, Hamilton paths, minimum spanning trees, and shortest paths;
- understand and apply vertex coloring to solve problems related to avoiding conflicts;
- use algorithmic thinking to solve problems related to vertex-edge graphs;
- use vertex-edge graphs to solve optimization problems.

In grades 9–12, all students should—

- understand and apply vertex-edge graph topics, including Euler paths, Hamilton paths, the traveling salesman problem (TSP), minimum spanning trees, critical paths, shortest paths, vertex coloring, and adjacency matrices;

- understand, analyze, and apply vertex-edge graphs to model and solve problems related to paths, circuits, networks, and relationships among a finite number of elements in real-world and abstract settings;
- devise, analyze, and apply algorithms for solving vertex-edge graph problems;
- compare and contrast topics in terms of algorithms, optimization, properties, and types of problems that can be solved;
- extend work with adjacency matrices for graphs through such activities as interpreting row sums and using the nth power of the adjacency matrix to count paths of length n in a graph.

Overview of Iteration and Recursion in Prekindergarten–Grade 12

Iteration and recursion constitute the third main discrete mathematics topic that *Principles and Standards for School Mathematics* recommends. Iteration and recursion are powerful tools for representing and analyzing regular patterns in sequential step-by-step change, such as day-by-day changes in the chlorine concentration in a swimming pool, year-by-year growth of money in a savings account, or the rising cost of postage as the number of ounces in a package increases.

As previously mentioned, to iterate means to repeat, so iteration is the process of repeating the same procedure or computation over and over again, like adding 4 each time to generate the next term in the sequence 4, 8, 12, 16, …. Recursion is the method of describing a given step in a sequential process in terms of the previous step or steps. A recursive formula provides a description of an iterative process. For example, the recursive formula NEXT = NOW + 4, or $s_{n+1} = s_n + 4$, with $n \geq 1$ and $s_1 = 4$, describes the pattern in the preceding sequence. The cluster of symbols s_n, which we read as "s sub n," provides a name for an arbitrary term, the nth term, of sequence s. Thus, s_4 is the fourth term, s_{10} is the tenth term, and so on. The equation $s_{n+1} = s_n + 4$ indicates that the $(n + 1)$st term of the sequence is 4 more than the nth term of the sequence; it has the same meaning as the equation NEXT = NOW + 4.

Iteration and recursion are two sides of the same coin. You can think of recursion as moving backward from the current step to previous steps, whereas iteration moves forward from the initial step. Both iteration and recursion are powerful tools for analyzing regular patterns of sequential change. (Computer science uses precise technical definitions for *iteration* and *recursion*, but this volume uses the terms in the more informal sense just described.)

As in the case of other topics, the students' work with iteration and recursion in the early grades is concrete and exploratory. The representation and analysis become more abstract and formal as the students progress through the grades. For example, in prekindergarten–grade 2, they should explore sequential patterns by using physical, auditory, or pictorial representations, like a pattern of handclaps that increases by two each time. In grades 3–5, students might describe a pattern of

"Mathematics topics such as recursion, iteration, and the comparison of algorithms are receiving more attention in school mathematics because of their increasing relevance and utility in a technological world." (NCTM 2000, p. 16)

Counting by 3s, as in 1, 4, 7, 10 …, is a familiar example of iteration and supports Curriculum Focal Points identified for the early grades.

adding two each time as NEXT = NOW + 2. In middle school, they can begin using subscripts in a very basic way—for example, to describe the add-2 pattern with the recursive formula $T_{n+1} = T_n + 2$. In high school, students can take a recursive view of functions, recognizing, for example, that NEXT = NOW + 2 can represent a linear function with slope 2.

In middle school and high school, students should also compare and contrast recursive formulas and explicit, or closed-form, formulas. For example, they might describe the sequence 5, 8, 11, 14, 17, … by using the recursive formula $s_{n+1} = s_n + 3$, with the initial term $s_0 = 5$, or by using the explicit formula $s_n = 5 + 3n$, for $n \geq 0$. The recursive formula describes the step-by-step change and gives a formula for the next term, s_{n+1}, in terms of the current term, s_n. In contrast, the explicit formula gives a formula for any term s_n in the sequence, without requiring knowledge of the previous term. Both representations have merit. The recursive formula more clearly shows the pattern of adding 3 each time, but the explicit formula is more efficient for computing a term far along in the sequence, such as s_{50}.

All the NCTM Standards include the ideas of iteration and recursion. In support of this integration, the following recommendations suggest how to develop iteration and recursion across the grades.

Recommendations for Iteration and Recursion in Prekindergarten–Grade 12

In prekindergarten–grade 2, all students should—

- describe, analyze, and create a variety of simple sequential patterns in diverse concrete settings;
- explore sequential patterns by using physical, auditory, and pictorial representations;
- use sequential patterns and iterative procedures to model and solve simple concrete problems;
- explore simple iterative procedures in concrete settings by using technology, such as Logo-like environments and calculators.

In grades 3–5, all students should—

- describe, analyze, and create a variety of sequential patterns, including numeric and geometric patterns, such as repeating and growing patterns, tessellations, and fractal designs;
- represent sequential patterns by using informal notation and terminology for recursion, such as NOW, NEXT, and PREVIOUS;
- use sequential patterns, iterative procedures, and informal notation for recursion to model and solve problems, including those in simple real-world contexts, such as growth situations;
- describe and create simple iterative procedures by using technology, such as Logo-like environments, spreadsheets, and calculators.

In grades 6–8, all students should—

- describe, analyze, and create simple additive and multiplicative sequential patterns (in which a constant is added or multiplied at

Both recursive and explicit representations have merit. A recursive formula gives the next term as a function of the current term. An explicit formula gives any term in the sequence without requiring knowledge of the previous term.

each step), as well as more complicated patterns, such as Pascal's triangle (in which each row of numbers, except the first two rows, is constructed from the previous row) and the Fibonacci sequence 1, 1, 2, 3, 5, 8, … (in which each term, except the first two terms, is the sum of the previous two terms);

- use iterative procedures to generate geometric patterns, including fractals like the Koch snowflake and Sierpinski's triangle;

- use informal notation such as NOW and NEXT, as well as subscript notation, to represent sequential patterns;

- find and interpret explicit (closed-form) and recursive formulas for simple additive and multiplicative sequential patterns and translate between formulas of these types;

- use iterative procedures and simple recursive formulas to model and solve problems, including those in simple real-world settings;

- describe, create, and investigate iterative procedures by using technology, such as Logo-like environments, spreadsheets, calculators, and interactive geometry software.

In grades 9–12, all students should—

- describe, analyze, and create arithmetic and geometric sequences and series;

- create and analyze iterative geometric patterns, including fractals, with an investigation of self-similarity and the areas and perimeters of successive stages;

- represent and analyze functions by using iteration and recursion;

- use subscript and function notation to represent sequential patterns;

- investigate more complicated recursive formulas, such as simple nonlinear formulas; formulas in which the added quantity is a function of n, such as $S(n) = S(n - 1) + (2n + 1)$; and formulas of the form $A(n + 1) = rA(n) + b$, recognizing that the resulting sequence is arithmetic when $r = 1$ and geometric when $b = 0$;

- use finite differences tables to find explicit (closed-form) formulas for sequences that can be represented by polynomial functions;

- understand and carry out proofs by mathematical induction, recognizing a typical situation for induction proofs, in which a recursive relationship is known and used to prove an explicit formula;

- use iteration and recursion to model and solve problems, including those in a variety of real-world contexts, particularly applied growth situations, such as population growth and compound interest;

- describe, analyze, and create iterative procedures and recursive formulas by using technology, such as computer software, graphing calculators, and programming languages.

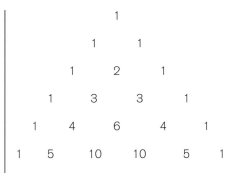

Rows 0–5 of Pascal's triangle

Stage 0　　Stage 1　　Stage 2

Stages 0–2 of the Koch snowflake

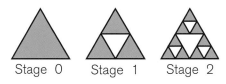

Stage 0　　Stage 1　　Stage 2

Stages 0–2 of Sierpinski's triangle

Conclusion

This introduction has presented an overview of the three topics of discrete mathematics that *Principles and Standards* recommends for study in prekindergarten–grade 12: combinatorics (systematic listing and counting), vertex-edge graphs, and iteration and recursion. It has also provided specific recommendations for developing these important topics across the grades from prekindergarten–grade 12. The chapters that follow discuss each of these topics as they might be presented in pre-K–grade 2 and grades 3–5. The development of an understanding of discrete mathematics in the subsequent years is the focus of the companion volume, *Navigating through Discrete Mathematics in Grades 6–12* (Hart et al. 2008).

NAVIGATIONS SERIES

PRE-K–GRADE 5

NAVIGATING *through* DISCRETE MATHEMATICS

Chapter 1
Systematic Listing and Counting in Pre-K–Grade 2

All students in pre-K–grade 2 should—

- *sort, organize, and count small numbers of objects;*

- *informally use the addition principle of counting;*

- *list all possibilities in counting situations;*

- *sort, organize, and count objects by using Venn diagrams.*

When children learn how to count, they are eager to count everything, from the noodles on their plates to the numbers of steps that they take when walking to the car. Teachers and parents should encourage these activities because repeated counting experiences build children's concepts of number. Similarly, to develop counting skill in more complicated situations, young children should participate in activities that introduce them to listing and counting systematically.

Activities in prekindergarten through second grade should involve students in sorting, organizing, and counting concrete objects. Buttons are good items for such activities because they come in many different sizes, colors, and shapes and have various numbers of holes. Teachers can ask children to sort a small pile of buttons by color and count the number of buttons of each. Students who are able to add the numbers can find the total number of buttons in their pile. This activity can help them see that they can break a counting problem into smaller, more manageable problems and then add the solutions to find the solution to the original problem. Activities like these can introduce students to the addition principle of counting, a principle that this book subsequently presents in a more formal manner and that comes into play at all grade levels.

Students should use Venn diagrams to sort objects according to two attributes simultaneously—for example, color and size. If the labels on two circles in a Venn diagram are "blue" and "big," as in figure 1.1, students should be able to place any button in the appropriate region, depending on whether it is blue and big, blue and not big, not blue and big, or not blue and not big. In this situation, they can find the total

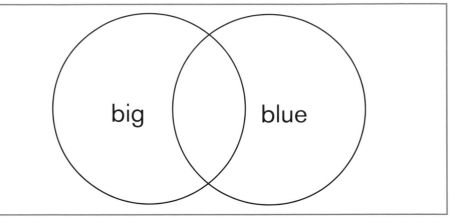

Work with systematic listing and counting has connections with the Curriculum Focal Points for grades K–2. In the investigation Bucket of Buttons, students build various sets of buttons, sort and organize buttons by attributes, count the buttons in the sets, combine groups of buttons, and separate groups into smaller groups, all of which help develop students' understanding of whole numbers and their ability to solve problems with them.

Addition Principle of Counting: If it is possible to partition the items to be counted into separate groups (call them A, B, C, and so on), with each item appearing in exactly one of these groups, and if group A has *a* items, group B has *b* items, group C has *c* items, and so on, then the total number of items is $a + b + c + \ldots$.

number of buttons by taking the sum of all four numbers, and they can find the number of big buttons by adding the number of blue and big buttons and the number of big and not blue buttons. These activities are all examples of the use of the addition principle of counting.

Venn diagrams are also useful in prekindergarten through second grade for making comparisons between two familiar children's stories. For example, if the labels on the circles are "Snow White" and "Cinderella," as in figure 1.2, the students can place storybook features (like "wicked stepmother" or "fairy godmother") in the appropriate regions. An additional example—this one for gathering data—can have circles labeled "have a brother" and "have a sister," as in figure 1.3. Each student can place his or her own name in the appropriate region.

Counting problems for young children should involve concrete objects and relatively small numbers, as in the preceding examples.

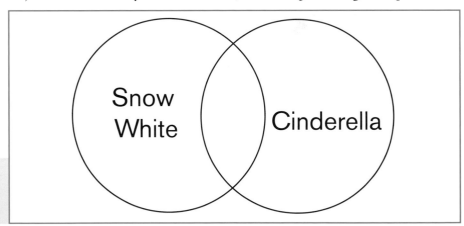

Fig. **1.2.**

A Venn diagram that helps students compare characters in two familiar stories

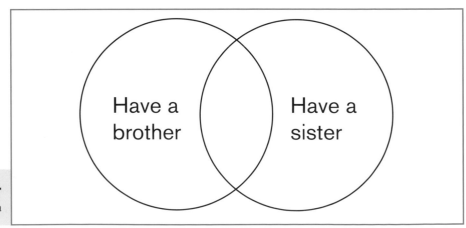

Fig. **1.3.**

A Venn diagram for gathering student data

Another important type of problem involves a question such as, "How many different outfits can you put together that use one of three shirts and one of two pairs of shorts?" For this problem, you can present young students with a number of cutout shirts in three different colors (say red, blue, and yellow) and shorts in two colors (say black and green) and a number of figures to which the students can attach those shirts and shorts.

If you ask students how many different outfits they can make, they typically attack this activity vigorously but randomly. As a result, they are likely to have a number of figures wearing the same outfit, or they may omit an outfit altogether. Give your students a reasonable amount of time to experiment with these activities and then ask them which outfits have yellow shirts, which have red shirts, which have blue shirts, and how many outfits are possible with each. Such questions can help the students detect duplicates and discover omissions. Once they are able to group the outfits, they will see that the set of all outfits consists of two groups of three outfits—one group with three black shorts and the other group with three green shorts—or they can see the set as three groups of two outfits—one with blue shirts, one with red shirts, and one with yellow shirts. They will then conclude that there are six outfits altogether, perhaps after organizing them as in figure 1.4. They may also see that each outfit results from selecting one shirt from the group of three shirts and one pair of shorts from the group of two pairs of shorts. Looking at the problem in this way serves as an introduction to the multiplication principle of counting that the next chapter informally introduces for students in grades 3–5.

Young students can use the applet Bobbie Bear to create as many different outfits as possible. Students click and drag an outfit (shirt and pants) from Bobbie Bear's closet to put it on Bobbie. The applet makes a visual record of all outfits so that students can decide whether they have found all possibilities. The number of possible shirts ranges from one to five, and the number of possible pants ranges from one to four.

John Venn was a nineteenth-century British mathematician and logician who in 1881 used diagrams with overlapping circles to represent groups of items that share common attributes; these diagrams became known as Venn diagrams.

 *Students can explore systematic listing and counting by using the applet Bobbie Bear on the accompanying CD-ROM.*

Fig. **1.4.**

Students may organize the outfits as two groups of three outfits (as in the rows), as three groups of two outfits (as in the columns), or they may organize the outfits in both ways simultaneously, as pictured here.

Multiplication Principle of Counting: If each item to be counted involves selecting one from group A, then one from group B, then one from group C, and so on, with *a* selections in group A, *b* selections in group B, *c* selections in group C, and so on, then the total number of items is $a \times b \times c$ ....

Given some number of shirts and pants in the closet, the students guess in advance the number of different outfits that they can create.

Doing concrete activities like these in prekindergarten through second grade helps prepare students to extend their use of the addition principle in grades 3–5 and helps them create systematic lists, more complex diagrams, and charts showing all possibilities, all of which will prepare them to start using the multiplication principle of counting in grades 3–5.

Bucket of Buttons

The investigation Bucket of Buttons consists of a rich set of mathematical activities with variations that are suitable for students at all grade levels from prekindergarten through grade 2. In using these explorations in sorting and counting, you will give your students a plastic bucket or another suitable container that holds buttons. You will ask them to sort the buttons, discuss their rules for sorting, count the number of buttons in a particular category or categories, and systematically organize the collection. The number and types of buttons and the questions that you ask will depend on the grade level of your students.

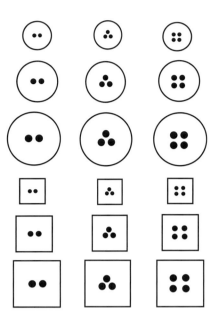

The Bucket of Buttons activities involve up to 72 different buttons. The students consider four attributes—color, shape, size, and number of holes—and each button represents one of 72 possible combinations of these attributes. The color can be blue, red, yellow, or green; the shape can be either circular or square; the size can be small, medium, or large; and the number of holes can be two, three, or four.

The total number of buttons, 72, is a consequence of the multiplication principle of counting. Because there are four colors, two shapes, three sizes, and three different numbers of holes and because each button represents one combination of these four attributes, the total number of buttons is $4 \times 2 \times 3 \times 3$, or 72. Ignoring color and focusing only on shape, size, and number of holes gives $2 \times 3 \times 3$, or a total of 18, different buttons.

The blackline masters include the template "Buttons for the Bucket," which presents these 18 buttons for you to reproduce on card stock and cut out. If you copy the 18 buttons onto four different-colored sheets of card stock (blue, red, yellow, and green) and cut out all the buttons on these four sheets, then you will have the complete set of 72 buttons. You should place the buttons in a suitable container, which this investigation calls a bucket, and the class will be ready for any of the Bucket of Buttons activities.

Students at any level from pre-K–grade 2 can carry out the activities in this investigation, but the full set of 72 buttons may be appropriate only for second-grade classes. Students at lower levels can complete the preliminary activities (designed for students in prekindergarten through grade 1) and then continue to the numbered activities with smaller sets of buttons. For example, they might use only the blue buttons (18 buttons), the blue and red buttons (36 buttons), the large buttons (24 buttons), or the round buttons (36 buttons). Ziemba and Hoffman (2006; available on the CD-ROM) provide other examples of activities for younger students.

Goals

- Sort, organize, and count small numbers of objects
- Informally use the addition principle of counting
- List all possibilities in counting situations
- Sort, organize, and count objects by using Venn diagrams

Materials and Equipment

Preliminary Activities

For each student—

pp. 164, 165, 166

- Buttons from the template "Buttons for the Bucket" as specified below in the text
- A copy of the activity sheet "Bucket of Round Blue Buttons"
- A copy of the activity sheet "More Buttons in the Bucket"
- A bucket or another suitable container for buttons
- Crayons
- Scissors

Activity 1—Counting Buttons

For each team of three or four students—

p. 164

- A bucket or other suitable container
- A small paper bag
- Buttons made from four different-colored copies of the template "Buttons for the Bucket" (blue, red, yellow, and green)

Activity 2—Sorting Buttons

For each team of students—

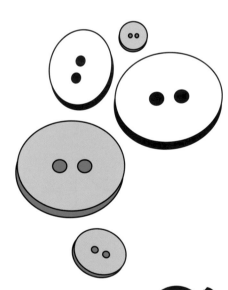

- The bucket of buttons from activity 1
- Six 36-inch lengths of heavy string or twine, each with the ends tied, to be arranged in a circle
- Twelve blank rectangular strips of paper, 6 inches by 3 inches

Activity 3—Listing Buttons

For each team of students—

- The bucket of buttons from activity 1

For each student—

- A blank sheet of paper
- A blue crayon, colored pencil, or marker

Activity 4—Big Blue Buttons

For each team of students—

p. 167

- The bucket of buttons from activity 1
- Two pieces of string, each with the ends tied
- Two blank rectangular strips of paper, 6 inches by 3 inches

For each student—

- A copy of the activity sheet "Handful of Buttons"

Activity 5—Crazy Shirts

For each pair of students—

pp. 168, 169

- A copy of the template "Shirt Buttons"

- Three copies of the activity sheet "Crazy Shirts"

For each student—

- A pair of scissors
- A blue crayon or marker

Prior Knowledge

Students should be able to—

- identify colors, shapes, and sizes of buttons, as well as numbers of buttonholes;
- distinguish attributes that are the same and different;
- count from 1 to 72 (students who cannot yet count to 72 should work with fewer buttons); and
- color pictures so that regions colored with specific colors are identifiable.

Preliminary Activities

Either in previous grades or in preparation for this activity, students should have completed simple counting and sorting activities, such as the following:

Preliminary Activity 1—Bucket of Six Blue Buttons

- Fill each student's bucket with the six blue medium-sized buttons (see figure 1.5).
- Have students sort the buttons by shape. Ask them how many groups they have and how many buttons are in each group. (The students should respond that they have two groups, with three buttons in each group.)
- Ask students how many buttons they have altogether. (They should answer that they have six buttons.)
- Ask the students to sort the buttons by the number of holes. Ask them how many groups they have and how many buttons are in each group. (They should state that they have three groups, each with two buttons.)
- Again ask them how many buttons they have altogether. (They should realize that they still have a total of six buttons.)

Remind the students that the number of buttons stays the same, no matter how they sort them. If you are using this activity with first or second graders who are familiar with addition, you can represent the first count of the number of buttons by 3 + 3 and the second count by 2 + 2 + 2; to represent the fact that the two counts are equal, write

$$3 + 3 = 2 + 2 + 2.$$

Preliminary Activity 2—Bucket of Round Blue Buttons

The next preliminary activity uses the nine round buttons shown at the bottom of the activity sheet "Bucket of Round Blue Buttons" (see fig. 1.6). To begin this activity, give each student one copy of the activity sheet and have the students color all nine buttons blue

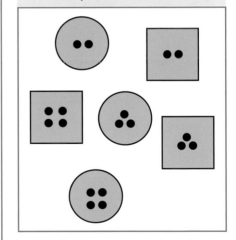

Fig. **1.5.**

Ask students to sort the six blue medium-sized buttons first by shape and then by number of holes.

(alternatively, of course, you can copy the activity sheet on blue paper). Ask the students to cut out the buttons and place them in their buckets. Have the students sort them by the number of holes.

Photo by Colette DeLeo; all rights reserved

Fig. **1.6.**

How can students sort these round blue buttons?

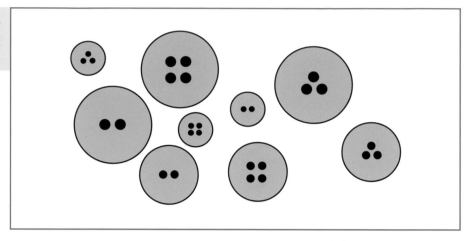

A kindergarten student colors buttons for the preliminary activity 2, Bucket of Round Blue Buttons.

- Ask the students how many groups they have. (They should respond that they have three groups.)
- Ask them how many buttons are in each group. (They should answer that they have three buttons in each group.)

The activity sheet "Bucket of Round Blue Buttons" includes additional questions.

Next, let the bucket contain the twelve blue buttons that are either medium-sized or large, as shown in figure 1.7. Ask the students to sort them by size and shape.

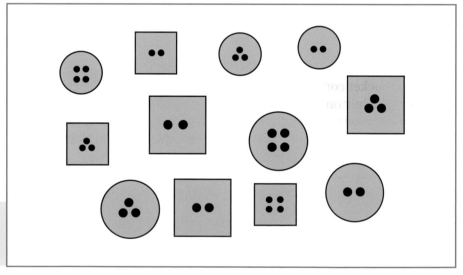

Fig. **1.7.**

Twelve blue buttons to sort by size, shape, and number of buttonholes

- Ask the students how many groups they have. (They should have four groups.)
- Ask them how many buttons are in each group. (They should have three buttons in each group.)

Next, the bucket should contain fifteen randomly chosen blue buttons. Have students sort them by size, by number of holes, and by shape, and answer various counting questions.

Navigating through Discrete Mathematics in Prekindergarten–Grade 5

Preliminary Activity 3—More Buttons in the Bucket

The students work with the twenty-four small buttons in this activity, as shown in figure 1.8. To begin, give each student one copy of the activity sheet "More Buttons in the Bucket." Have the students color the twenty-four buttons blue, red, yellow, and green, as the sheet directs, and then ask them to cut out the buttons and place them in their bucket. Ask the students to sort the buttons by color, by shape, and by the number of holes and answer various counting questions like those on the activity sheet.

Next, let the bucket contain the thirty-six round buttons. Have students remove the small buttons, leaving the medium and large buttons in the bucket.

- Ask the students how many buttons are small. (They should indicate that twelve buttons are small.)

- Ask them how many buttons are not small. (They should realize that twenty-four buttons are not small.)

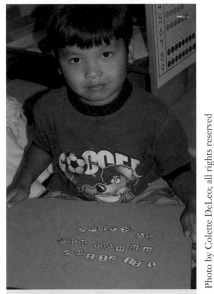

A preschool student shows the twenty-four small buttons sorted by the numbers of holes.

Photo by Colette DeLeo; all rights reserved

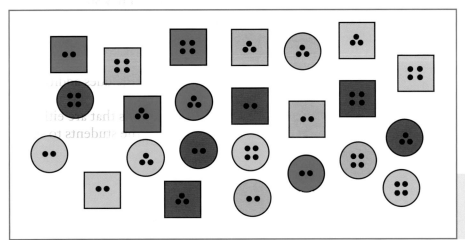

Fig. 1.8.

Twenty-four small buttons to sort by color, shape, and number of holes

Let the bucket contain thirty randomly chosen buttons. Have students sort the buttons by the number of holes and answer various counting questions. Ask teams of students to design their own kinds of buttons to sort and count—they can, for example, use shapes other than circles or squares, other colors, or even other attributes—and create their own sorting and counting problems. After the teams have solved their own problems, ask each team to share its buttons and counting problems with another team.

Activities

The investigation Bucket of Buttons consists of a sequence of five activities. Students explore different ways of counting a group of buttons when they do activity 1, Counting Buttons. In activity 2, Sorting Buttons, they sort a large group of buttons into smaller groups according to various attributes of the buttons. As in activity 1, they informally explore the addition principle of counting. When students work on activity 3, Listing Buttons, they try to imagine all the possible buttons with certain properties. In activity 4, Big Blue Buttons, they begin to use Venn diagrams to sort and count buttons and then learn how to use Venn diagrams in other contexts. In activity 5, Crazy

Shirts, students find as many shirts as possible that use two types of buttons.

Give each team of three or four students a paper bag and a bucket containing all the buttons. To ensure that the teams of students have different numbers of buttons in the initial activities, ask each team to designate one person to remove a handful of buttons from the bucket, put them in the paper bag, close it, and set it aside until later. Ask each team of students to pour out the buttons that remain in its bucket, forming a pile that each team member can reach.

Activity 1—Counting Buttons

Ask the students to imagine that they work for a sewing company that has just received a large shipment of buttons—the buttons in the bucket. Their first task is to determine the total number of buttons that they have received. Ask each team to count the number of buttons in the bucket. After all the teams have completed this task, ask one member of each team to explain how the team counted its buttons. The following are possible ways in which the team members might have counted the buttons:

- They might may have separated the buttons into small piles, with each team member counting one of the piles. Afterward, the students could have added all the totals together to arrive at a grand total.

- They might have worked together to divide the buttons into groups of ten and then counted the number of tens and the number of extra buttons.

- One team member might have counted all the buttons while the others verified that the counting was accurate.

- The team members might have separated the buttons into groups by color or by another attribute. Each team member might have counted one of the smaller piles, and then the students might have added the totals together.

After each of the teams has described its strategy, conduct a discussion of the different approaches and the advantages and disadvantages of each. Include in the discussion a description of any of the preceding strategies that the students did not mention. Discuss with the students why counting a large collection of buttons is sometimes easier if they break it into smaller groups, have a different person count each group, and then add the totals. One disadvantage of counting all the buttons is that one person has to do it all; if each person has a small group to count and the students then add the amounts, they can find the total faster. Even if only one person is counting all the buttons, breaking the whole collection group into smaller groups and counting each one separately is useful. A person who is distracted while counting a small group just has to recount that group and does not have to start over from the very beginning.

Note that the fourth strategy in the preceding list is similar to the first strategy, except that the fourth strategy creates the smaller groups deliberately instead of randomly. Although separating the items by some attribute may be useful, make sure that your students understand

To draw an extra set of round blue buttons, a kindergarten student first draws all the sets of holes and then draws three sizes of buttons around them.

Photo by Colette DeLeo; all rights reserved

that it does not make counting the smaller groups any easier. The second method probably is the quickest because it distributes the task among the team members and it does not involve adding two-digit numbers at the end.

Activity 2—Sorting Buttons

For a slightly different scenario, ask the students to suppose that the button manufacturer mailed all the buttons in the same package instead of shipping them by button type, and this mailing strategy has caused major problems for the sewing company. Tell the students that their task is to sort the buttons into different bins so that machine operators can quickly find the type of button that they need. Distribute six 36-inch lengths of string, each tied in a loop, to each group of students. Tell the students to arrange the strings in circles that do not overlap and imagine that each circle is a bin for buttons. The students have more bins than they need. If they ask, tell them that they do not need to use all the bins. However, telling them in advance how many bins to use limits their consideration of their sorting options. This activity is deliberately open-ended. The students must determine for themselves the attributes by which they wish to sort the buttons.

Ask each team to (1) keep track of how its members sorted the buttons, (2) count the buttons in each bin, (3) and make a descriptive label for each bin. Give each team of students twelve rectangular strips of paper to use for the labels. Each label should explain the kind of buttons that the bin contains. After the students have finished these tasks, ask each team to share its results. Also ask the team members to determine the total number of buttons that were in their bucket (after they put aside the paper bag).

Discuss the different ways in which the teams chose to sort their buttons (by color, by shape, by size, or by number of holes) and the number of bins that different teams used. Some teams may have sorted the buttons into two bins (for example, if they chose to sort by shape), some into three bins (if they sorted by size or number of holes), and some into four bins (if they sorted by color). Some teams may have used still other criteria or different numbers of bins.

Ask the students to sort the buttons into exactly three bins. If they previously used three bins, ask them to find a different way to group the buttons in three bins. Allow students to decide what attribute they will use to sort. To obtain exactly three groups, students can choose to sort either by number of holes or by size. In each situation, they create three different groups. Again, ask teams to share what they did. Call students' attention to the fact that sorting either by number of holes or by size involves exactly three different bins.

Ask the students to put all the buttons that were in their team's bins back into a single collection. Tell the students that now they are interested only in one particular kind of button, and they want to put those buttons into a separate bin and leave the rest jumbled together. Ask them to put all the buttons with two holes into a bin, label it "two-hole buttons," and count the number of buttons in the bin.

Ask the students how many buttons are not two-hole buttons. Also ask them whether they can find another way of figuring out the number. After a suitable pause, ask them for their answers and explanations of how they determined them. They may have solved this problem in many different ways, and the class should discuss each method that students used, as well as the following three ways to determine the number:

- Subtracting the number of two-hole buttons (found previously) from the total number of buttons that they determined in activity 1
- Counting all the buttons that do not have two holes
- Counting the three-hole buttons and the four-hole buttons and adding the two numbers

Before proceeding to activity 3, ask each team of students to put all the buttons back into the bucket, including the handful of buttons that they previously placed in the paper bag. As a result, each team will now have a full set of 72 buttons in the bucket, and all teams should obtain the same answers to the counting questions in activities 3 and 4.

Activity 3—Listing Buttons

Provide each student with a sheet of paper, and ask the students to draw pictures, without looking at the buttons in the bucket, of all the small blue buttons that have two or three holes. Each student should work with a blue crayon, marker, or colored pencil. Some students may not be able to draw all the possibilities. However, if you call on individual students and ask each of them to describe one button that he or she drew, you should be able to elicit all four types of buttons from the class—one is round with two holes, one is round with three holes, one is square with two holes, and one is square with three holes, as shown in figure 1.9.

Next, ask the students to draw pictures of all the blue buttons in the bucket that have two holes. The students should find that the number of possibilities is six. Three buttons are round—one of them is large, one is medium-sized, and one is small; and three buttons are square—one is large, one is medium-sized, and one is small, as shown in figure 1.10.

Drawing pictures of all the buttons that are blue and round is a harder problem. The number of possibilities is nine, as shown in figure 1.11. An even more difficult problem is drawing pictures of all the buttons that are round and have two holes; now the number of possibilities is twelve, as indicated in figure 1.12.

After the students solve each problem, ask them to check their answers by looking through the bucket to see whether they find any qualifying buttons in addition to those whose pictures they have drawn.

Activity 4—Big Blue Buttons

Next, ask each team to put aside all the yellow and green buttons, so that the bucket of buttons that the students have for this part of the activity holds only blue and red buttons. The total number of blue and red buttons is thirty-six. Ask each team of students to count the blue

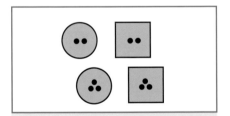

Fig. 1.9.

Students identify four types of small buttons.

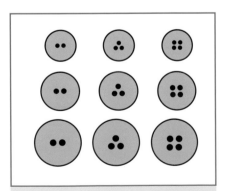

Fig. 1.11.

The buttons that are blue and round

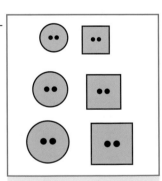

Fig. 1.10.

The blue buttons with two holes

buttons (eighteen) and the big buttons (twelve). Give each team two string loops to place together so that they overlap, as shown in figure 1.13. Ask the students how many different regions the two circles form. They will probably answer that they have three regions—an "oval" in the middle and two crescents (that look like a crescent moon) on the two sides of the oval. Point out that there is actually a fourth region—all the space outside the circles.

Tell the students that they are next going to place each of the thirty-six buttons in one of the four regions. Give them strips of paper to use to label the circle at the left "blue buttons" and the circle at the right "big buttons." This activity refers to these circles as bins since students will place buttons inside them.

The oval in the middle is part of both the blue-button bin and the big-button bin, so the buttons that belong inside the oval are those that are both big and blue. Take such a button, and place it in this region in the bins of one team. The crescent on the right is for buttons that are big but not blue; place such a button there. Ask the children what kind of button they should place in the other crescent (they should answer that the buttons in that crescent are blue but not big), and place an appropriate button there. Ask the children what kind of button goes outside the two circles (they should recognize that the region outside the circles is for buttons that are not blue and not big), and place an appropriate button there. Then pick one button at a time (without looking) from the bucket, and ask the students where you should place that button. Continue until all the students realize that buttons that are both big and blue should go in the oval, those that are blue but small or medium-sized should go in the left crescent, those that are big but red should go in the right crescent, and finally, those that are neither blue nor big should go outside the bins. Then have each group do the activity on its own until the teams have placed all thirty-six buttons in one of the four regions.

Ask the children to count the number of buttons in each of the regions, as shown in figure 1.14. Record the answers on the board in a chart similar to the one shown in figure 1.15. All groups should agree that twelve buttons are in the crescent at the left (blue but not big), six big blue buttons are in the central oval region, six buttons are in the crescent at the right (big but not blue), and twelve buttons are in the outer region (neither blue nor big). They should confirm that the total number of blue buttons (eighteen) that they counted previously equals the number of big blue buttons plus the number of not-big blue buttons.

Ask the students how many buttons are either big or blue but not both big and blue. The answer is 6 + 12, or 18. Next, ask them how many are big or blue or both big and blue. The answer is 12 + 6 + 6, or 24. Also ask how many buttons are blue but not big (twelve) and how many are not big and not blue (twelve).

Next, ask the groups to take out the yellow buttons that they previously put aside. Ask them to count their yellow buttons (they should have eighteen) and place each of them in the appropriate region. Then ask them to count the number of yellow buttons in each region. Ask them how many yellow buttons are in the left crescent (zero), how many are in the oval region (zero), how many are in the right crescent

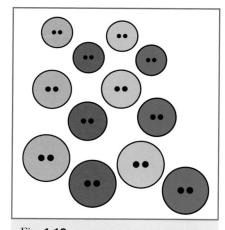

Fig. **1.12.**

The round buttons with two holes

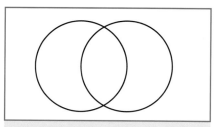

Fig. **1.13.**

Students place two string loops so that they overlap.

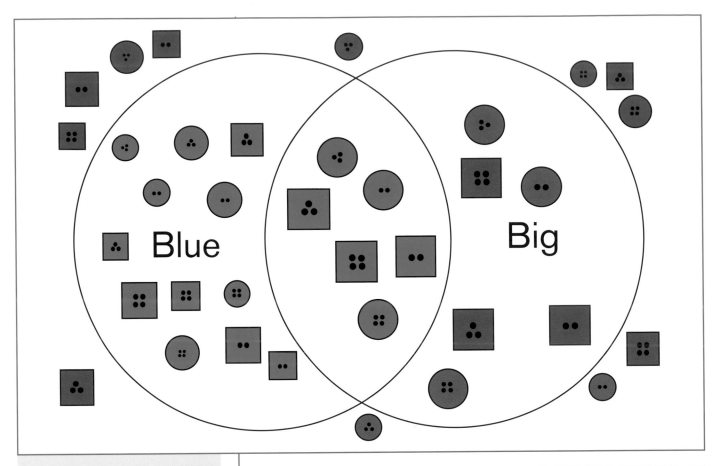

Fig. **1.14.**

Students use a Venn diagram to sort the buttons (gray indicates red buttons).

Fig. **1.15.**

Students categorize the blue and red buttons.

	Left Crescent	Oval	Right Crescent	Outside
Blue and red	12	6	6	12
Yellow				
Green				
Totals				

(six), and how many are in the outside region (twelve). Record these answers on the board, as shown in figure 1.16.

Then ask the students to imagine that all the teams have placed each green button in the appropriate region and ask how many buttons they would place in each of the four regions. They should answer that they would find the same numbers for the green buttons that they found for the yellow buttons, since the number of the buttons of any one color is the same as the number of buttons of any other color. Record these answers on the board, as in figure 1.16.

Next, ask each group to imagine that the teams have taken all the buttons in the original bucket of buttons and placed each button in the appropriate region. Ask the students how many buttons would be in each of the four regions. This preparation should enable each group of students to realize that to determine the number of buttons in each of the regions, the group should simply add the numbers in figure 1.16. The number of buttons in the outside region, for example, is the number of blue and red buttons in the outside region (the 12 in the first row of the figure), plus the number of yellow buttons in the outside

	Left Crescent	Oval	Right Crescent	Outside
Blue and red	12	6	6	12
Yellow	0	0	6	12
Green	0	0	6	12
Totals				

Fig. **1.16.**

Students categorize the yellow and green buttons.

region (the 12 in the second row), plus the (imagined) number of green buttons in the outside region (the 12 in the third row), for a total of thirty-six buttons. Record these answers on the board, as shown in figure 1.17.

	Left Crescent	Oval	Right Crescent	Outside
Blue and red	12	6	6	12
Yellow	0	0	6	12
Green	0	0	6	12
Totals	12	6	18	36

Fig. **1.17.**

Students find the number of buttons in each region of a Venn diagram.

Have the students return all the buttons to the bucket, and then ask each student to take a handful of buttons (about twenty) from the bucket. Distribute copies of the activity sheet "Handful of Buttons" and ask the students to repeat the preceding activity individually by answering the questions on the sheet. Different students will of course find different answers. After everyone finishes, have each student select a partner and check each other's work.

Use the following process to show the students two additional situations that use Venn diagrams:

- Draw two overlapping circles on the board. Label one circle "have a brother" and the other "have a sister," as shown in figure 1.3. Ask each child to come up to the board and write his or her name in the appropriate place and explain its location. Afterward, count and discuss the results.

- Draw two overlapping circles on the board. Label one circle "Snow White" and the other "Cinderella," as shown in figure 1.2, or use characters from two other stories that the children have recently read or heard. Explain that the class will use this Venn diagram to sort the features of the two stories—any feature that one story has and that the other story lacks will go in one of the crescent shapes, any feature that both stories share (for example, a wicked step-mother) will go into the oval shape, and any feature that neither story has (for example, a cowardly lion) will go outside the circles.

Activity 5—Crazy Shirts

In this activity, pairs of students work together to use two types of buttons to create as many different shirts as possible on the activity sheet "Crazy Shirts." Give each pair of students a copy of the template "Shirt Buttons." Ask students to color all twenty-four buttons blue. They can color them quickly, without attempting to stay inside the

Photo by Colette DeLeo; all rights reserved

A preschool student places buttons on shirts.

lines, because their next task will be to cut them out. Each student in the pair should cut out half the buttons and place them faceup on his or her desk. When students have completed this task, ask them how many different types of buttons they have (they have two types of buttons) and ask them to describe the two types of buttons (one type is blue and round and has two holes and the other type is blue and square and has two holes).

Next, distribute three copies of the activity sheet "Crazy Shirts" to each pair of students, and ask that they place all three sheets faceup on their desks. Point out to the students that each shirt has three button-holes but no buttons on the other side. Have them imagine that they are workers in a sewing company that has so many of these extra buttons that they are going to use them to make "crazy shirts." A crazy shirt is any shirt that mixes or matches the two button types. For example, students can make a crazy shirt by placing a square button in the top position, a round button in the middle position, and a square button in the bottom position. Another possibility is to use round buttons in each of the three positions. Ask your students to work together to make all the possible crazy shirts that this sewing company can make with the available buttons. The students have received more buttons and shirts than they need, so that the materials provided do not suggest a solution to the problem. Students should discover, not be told, the total number of possible shirts.

After the students have completed this task, ask them to compare their answers with those of another team and decide on the total number of possible shirts. Students should try to convince everyone in their group that they have actually found all the different possible shirts.

Teachers should not expect their students to generate these shirts in an orderly fashion. Indeed, young children often use a random process to generate all the possible shirts. However, many will also invent the strategy of "opposites." This strategy considers a round button and a square button to be "opposites." For example, students who randomly generate the shirt shown on the left side of figure 1.18 may next generate the shirt shown on the right side of figure 1.18 as its opposite shirt. In every position where a round button appears on one shirt, a square button appears in the same position on the opposite shirt; and in every position where a square button appears on one shirt, a round button appears in the same position on the opposite shirt.

Figure 1.19 shows the complete list of eight crazy shirts, organized by using an opposite strategy. Your students may not organize them by opposites, and even if they do, they may list the shirts in a different order than that shown in figure 1.19 and may reverse some pairs, so that, for example, shirt 3 and its opposite may be the first pair of shirts in a student's list, or students may show shirt 3's opposite as the first shirt.

A student may say something similar to, "What's so crazy about a shirt with all round buttons? Isn't a shirt crazy only if it has both round and square buttons?" You can respond by saying something like, "That's true, but since we're counting all the possibilities for the buttons, we need to include the shirt that has only round buttons and the shirt that has only square buttons in our count. But now that we've found that the total number of shirts is eight and you think that

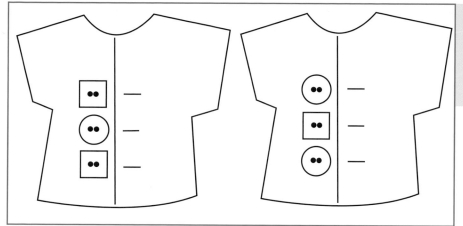

Fig. **1.18.**

To find all possible arrangements, children invent strategies such as an "opposite strategy," in which they create a shirt and then use the "opposite" choice of buttons for the next shirt.

Fig. **1.19.**

The set of all eight crazy shirts

Shirt 1	Shirt 1's Opposite	Shirt 2	Shirt 2's Opposite	Shirt 3	Shirt 3's Opposite	Shirt 4	Shirt 4's Opposite

the shirts that have only round buttons and that have only square buttons are not crazy, how many shirts are really crazy?" The answer, of course, is six.

When asked to list all the possibilities, many children first think in random ways. As their organizational skills develop, so too does their systematic thinking. In pre-K–grade 2, it is too early to insist that students think systematically; the goal, however, is to assist in developing systematic thinking. The point is just to be sure that the students understand the two tasks involved: obtaining all the possibilities and explaining how they know that they have indeed obtained them. In grades 3–5, students can continue to develop their systematic thinking in activities like those in the investigation Bindu Bear, which appears in the next chapter.

The task of counting all the crazy shirts can also help students appreciate the difficulty of determining whether they have found all the possibilities if their method for generating possibilities is essentially random. The questions, "Do you have them all?" and "How do you know?" will help students recognize the need to organize the different possibilities, even if they are now unable to answer these questions fully. Giving students these kinds of experiences will make it easier for you to motivate them to think systematically.

The Mathematics in the Investigation

This investigation focuses on sorting and counting. Sorting involves first organizing a large group of objects by dividing them into a number of smaller groups according to a single attribute; for example, if the attribute is color, then the students sort the objects into separate groups of blue buttons, red buttons, yellow buttons, and green buttons. In the investigation Bucket of Buttons, the students at different times sort the buttons according to four different attributes—size, color, shape, and number of holes. When sorting by one attribute—color, for example— making one group for each color is appropriate. However, students can also sort by two attributes simultaneously by using a Venn diagram with two circles. For example, if they are sorting by color and size, then the four groups can represent big and blue, big and not blue, blue and not big, and not big and not blue. You can also let your students use Venn diagrams to sort by three attributes. This volume's companion book, *Navigating through Discrete Mathematics in Grades 6–12* (Hart et al. 2008), presents examples of such activities in chapter 1, "Systematic Listing and Counting in Grades 6–8," but teachers may initially present and discuss such activities at grades 4 and 5.

Counting involves enumerating the objects in the various groups. By second grade, it also involves the students in recognizing that they can find the number of buttons in certain groups by separating the buttons into smaller groups, finding the number of buttons in each, and adding those numbers together. This process uses the addition principle of counting, which this volume does not formally introduce until third grade. However, students should use it in grade 2, even if they do not use it explicitly or use its name. Thus, for example, in activity 4, Big Blue Buttons, students learn that they can find the number of buttons that do not have two holes by adding the number of buttons with three holes and the number of buttons with four holes. In activity 5, Crazy Shirts, they learn that they can find the number of buttons that are either blue or big or both by adding three numbers—the number of big blue buttons, the number of big buttons that are not blue, and the number of blue buttons that are not big.

PRE-K–GRADE 5

NAVIGATING *through* DISCRETE MATHEMATICS

Chapter 2
Systematic Listing and Counting in Grades 3–5

All students in grades 3–5 should—

- *represent, analyze, and solve a variety of counting problems by using arrays, systematic lists, tree diagrams, and Venn diagrams;*

- *use and explain the addition principle of counting;*

- *informally use the multiplication principle of counting;*

- *understand and describe relationships among arrays, systematic lists, tree diagrams, and the multiplication principle of counting.*

In grades 3–5, children should learn how to solve a variety of counting problems by using three essential counting strategies—arrays, organized lists, and tree diagrams—and they should understand the connections among these strategies. They should be able to use them in a variety of contexts—for example, to count systematically the number of different outfits that they can make from three shirts (say, a green one, a purple one, and a yellow one) and two types of pants (say, dotted and striped). They should also understand how all three strategies can yield the same list of six outfits.

Students in grades 3–5 should also be able to apply the addition principle of counting and the multiplication principle of counting to a variety of counting problems. They should have informally used the addition principle of counting in previous grades, and they should now be able to explain its use explicitly. When they are familiar with multiplication, students in grades 3–5 should be able to make informal use of the multiplication principle of counting. For example, students may say, "There are five ways of doing this and then four ways of doing that, so altogether there are five times four ways of doing this and then that." Using the multiplication principle of counting to find the number of items in an array can also help reinforce the array model of multiplication that students learn in third grade. As in the preceding example, students should refer to the multiplication principle informally. When they move on to grades 6–8, they will formally express the addition and multiplication principles by using algebraic notation.

Addition Principle of Counting: If it is possible to partition the items to be counted into separate groups (call them A, B, C, and so on), with each item appearing in exactly one of these groups, and if group A has *a* items, group B has *b* items, group C has *c* items, and so on, then the total number of items is
$$a + b + c + \dots$$

Multiplication Principle of Counting: If each item to be counted involves selecting one from group A, then one from group B, then one from group C, and so on, and if *a* selections are possible in group A, *b* selections are possible in group B, *c* selections are possible in group C, and so on, then the total number of items is
$$a \times b \times c \times \dots$$

Systematic Listing and Counting has connections with the Curriculum Focal Points for grades 3–5. Solving problems that involve arrays, organized lists, and tree diagrams, as well as using the addition and multiplication principles of counting, serve to strengthen students' understanding of multiplication through the use of those representations.

Tree diagrams are particularly important in grades 3–5 because visualizing and constructing systematic lists and arrays becomes more difficult when the problems become more complex. For example, the array that you would use for a problem involving three shirts, two pairs of pants, and four hats would be three-dimensional. However, extending each of the six branches of a tree diagram (used for three shirts and two pairs of pants) in four ways (if you add four hats) is easy to visualize and provides a way to generate a systematic list. Tree diagrams are also useful at this grade level to explore problems in probability informally.

The use of Venn diagrams should be more sophisticated at these grade levels than at the earlier ones. Students can organize objects according to three attributes rather than just two, and more important, they can solve simple numerical problems that are based on Venn diagrams. For example, ask each student in the class whether he or she likes to play soccer, softball, or basketball. Students can write their names on small pieces of paper and place them in the appropriate regions of a Venn diagram that has three overlapping circles labeled with the three sports, as shown in figure 2.1. They can then answer simple questions such as, "How many students like both soccer and softball but not basketball?" Although the investigation in this chapter does not discuss Venn diagrams, teachers can present and discuss problems involving three attributes with students in grades 3–5. *Navigating through Discrete Mathematics in Grades 6–12* (Hart et al. 2008), presents other Venn diagram activities in chapter 1, "Systematic Listing and Counting in Grades 6–8."

In general, the counting situations and strategies used in grades 3–5 are transitional, moving from simple, concrete situations and implicit, informal strategies in the earlier grades toward the more complex, abstract situations and more formal algebraic strategies in grades 6–12. For additional counting activities for children in grades 3–5, see "Squares on the Geoboard" (Kring 1999) and "The Orange Game" (Sakshaug 1999) on the accompanying CD-ROM.

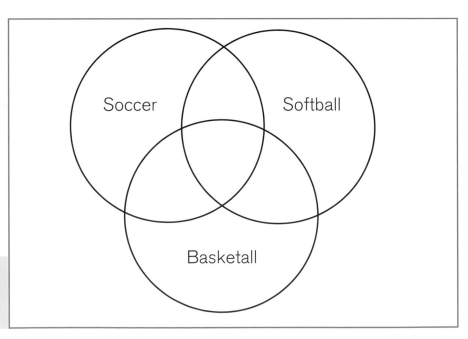

Fig. 2.1.

Students write their names on slips of paper, then place them in the appropriate regions of the Venn diagram.

Bindu Bear's Boutique

The investigation Bindu Bear's Boutique consists of a sequence of mathematical activities in which students count the number of outfits that they can create with specified items. The investigation highlights the value of counting in an organized way. Students can use the applet Bobbie Bear to create as many different outfits as possible by clicking on and dragging an outfit (shirt and pants) from Bobbie's closet to put it on Bobbie. The applet gives students a visual record of the outfits so that they can determine whether they have all possibilities. The number of possible shirts ranges from one to five, and the number of possible pants ranges from one to four. Children guess in advance the number of different outfits that they can create from some number of shirts and pants in the closet.

Although the task of finding all the outfits and determining how many there are is easy when the number of items is small, more sophisticated methods become necessary as the number of possibilities increases. By the end of this sequence of activities, students should appreciate the power of the multiplication principle of counting, which activity 5, The Multiplication Principle of Counting, describes. However, to develop that appreciation, students must first look for all the different outfits that they can make, determine whether they have really found all the possibilities, learn how to organize their initially random efforts, and begin counting in a systematic fashion. After completing this sequence of activities, they can understand and use the multiplication principle of counting and apply it to count the number of possibilities in situations in which that number is large. Teachers should present students with the multiplication principle of counting only after students have had a variety of rich experiences in sorting and listing.

The initial activities in this investigation are appropriate for third-grade students. Subsequent activities may be more appropriate for fourth-grade students, and the final activities may be more suitable for students in the fifth grade.

Students can explore systematic listing and counting by using the applet Bobbie Bear on the accompanying CD-ROM.

Goals

- Represent, analyze, and solve a variety of counting problems by using arrays, systematic lists, and tree diagrams
- Use and explain the addition principle of counting
- Informally use the multiplication principle of counting
- Understand and describe relationships among arrays, systematic lists, tree diagrams, and the multiplication principle of counting

Materials and Equipment

Preliminary Activity

The students do not need any special materials.

Activity 1—Organizing Outfits for the First Week

For each student—

- One copy of the activity sheet "Outfits at Bindu Bear's Boutique"
- One copy of the activity sheet "Outfits for the First Week"

pp. 170, 171

- A sheet of paper
- Purple, yellow, and green crayons
- A pencil
- Scissors

Activity 2—Organizing Outfits for the Second Week

For each student—

- Two copies of the activity sheet "Bear Cutouts"
- One copy of the activity sheet "Shoe Cutouts"
- Purple, yellow, and green crayons
- A pencil
- Scissors
- A gluestick

For each team of three or four students—

- One large sheet of construction paper (about 17 inches by 12 inches)

pp. 172, 173

Activity 3—Creating a Systematic List

For each student—

- Two sheets of lined paper

For the teacher—

- (Optional) Eighteen 3×8 cards

Activity 4—Tree Diagrams

The students do not need any special materials.

Activity 5—The Multiplication Principle of Counting

The students do not need any special materials.

Prior Knowledge

Students should be able to—

- sort by attributes;
- use Venn diagrams with two attributes; and
- count informally by using the addition principle of counting.

Students should have had experiences with sorting and counting a variety of objects, including those in the Bucket of Buttons investigation in chapter 1. They should be familiar with the addition principle of counting and its use in ordinary activities—for example, when someone in each group of students counts the number of students in his or her group, and the teacher counts the number of children in the class by adding together all the reported numbers.

Preliminary Activity

The following preliminary activity involves using the addition principle of counting in a setting that may be more mathematical than those that students have encountered in earlier counting activities. It can help reinforce the addition principle of counting for students in grades 3–5.

Draw the three-by-three grid shown in figure 2.2 on the board, and ask your students how many squares they can find in the diagram. Although they may initially answer that the diagram has nine squares—since those squares are clearly visible—you should persist and ask whether anyone sees any other squares in the diagram. A student will probably observe that in addition to those nine squares, there is a large square. Ask the student to go to the board and outline that square.

Then one of your students may observe (perhaps with some prompting) that the figure also includes squares of intermediate size. The nine small squares are all one-by-one squares, and the large square is a three-by-three square, but the figure also contains intermediate squares whose dimensions are two by two. How many of these squares does the figure have? After showing your students one such square (see figure 2.3), ask them to work in pairs to find the others. Each pair should find four two-by-two squares. The class can then find the total number of squares in figure 2.2 by adding the number of small squares, the number of intermediate squares, and the number of large squares to obtain 9 + 4 + 1, or 14, squares in all.

By third grade, students should have seen enough of these kinds of counting examples that they are able to recognize and use the addition principle of counting, as well as refer to it when they use it. They should also be able to explain how and when to use it and be able to make up their own examples of counting situations to which it applies.

Activities

The story line for this investigation, which you should share with your students before beginning, is that Bindu Bear is the owner of Bindu Bear's Boutique, and she wants to arrange her store's front window to show off the new outfits for the month. Every week, she plans to display all the different outfits that she can put together by using specific items in her store. She will display each outfit on a bear mannequin. She wants to find out how many different outfits she should plan to display.

In activity 1, Organizing Outfits for the First Week, students find all outfits that they can make by using three different shirts and two different pairs of pants. They also begin to discuss how to list the outfits systematically, by using a chart or array. When students work on activity 2, Organizing Outfits for the Second Week, they create different outfits by using three types of shoes as well as the three shirts and two pairs of pants from activity 1. For this activity, the students need to discuss other ways to list the outfits systematically. In activity 3, Creating a Systematic List, they generate and examine various ways to list items systematically, including alphabetical listing, in which they make decisions about what to list first on the basis of alphabetical order. Activity 4, Tree Diagrams, uses tree diagrams to represent all the possible outfits and to create systematic lists of the outfits. Finally, in activity 5, The Multiplication Principle of Counting, the students use tree diagrams to count all the possibilities without actually having to list them all.

Activity 1—Organizing Outfits for the First Week

Give each student a copy of the activity sheet "Outfits at Bindu Bear's Boutique," which contains twelve copies of the bear mannequin. Explain that each of Bindu Bear's outfits consists of a shirt and a pair of

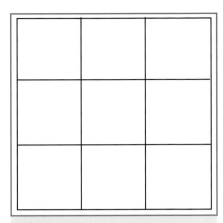

Fig. **2.2.**

How many squares can you find in this diagram?

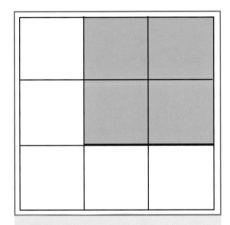

Fig. **2.3.**

An example of a two-by-two square

*Students should discover,
instead of being told, the
total number of possible
outfits.*

pants. Bindu Bear's shirts are green, purple, or yellow; and her pants have either dark gray dots or dark gray stripes. Ask students to make all the possible outfits on the bear mannequins by using crayons for the shirts and a pencil for the pants. The number of mannequins on this activity sheet is more than the students need, so it does not suggest a solution to the problem. Students should discover, instead of being told, the total number of possible outfits.

After the students have finished coloring the bears, assign each student to compare answers with a partner and decide on the total number of possible outfits. Students should try to convince their partners—and themselves—that they have actually found all the different possible outfits.

You should not expect students to generate these outfits in an organized fashion. Indeed, the complete list of six outfits that follows is in a random order to give an idea of the students' initial solutions.

- Purple shirt with dotted pants
- Yellow shirt with striped pants
- Purple shirt with striped pants
- Green shirt with striped pants
- Green shirt with dotted pants
- Yellow shirt with dotted pants

This chapter focuses on listing these possibilities in a systematic way. For now, however, just be certain that the students understand the two tasks involved:

- Obtaining all possibilities
- Explaining how they know that they have indeed obtained all the possibilities

An additional goal of this activity is to give the students an appreciation of the difficulty of determining whether they have found all possibilities when they use an essentially random method for generating them. The questions, "Do you have them all?" and "How do you know?" can help students recognize the need to organize the different possibilities, even if they are unable to answer the two questions fully. Giving students these kinds of experiences makes it easier for you to motivate them to think systematically.

Explain to the students that one way to verify that they have found all possible arrangements is to organize the information in a chart or an array. Although the word *array* may be too sophisticated for students in these grades, you should introduce it if it is appropriate for your students. This way of organizing information is particularly helpful when you have two items—for example, shirts and pants—each available in a variety of types.

Give each student a copy of the activity sheet "Outfits for the First Week." Explain to the students how the chart is organized and how they can read and obtain information from a chart. Introduce the terms *rows* and *columns* and explain what they mean—rows go across the chart, and columns go up and down. Rows are horizontal, like a person lying down, and columns are vertical, like a person standing. The body of this chart has three rows (one for each type of shirt) and two columns

	Dotted Pants	Striped Pants
Green Shirt		
Purple Shirt		
Yellow Shirt		

Outfits for the First Week

(one for each type of pants). A bear mannequin occupies each cell in the chart. The chart shows all the outfits, and it puts each one in a particular spot. For example, the cell at the bottom right is the place for the outfit consisting of a yellow shirt and striped pants.

Have the students color one outfit together as a class, and then ask them to color the remaining five outfits according to each bear's position in the chart. Review the entire chart as a class, and have students compare the results in the chart with their results for the activity sheet "Outfits at Bindu Bear's Boutique." They should note that the chart includes all the outfits that they found previously.

After the students have completed their charts, point out that the chart makes it easy for them to write a list of all the outfits. That is, if they go through the chart, from top to bottom, one row at a time, and read each row from left to right, they have the following list of all outfits:

1. Green shirt, dotted pants
2. Green shirt, striped pants
3. Purple shirt, dotted pants
4. Purple shirt, striped pants
5. Yellow shirt, dotted pants
6. Yellow shirt, striped pants

Generate this list with your students. Point out (or have the students point out) that this list first shows all the outfits with green shirts, then all the outfits with purple shirts, and finally all the outfits with yellow shirts. They should recognize that there are three groups of two (represented as rows in the chart) and that within each group, the same pattern always occurs—dotted pants and then striped pants. Be sure that your students recognize the three groups of outfits in the list and the organization of outfits within each group.

Explain to the students that a list like this one is a *systematic list,* since it includes all the possibilities and organizes them by using a pattern, or system. The pattern here is all outfits with green shirts, then all outfits with purple shirts, and then all outfits with yellow shirts, with dotted pants first, followed by striped pants, in each group. Doing this activity (and others like it) can help your students recognize when a list is systematic and when it is not and can help them in the future when they use multiplication to count the number of outfits.

Next, give each student a blank piece of paper to make a large chart that has two rows and three columns, with room at the left and the top for labels for the rows and columns. The students should label the two rows "dotted pants" and "striped pants," and the three columns "green shirt," "purple shirt," and "yellow shirt." Next, ask the students to cut out the six mannequins that they colored from the activity sheet "Outfits at Bindu Bear's Boutique," with each one wearing a different outfit. Tell the students to place each bear in its appropriate position in the chart that they just made. Then ask the students to make a systematic list of outfits. Again moving across the rows, they should organize their list as follows:

1. Dotted pants, green shirt
2. Dotted pants, purple shirt

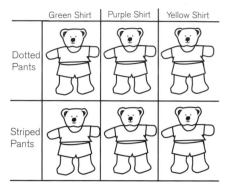

A 2×3 Chart of the Outfits for the First Week

3. Dotted pants, yellow shirt
4. Striped pants, green shirt
5. Striped pants, purple shirt
6. Striped pants, yellow shirt

Discuss with your students whether this list is the same as the first list that they made. Although the two lists have exactly the same outfits, they are different lists because the outfits are in a different order.

This list includes two groups of three items (represented as rows in the chart). Within each group, the same pattern always occurs—green shirt, then purple shirt, and then yellow shirt. Point out that the first chart is called a three-by-two chart, since it has three rows and two columns; and the second chart is called a two-by-three chart, since it has two rows and three columns. Ask the students the following questions:

- "How many rows are in a four-by-seven chart?" (Four)
- "How many columns are in a four-by-seven chart?" (Seven)
- "What would you call a chart that has three columns and five rows?" (A five-by-three chart, since the first number always refers to the number of rows)
- "What is the number of cells in a three-by-two chart?" (Six)
- "How many bear mannequins would be in a four-by-seven chart?" (Twenty-eight)

Students should initially find the number of cells in a three-by-two chart or a four-by-three chart by counting all the cells or by repeated addition; that is, they should notice that each row in a three-by-two chart has two cells, so that the total number of cells in a three-by-two chart is 2 + 2 + 2, or 6, cells, and the total number of cells in a four-by-three chart is 3 + 3 + 3 + 3, or 12, cells.

However, once students have learned about multiplication, they should be able to determine that the number of cells in a three-by-two chart is 3 × 2, or 6, cells, and that the number of cells in a four-by-three chart is 4 × 3, or 12, cells. Thus, once they have learned about multiplication, they should be able to answer these questions by using counting, repeated addition, or multiplication. Answering these questions by using multiplication helps prepare students for the multiplication principle of counting.

This activity is appropriate for introducing students to the array model of multiplication or for reinforcing their understanding of it. In the array model of multiplication, students typically see a rectangular array of dots, like that in figure 2.4, as representing a product: four dots are on the side of the rectangle and five dots are on the bottom, so the total number of dots in the array is 4 × 5, or 20. Similarly, a three-by-two array of dots represents 3 × 2 = 6, a four-by-three array of dots represents 4 × 3 = 12, and a four-by-seven array of dots represents 4 × 7 = 28. Although the charts in this activity are not the same as arrays of dots, each chart contains an array of outfits on bear mannequins, so the number of outfits in a four-by-three chart is the same as the number of dots in a four-by-three array, and the number of outfits in a four-by-seven chart is the same as the number of dots in a four-by-seven array.

As a result, you can present finding the number of cells in a chart to the students as an activity that is similar to finding the number of dots in an array.

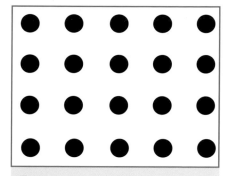

Fig. **2.4.**

An array model of dots for multiplying 4 × 5

Activity 2—Organizing Outfits for the Second Week

For this activity, give each student two copies of the activity sheet "Bear Cutouts," one copy of the activity sheet "Shoe Cutouts," a box of crayons, a pair of scissors, a pencil, and a gluestick. Ask each student to cut along the dashed lines of the templates so that they have twenty-four separate bears and twenty-four pairs of shoes. Explain that the students are now going to work on Bindu Bear's outfits for the second week. Bindu has just received a new line of shoes—boots, loafers, and sneakers. This week, she again wants to display all the different outfits that she can make with the shirts, pants, and shoes that she has for sale. How many outfits can the students find? Allow them to work independently to create outfits by coloring each shirt with a green, purple, or yellow crayon; drawing dots or stripes on the pants with a pencil; and taking a pair of shoes and gluing them onto the bear's feet.

After each student has found about ten outfits, create teams of three or four students to share the outfits that they have found and see whether they can find any more outfits as a team. Distribute a large sheet of construction paper to each team, and ask students to place one copy of each different outfit on that page so that they can organize the outfits that they have created. Because children will vary in their coloring techniques, two children's versions of the same outfit may look quite different. Emphasize that for the purposes of this activity, two outfits are the same if they have shirts of the same color, the same type of pants, and the same type of shoes.

Students should not glue the bears to the construction paper at this point, because they will need to move the bears to sort them. After each team has had an opportunity to generate the outfits and figure out how many they have, ask the students what strategy they used to find the different outfits. Typically, most students generate the outfits randomly and do not find all of them.

Some of the teams, however, may apply the ideas introduced in activity 1 and attempt to create a chart or an organized list, and they may be partially successful. For example, they may try to make a chart similar to the chart "Outfits for the First Week" and put three outfits in each cell—that is, all the outfits with the same shirts and pants but the three different styles of shoes. Or they may create three copies of such a chart and use the first for all the outfits involving boots, the second for all the outfits involving loafers, and the third for all the outfits involving sneakers.

Ask the students how they know whether they have listed every possible outfit. In fact, most of the teams probably will not find all eighteen outfits. Explain that finding all the different outfits can be tricky, especially when there are a lot of outfits. Tell them that when counting problems are difficult—that is, when the number of possibilities is large—having a systematic way of counting is important so that they can be sure that they have counted all the different possibilities.

Ask the students to look at all the outfits that they have created on the mannequins and try to organize these outfits in a systematic way. That is, have them sort the outfits into several groups so that the outfits

in each group have something in common. Ask the students to explain how many groups they have and how they organized the outfits within each group.

If the students have not generated all eighteen outfits, do not tell them what outfits are missing. Allow them to discover any additional outfits while they organize their groups of outfits and discover which outfits they have missed. This step is an important one in helping students become independent problem solvers. They need to experience self-assessment and self-correction while working on difficult problems. When a team has found and organized all eighteen outfits, ask the team members to glue the bears on the construction paper so that the other students can see how they organized their outfits. Have each team report on its method of organization to the entire class. Summarize and list on the board the different ways that your groups of students organized the outfits.

Some teams may organize the outfits by shirt color and realize that they need to have six outfits for each color. Other teams may organize the outfits by shoes, so they should have six outfits for each shoe style; others may organize the outfits by pants, in which case they should have nine outfits for each pants type. As you go around the room, ask the members of each team how they can organize each of the smaller groups of outfits. For example, ask teams that organized the outfits by shirt color (or by shoe style) how they can organize each of the three smaller groups of outfits, and ask teams that organized by pants type how they can organize each of the two smaller groups of outfits. Then ask the teams to report again on how they organized the outfits. By this point they should have found all eighteen outfits. Each team's report should indicate that the members organized all the outfits first by one item of clothing (shirt color, pants type, or shoe style) and then by a second item of clothing—for example, first by shirt color and then by shoe style.

The students may have organized their outfits in any of six ways:

- By shirt and then by shoes
- By shirt and then by pants
- By shoes and then by shirts
- By shoes and then by pants
- By pants and then by shirts
- By pants and then by shoes

All these solutions are good ways to organize the eighteen outfits. The next task is to create a systematic list.

Activity 3—Creating a Systematic List

This activity helps you guide your students in generating a systematic list of all eighteen outfits discussed in activity 2. This work is likely to occur in stages. Figures 2.5 through 2.9 record progress along a path toward a fully systematic list. Each list is more systematic than the previous one. The captions of these five figures indicate the extent to which each list is completely systematic. The list in figure 2.8 is fully systematic, although those in figures 2.5, 2.6, and 2.7 are not. There are, however, many fully systematic lists for the problem in activity 2.

Students need to experience self-assessment and self-correction while working on difficult problems.

The systematic list in figure 2.9 has a special feature that makes it unique. Going through this activity takes some time, but it can provide students with good insights into systematic listing and counting.

Ask your students to take out a sheet of lined paper, write the numbers from 1 to 18 on eighteen successive lines, and make a list of the eighteen outfits in activity 2. The students' lists should reflect the way that they have organized the outfits. Figure 2.5, for example, is a list that a team of students might produce if the team organized the outfits first by shirts, then by pants.

1.	Green shirt, dotted pants, loafers
2.	Green shirt, dotted pants, sneakers
3.	Green shirt, dotted pants, boots
4.	Green shirt, striped pants, boots
5.	Green shirt, striped pants, sneakers
6.	Green shirt, striped pants, loafers
7.	Yellow shirt, striped pants, loafers
8.	Yellow shirt, dotted pants, sneakers
9.	Yellow shirt, striped pants, boots
10.	Yellow shirt, dotted pants, boots
11.	Yellow shirt, striped pants, sneakers
12.	Yellow shirt, dotted pants, loafers
13.	Purple shirt, striped pants, loafers
14.	Purple shirt, striped pants, boots
15.	Purple shirt, striped pants, sneakers
16.	Purple shirt, dotted pants, sneakers
17.	Purple shirt, dotted pants, loafers
18.	Purple shirt, dotted pants, boots

Fig. **2.5.**

A list that is fully organized by shirts, partially organized by pants, and not organized by shoes; version 1

Different teams of students will produce different lists, and even if a team organized its list first by shirts and then by pants, its list might not be identical to the list in figure 2.5. Before focusing on the lists that your students have made on their sheets of lined paper, present the list that is in figure 2.5 as a classroom example.

Display the list, and ask the students whether they can identify groups of outfits. They should recognize that the list shows three groups, each with six outfits—the outfits with green shirts, the outfits with yellow shirts, and the outfits with purple shirts. Draw a line under items 6 and 12 to separate and highlight these three groups.

Next, ask the students whether they can determine how each of those three groups is organized. They should be able to identify an organizational pattern for each of the groups. In the first group of six outfits, the organization is by pants type, with three outfits that have dotted pants followed by three outfits that have striped pants. The pattern of the second group of six outfits is that the pants types alternate—striped, dotted, striped, dotted, striped, dotted. In the third group of outfits, the organization is by pants type, with three outfits that have striped pants followed by three outfits that have dotted pants. Thus, the organization of each group of outfits follows a pattern.

However, although the list in figure 2.5 is fully organized by shirts, it is only partially organized by pants. To organize the list fully by pants would require that all the outfits with yellow shirts (the second group in figure 2.5) that also have striped pants be grouped together, and all the outfits with yellow shirts that also have dotted pants be grouped together. Figure 2.6 displays such a list; it has three groups, each with six outfits, and within each group are three outfits with striped pants grouped together and three outfits with dotted pants grouped together.

Fig. **2.6.**	
A list that is fully organized by shirts, partially organized by pants, and not organized by shoes; version 2	1. Green shirt, dotted pants, loafers 2. Green shirt, dotted pants, sneakers 3. Green shirt, dotted pants, boots 4. Green shirt, striped pants, boots 5. Green shirt, striped pants, sneakers 6. Green shirt, striped pants, loafers 7. Yellow shirt, striped pants, loafers 8. Yellow shirt, striped pants, sneakers 9. Yellow shirt, striped pants, boots 10. Yellow shirt, dotted pants, boots 11. Yellow shirt, dotted pants, loafers 12. Yellow shirt, dotted pants, sneakers 13. Purple shirt, striped pants, loafers 14. Purple shirt, striped pants, boots 15. Purple shirt, striped pants, sneakers 16. Purple shirt, dotted pants, sneakers 17. Purple shirt, dotted pants, loafers 18. Purple shirt, dotted pants, boots

Ask the students whether the three groups use the same pattern. They should recognize that although a pattern appears within each group, no pattern occurs across the groups. In the first group of six outfits, the pants are dotted and then striped; in the second and third groups, the pants are striped and then dotted. In a systematic list, the same patterns must reappear throughout the list. Thus, the caption of figure 2.6 indicates that the list is only partially organized by pants.

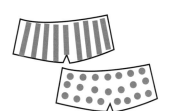

Have the students take another sheet of lined paper, write the numbers 1 to 18 on successive lines, and on the basis of the list in figure 2.6, make a list in which the pattern of the types of pants is the same each time. One possibility for such a list appears in figure 2.7. In that list, the dotted pants precede the striped pants in each group; the reverse is also possible. This list is fully organized by shirts and then fully organized by pants.

Ask the students whether this list is also organized by shoes (it is not) and whether they can arrange the eighteen outfits so that the shoes also follow a pattern—more specifically, so that all the groups of shoes follow the same pattern. Ask them to use the same sheet of paper for this list and replace some pairs of shoes with others. They can, for example, make the order of the shoes in all six groups the same as the order of the shoes in the first group (the "green shirt, dotted pants" group). They might then come up with the list in figure 2.8, which is fully organized—first by shirts, then by pants, and then by shoes.

Ask the students to take out their first sheet of lined paper—the one on which they organized the eighteen outfits—and on a third sheet of lined paper, use their own organization to create a list that is fully organized—that is, in which the shirt colors, pants types, and shoe styles have the same patterns throughout the list. Point out to the students that many different ways exist to organize the eighteen outfits systematically;

1.	Green shirt, dotted pants, loafers
2.	Green shirt, dotted pants, sneakers
3.	Green shirt, dotted pants, boots
4.	Green shirt, striped pants, boots
5.	Green shirt, striped pants, sneakers
6.	Green shirt, striped pants, loafers
7.	Yellow shirt, dotted pants, boots
8.	Yellow shirt, dotted pants, loafers
9.	Yellow shirt, dotted pants, sneakers
10.	Yellow shirt, striped pants, loafers
11.	Yellow shirt, striped pants, sneakers
12.	Yellow shirt, striped pants, boots
13.	Purple shirt, dotted pants, loafers
14.	Purple shirt, dotted pants, boots
15.	Purple shirt, dotted pants, sneakers
16.	Purple shirt, striped pants, sneakers
17.	Purple shirt, striped pants, loafers
18.	Purple shirt, striped pants, boots

Fig. 2.7.

A list that is fully organized by shirts, fully organized by pants, and not organized by shoes

1.	Green shirt, dotted pants, loafers
2.	Green shirt, dotted pants, sneakers
3.	Green shirt, dotted pants, boots
4.	Green shirt, striped pants, loafers
5.	Green shirt, striped pants, sneakers
6.	Green shirt, striped pants, boots
7.	Yellow shirt, dotted pants, loafers
8.	Yellow shirt, dotted pants, sneakers
9.	Yellow shirt, dotted pants, boots
10.	Yellow shirt, striped pants, loafers
11.	Yellow shirt, striped pants, sneakers
12.	Yellow shirt, striped pants, boots
13.	Purple shirt, dotted pants, loafers
14.	Purple shirt, dotted pants, sneakers
15.	Purple shirt, dotted pants, boots
16.	Purple shirt, striped pants, loafers
17.	Purple shirt, striped pants, sneakers
18.	Purple shirt, striped pants, boots

Fig. 2.8.

A list that is fully organized by shirts, then by pants, then by shoes

all their lists are likely to be different from the list developed in figures 2.5 through 2.8. Their organization may follow a different order—for example, first by pants, then by shoes, then by shirts. Within each group, they may organize the outfits in a different order; for example, although the list in figures 2.5 through 2.8 proceeds from green to yellow to purple, their shirts may go from purple to green to yellow. However, as you examine each team's list, do the following to guarantee that the lists are parallel to the list described in the examples:

1. Ensure that the students have divided the eighteen outfits into groups—for example, green shirts, purple shirts, and yellow shirts.

2. Ensure that within each of those groups, the students have organized the outfits. Be prepared for the fact that the organization of the outfits in one group may differ from the organization of the outfits in another group; for example, the outfits in one group all may have dotted pants, then all striped pants, but in another group, the outfits may alternate between dotted pants and striped pants, as in figure 2.5.

3. Ensure that the students have organized the outfits in each of the groups into subgroups. For example, all groups of different-colored shirts have the subgroups of all dotted pants and then the subgroup of all striped pants, as in figure 2.6.

4. Ensure that within each group, the students have organized the subgroups in the same way; for example, all three groups have the subgroup of all dotted pants, then the subgroup of all striped pants, as in figure 2.7.

5. Ensure that within each of the subgroups, the students have organized the outfits the same way; for example, for each color of shirt and each type of pants, the shoes are organized loafers, sneakers, and boots, as in figure 2.8.

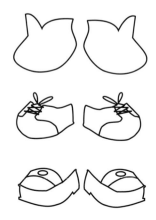

You may want to prepare in advance eighteen 3 × 8 cards, on each of which you have identified a different one of the eighteen possible outfits. With these cards in hand, write the numbers 1 to 18 on the blackboard. As the students give you the possibilities on their initial list, you can tape the cards next to the numbers. Then, while you go through the preceding steps, you can move the cards so that they are fully organized at the end. Note, however, that the cards prepared in advance will work only for a list of outfits that the students generate and organize in the same general way that you organized them on your cards—for example, first by pants, and then by shoes, and then by shirts. To be fully prepared, you would need six such sets of cards!

After each team has organized its outfits systematically, review the different lists with the class and highlight the many different patterns that the students have produced. Ask the students to compare their lists. Although two teams may have exactly the same list, that possibility is unlikely. Ask the students whether one list is better than the others, and remind them that this is not the case. Point out that one possible list has a special feature that makes it unique. In that list, the pattern is created automatically when students make all choices on the basis of alphabetical order.

Organizing the list on this basis means that when students decide the order in which the items appear, they always decide alphabetically. Thus, the different styles of shoes appear in the following order: boots come before loafers, and loafers come before sneakers, since *B* precedes *L*, which precedes *S*. The order of the shirts is green, then purple, then yellow, since *G* precedes *P*, and *P* precedes *Y*; and the dotted pants appear before the striped pants, since *D* comes before *S*. Next, ask the students to organize their lists alphabetically and compare them with those of the other students. Every team should create the list shown in figure 2.9.

> *Students should realize that they may be able to organize the same list systematically in many different ways and that each of these ways is a good solution to the problem.*

Fig. **2.9.**

A list that is fully organized by shirts, and then by pants, then by shoes—an alphabetical list

1. Green shirt, dotted pants, boots
2. Green shirt, dotted pants, loafers
3. Green shirt, dotted pants, sneakers
4. Green shirt, striped pants, boots
5. Green shirt, striped pants, loafers
6. Green shirt, striped pants, sneakers
7. Purple shirt, dotted pants, boots
8. Purple shirt, dotted pants, loafers
9. Purple shirt, dotted pants, sneakers
10. Purple shirt, striped pants, boots
11. Purple shirt, striped pants, loafers
12. Purple shirt, striped pants, sneakers
13. Yellow shirt, dotted pants, boots
14. Yellow shirt, dotted pants, loafers
15. Yellow shirt, dotted pants, sneakers
16. Yellow shirt, striped pants, boots
17. Yellow shirt, striped pants, loafers
18. Yellow shirt, striped pants, sneakers

An important advantage of organizing lists alphabetically is that all teams of students finish with the same lists and can therefore compare their answers. Review with your students the patterns in this alphabetical systematic list. They should be able to see three groups of six (as defined by shirt color), and within each group they should see a pattern for the pants and then a pattern for the shoes. Make explicit that these same patterns repeat among the three groups. Hence, the list is systematic.

The students can see that generating systematic lists in this fashion can be hard work. Is there a more efficient way to find all the outfits? This is the question that the next activity helps the students explore.

Activity 4—Tree Diagrams

A more efficient way of finding all the outfits is by using a tree diagram, which, as in the previous activity, first considers shirt color, then pants type, and then shoe style. Create a tree diagram for the class in the following three stages:

- Represent the three possible choices for the shirt color by drawing three line segments that emerge from an initial vertex and labeling the vertices at the ends of the segments with the shirt colors. List the three shirt colors in alphabetical order, and tell the students that you are using this process because having everyone alphabetize is a way of making sure that everyone's list is the same as everyone else's, as the class discussed in activity 3.

- Remind the students that after someone selects a shirt color, he or she has two possible choices for the pants—dotted or striped. So draw two line segments that emerge from each vertex labeled with a shirt color, and label the vertices at their ends with the pants types. As before, label the vertices alphabetically.

- Finally, after choosing a shirt and a pair of pants, someone must choose a pair of shoes to complete an outfit. So for each vertex labeled with a pants type, draw three emerging line segments, and label the terminal vertices with the shoe styles. Again, label the vertices alphabetically. Your tree diagram should look like the one in figure 2.10.

After you have created this tree diagram, introduce the idea of "vertical levels" in the diagram. The first vertical level, to the right of the initial starting point, contains the three possible shirt colors. In the second vertical level are the two possible pants types—dotted and striped—repeated three times, once for each shirt color. In the third vertical level are the three shoe styles—boots, loafers, and sneakers—repeated six times, once for each shirt color and pants type. The three vertical levels are labeled "Shirt Color," "Pants Type," and "Shoe Style" in figure 2.10.

Focus the students' attention on the branches in the tree diagram. Explain that a *branch* is a path from the initial vertex of the tree diagram to a vertex that is in the last vertical level of the tree diagram. One branch in the tree diagram in figure 2.10 starts at the vertex at the left, goes to purple, then to dotted, and then to sneakers. This branch, of course, represents the outfit consisting of purple shirt, dotted pants, and sneakers.

Point out that you can generate the entire systematic list of figure 2.9 simply by following each branch of this tree diagram, starting at the top and working your way down. For example, when you follow the topmost branch, you pass three vertices labeled "Green," "Dotted, and "Boots." This branch represents the first outfit—green shirt, dotted pants, and boots—in figure 2.9. The next branch (or next outfit) has the

An efficient way of finding all the outfits is by using a tree diagram.

Fig. **2.10.**

A tree diagram as a way to generate a list

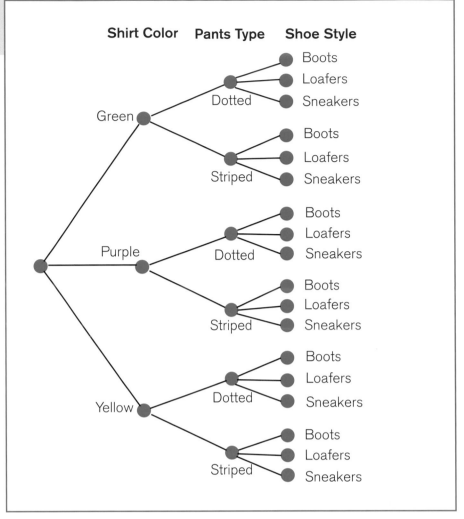

vertices "Green," "Dotted," and "Loafers" and corresponds to the second outfit in figure 2.9. Continue in this fashion until the students see that this tree diagram represents every outfit in the systematic list in figure 2.9.

Next, point out that the tree diagram is *uniform* because the branches that emerge from any two vertices that are in the same vertical level look the same. For example, what appears to the right of the upper vertex labeled "Dotted" is the same as what appears to the right of each vertex underneath that vertex, whether it is labeled "Dotted" or "Striped." Similarly, what appears to the right of the vertex labeled "Green" is exactly the same as what appears to the right of the vertex labeled "Purple" and what appears to the right of the vertex labeled "Yellow."

Emphasize that it is possible to generate every systematic list with a tree diagram. To illustrate this point, provide each team of students with the list in figure 2.11—a systematic list that includes the same eighteen outfits, organized in a different way. Ask students to work in teams to generate the tree diagram that corresponds to this systematic list. The tree diagram in figure 2.12 corresponds to the systematic list in figure 2.11.

Review the construction of the tree diagram in figure 2.12, and discuss how to use it to generate the systematic list.

1. Dotted pants, boots, green shirt	**Fig. 2.11.**
2. Dotted pants, boots, purple shirt	What tree diagram would generate this systematic list?
3. Dotted pants, boots, yellow shirt	
4. Dotted pants, loafers, green shirt	
5. Dotted pants, loafers, purple shirt	
6. Dotted pants, loafers, yellow shirt	
7. Dotted pants, sneakers, green shirt	
8. Dotted pants, sneakers, purple shirt	
9. Dotted pants, sneakers, yellow shirt	
10. Striped pants, boots, green shirt	
11. Striped pants, boots, purple shirt	
12. Striped pants, boots, yellow shirt	
13. Striped pants, loafers, green shirt	
14. Striped pants, loafers, purple shirt	
15. Striped pants, loafers, yellow shirt	
16. Striped pants, sneakers, green shirt	
17. Striped pants, sneakers, purple shirt	
18. Striped pants, sneakers, yellow shirt	

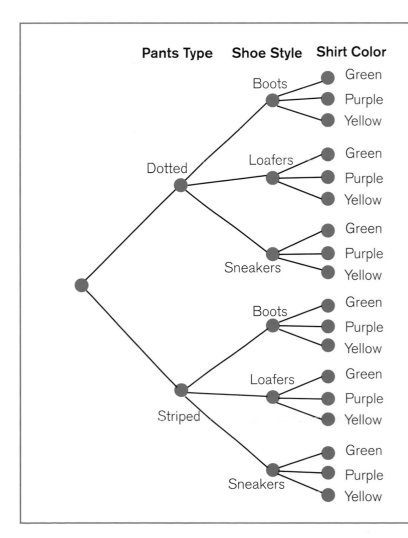

Fig. 2.12.

A tree diagram that generates the systematic list in figure 2.11

- The first vertical level, which contains the two types of pants, includes two groups of nine outfits (the top group includes all the outfits with dotted pants, and the bottom group includes all the outfits with striped pants).
- In the second vertical level are the shoe styles. Each of the groups of nine outfits in the first level now consists of three subgroups, each with three outfits (the top subgroup includes all three outfits with boots, the middle subgroup includes all three outfits with loafers, and the bottom subgroup includes all three outfits with sneakers).
- In the third vertical level are the shirt colors. Each of the subgroups of three outfits in this level is identical (one outfit with a green shirt, then one outfit with a purple shirt, then one outfit with a yellow shirt).

Also point out that the line segments that emerge from any vertex of the tree diagram have the same labels as the line segments that emerge from any other vertex at the same vertical level, so the part of the tree diagram that emerges from any vertex looks exactly the same as the part of the tree diagram that emerges from any other vertex at the same vertical level.

To summarize, compare the two tree diagrams in figure 2.10 and figure 2.12 by placing them next to each other so that the students can see them. Discuss the similarities and differences between the tree diagrams. Be sure to note that both tree diagrams represent exactly the same collection of outfits, although they are listed systematically in two different orders, and each of these lists has eighteen possible outfits (that is, eighteen terminal nodes). Next, place under each tree diagram the systematic list that corresponds to it. The list in figure 2.9 corresponds to the tree diagram in figure 2.10, and the list in figure 2.11 corresponds to the tree diagram in figure 2.12. Discuss the similarities and differences between the lists. Conclude that both of these solutions are excellent answers when someone has asked for a systematic list.

Since tree diagrams are very useful for generating systematic lists, this activity introducing them could have appeared as the first activity in the investigation. The students, however, would not have seen the power of tree diagrams if they had started using them before struggling on their own to generate a systematic list.

But what if someone asks only how many outfits are possible and does not ask for a systematic list? How can the students calculate the number eighteen directly? The next activity—the last in the investigation—helps them find out.

Activity 5—The Multiplication Principle of Counting

What is the underlying mathematical operation behind tree diagrams? Why can any of several different tree diagrams represent the same number of possibilities?

Reviewing their work in activity 4 and looking again at the tree diagram in figure 2.10 can help students answer the first question. In that activity, students created a tree diagram on the basis of a list that used the following sequence of items: shirts, then pants, and then shoes. Looking at the construction of this tree diagram reveals that from each of the three vertices for shirt color, two branches emerge—one for each

Students do not see the power of tree diagrams if they start using them before struggling on their own to generate a systemic list.

of the two types of pants. Hence, to know how many shirt-and-pants outfits exist, someone can simply multiply 3 × 2 and conclude that the number of outfits is 6. But for every vertex representing a pants type, three more branches emerge, representing the number of possible shoe styles. So the total number of possible shirt-pants-and-shoe outfits in this tree diagram is 3 × 2 × 3, or 18. Students need to recognize that the first 3 represents the number of possible shirt choices, the 2 represents the number of possible pants choices, and the second 3 represents the number of possible choices for shoes.

When students have a task (such as making an outfit) that consists of a sequence of steps (for example, first choose a shirt, then choose a pair of pants, and then choose a pair of shoes), they can multiply the number of possible ways to complete each step to determine the total number of ways to accomplish the task. This method of counting is the *multiplication principle of counting*. Although you can mention this principle to your students, they should not focus on memorizing the name or formally stating the principle. Rather, you should expect them to use multiplication to solve counting problems in the manner indicated by the multiplication principle of counting.

Next, ask the students to consider the tree diagram in figure 2.12. Remind them that in activity 4 they discovered that although they selected items in a different sequence (pants first, then shoes, and then shirt) to create each outfit, they still finished with the same total number of outfits and exactly the same outfits. Ask the students to generate the multiplication problem that represents the list of outfits in figure 2.12. Students should recognize that the description of each outfit in this systematic list represents selecting first pants, then shoes, and then a shirt. Because there are two types of pants, three shoe styles, and three shirt colors, the total number of outfits is 2 × 3 × 3, or 18, outfits.

To answer the second question—to explain why they can use any of several different tree diagrams to represent the same number of possibilities—students need to understand that they can multiply numbers in any order yet still arrive at the same answer. You should specifically relate this observation to the commutative and associative properties of multiplication, which fourth-grade students should be able to understand, use, and name. As students look at the tree diagram in figure 2.10 (the shirt-pants-shoes tree) from left to right, they can see that the number 18 comes from 3 × 2 × 3. However, they can also see that in the tree diagram in figure 2.12 (the pants-shirts-shoe tree) the number 18 comes from 2 × 3 × 3. Because

$$3 \times 2 \times 3 = 2 \times 3 \times 3,$$

the structures of the two tree diagrams may be different, yet they still yield the same number of possible outfits.

Group your students into teams of two, and ask the members of each team to pretend that they are fashion designers for Bindu Bear's Boutique and are responsible for choosing the items that the boutique will feature during the third week and for displaying all possible outfits. Each team should create outfits that consist of three or four types of items. One example might be outfits consisting of a hat, a shirt, and a pair of pants. A more complicated example might be outfits consisting of a hat, a dress, boots, and a purse. Of course, the teams should include two or more styles of each type of clothing. Ask each team to generate a tree diagram that represents all the outfits and to write a multiplication problem that answers the question, "How many bear mannequins would you need to display all the outfits in your fashion line at Bindu Bear's Boutique?

After all the teams have generated their own tree diagram and multiplication problem, have each team swap problems with another team and solve the other team's design problem by using both a tree diagram and the multiplication principle of counting. The two teams should then verify that each of them has correctly created a tree diagram that represents the other team's fashion line and that each team has found the correct number of outfits in that line.

Extension Activities

By the fifth grade, students should have seen enough examples that they are able to recognize and use the multiplication principle of counting, refer to the multiplication principle of counting when it is in use, explain how and when to use it, and devise their own examples of counting situations to which it applies. For example, they should recognize that they can find the number of buttons in chapter 1's investigation, Bucket of Buttons, by using the multiplication principle of counting: because there are two different shapes, three different numbers of holes, four different colors, and three different sizes, the total number of buttons is $2 \times 3 \times 4 \times 3$, or 72.

A more challenging and abstract activity is to count the number of possible systematic lists—for example, the total number of ways of systematically listing the shirt-and-pants outfits for the first week in activity 1. To solve this problem, students must ask themselves what choices they need to make to create a systematic list of the shirt-and-pants outfits. One decision is whether to start with shirts or whether to start with pants: the number of possibilities there is two. A second choice comes in deciding how to list the different pairs of pants, that is, whether striped or dotted comes first: the number of possibilities there is also two. A third choice comes in deciding how to list the three different shirts. The number of possibilities in this situation is six—listed alphabetically, they are green-purple-yellow, green-yellow-purple, purple-green-yellow, purple-yellow-green, yellow-green-purple, and yellow-purple-green. Since the students make each of these choices independently, the total number of ways of making these choices is $2 \times 2 \times 6$, or 24, so they actually have twenty-four possible ways of listing these outfits systematically.

The fact that there are six ways of listing the shirts is also a consequence of the multiplication principle of counting, since there are three possibilities for the shirt that is listed first, two for the shirt that is listed second, and one for the shirt that is listed last. Therefore, the total number of ways to list the shirts is $3 \times 2 \times 1$, or 6.

An even more challenging extension task is to find the total number of ways of systematically listing all the shirt-pants-shoes outfits. The number of possible lists is 432. How does the multiplication principle of counting help to determine that number? First, the number of possible ways of determining the shirt-pants-shoes order is six. (As in the preceding discussion, there are three possibilities for the items (shirt,

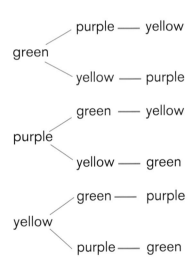

pants, or shoes) that appear first on the list, then two possibilities for the item that is second, and one possibility for the item that is last. The number of possibilities for the shirt-pants-shoes order is therefore 3 × 2 × 1, or 6). After someone has determined that number, he or she has six possible ways of listing the three styles of shoes, six possible ways of listing the three colors of shirts, and two possible ways of listing the types of pants. The multiplication principle of counting indicates that there are 6 × 6 × 6 × 2, or 432, ways altogether to make a systematic list of all outfits. Listed alphabetically, the six ways of determining the shirt-pants-shoes order are pants-shirt-shoes, pants-shoes-shirt, shirt-pants-shoes, shirt-shoes-pants, shoes-pants-shirt, and shoes-shirt-pants.

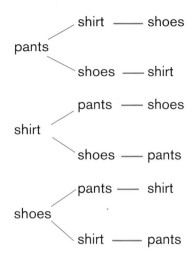

The Mathematics in the Investigation

The mathematical focus of this activity is systematic listing and counting—more specifically, it is moving students from thinking randomly to thinking systematically in carrying out tasks involving listing and counting.

By the end of grade 5, students should be able to recognize situations in which they can use the multiplication principle of counting; understand the multiplication principle of counting by representing situations using arrays, tree diagrams, and alphabetical lists; and apply the multiplication principle of counting to these situations. The development of this understanding should proceed along the following path:

1. Students should use the addition principle of counting to count a collection of objects by breaking the collection into coherent parts, counting each part, and then adding the results—for example, they may count the number of outfits that they can make by using three shirts (G = green, P = purple, and Y = yellow) and two pairs of pants (D = dotted and S = striped) by counting the three outfits with D and the three outfits with S and then adding the results to get 3 + 3 = 6. Alternatively, they may count the outfits with G, the outfits with P, and the outfits with Y and add the results to obtain 2 + 2 + 2 = 6. Students should have had a variety of informal experiences using the addition principle of counting in prekindergarten through grade 2 so that teachers can name and formalize this principle by grade 3.

2. Students should begin to list and count systematically and be able to find all possible ways of carrying out a counting task such as the preceding one by using the following three methods:

   • Arrays: students use a three-by-two chart to represent the possibilities in this example, and they note that the two column totals are the same, so they can multiply 3 × 2 to get 6.
   • Systematic lists: students develop a systematic list of all possibilities by listing all items in the first row of the chart, then listing all items in the second row in the chart, and so on. Alternatively, they can base the list on columns instead of rows.
   • Tree diagrams: students use a tree diagram to generate and organize all the possibilities.

3. Students should be able to generate systematic lists and use the multiplication principle of counting to count all possibilities:

- Students use a tree diagram to obtain a systematic list of the branches on the tree.
- Students develop an alphabetical list of possibilities by mentally visualizing the tree diagram without actually constructing it. Thus, they should be able to generate—without actually constructing the tree diagram—the two lists of all outfits (G-D, G-S, P-D, P-S, Y-D, Y-S, and D-G, D-P, D-Y, S-G, S-P, S-Y) for the previous situation, where, for example, G-D refers to the outfit with a green shirt and dotted pants.

4. By the end of grade 5, students should be able to use both the addition and multiplication principles of counting and recognize the types of situations to which the principles apply. They should be able to use these principles to answer questions like the following:

- "In how many different ways can you answer five questions on a true-false exam?" ($2 \times 2 \times 2 \times 2 \times 2$, or 2^5, or 32)

- "How many different outcomes are possible if you toss three dice?" ($6 \times 6 \times 6$, or 6^3, or 216)

- "In how many possible ways can you pick two cards from a 52-card deck?" (52×51, or 2,652)

Experience with such problems will prepare the student for investigating problems in probability as well as more advanced counting problems in subsequent grades.

NAVIGATING *through* DISCRETE MATHEMATICS

Chapter 3
Vertex-Edge Graphs in Pre-K–Grade 2

All students in pre-K–grade 2 should—

- *build and explore vertex-edge graphs by using concrete materials;*

- *explore simple properties of graphs, such as the numbers of vertices and edges, neighboring vertices and the degree of a vertex, and whole-number weights on edges;*

- *use graphs to solve problems related to paths, circuits, and networks in concrete settings;*

- *color simple pictures by using the minimum number of colors;*

- *follow and create simple sets of directions related to building and using graphs;*

- *concretely explore the notion of the shortest path between two vertices.*

Vertex-edge graphs are mathematical models that consist of a collection of vertices (represented by points or little circles) and edges (represented by line segments, which may be straight or curved). Each edge connects two vertices. Figure 3.1 shows a vertex-edge graph consisting of seven vertices and eight edges. Vertex-edge graphs can model many real-life applications in which a number of sites are connected or need to be connected, such as locations on a map or computers in a network. Vertex-edge graphs can help answer such questions as, What is the best route for a delivery truck to take to carry packages to particular locations?

Vertex-edge graphs offer an ideal environment in which young students can explore abstract mathematical topics, reason and communicate about mathematics, and make connections among mathematical ideas—all in the context of concrete, engaging problems and real-life applications. Because vertex-edge graphs can model networks, they themselves are sometimes called *networks*. However, this book provides approaches for using these graphs in classrooms with young students, so it does not refer to them as networks. *Vertex-edge graph* is itself a rather long and sophisticated term, so this book sometimes uses the simpler, shorter name *graph*.

In prekindergarten–grade 2, students should begin to learn about vertex-edge graphs by building them, by counting their vertices and edges, by exploring simple properties (for example, by identifying the number of neighbors at a vertex), and by solving simple problems (for instance, by finding the shortest path between two vertices). These early

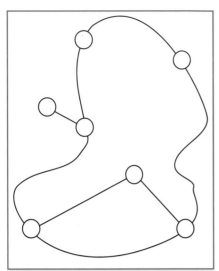

Fig. 3.1.

A graph with seven vertices and eight edges

Students can explore vertex-edge graphs by using the applet Graph Creator on the accompanying CD-ROM.

To read more about presenting vertex-edge graphs in the primary grades, see "Discrete Mathematics in K–2 Classrooms" (DeBellis 1997; available on the CD-ROM).

experiences can help reinforce the learning of basic skills—including counting, mastering addition facts, and following directions. Moreover, the process of finding all the different paths from one vertex to another can help develop combinatorial thinking (see activity 2, Let Me Count the Paths).

In fact, this chapter's investigation, From Here to There, addresses all but one of this book's recommendations for learning about vertex-edge graphs in prekindergarten–grade 2. The remaining recommendation—that students at these levels color simple pictures and maps by using the minimum number of colors—is easy to act on in the classroom. Young children spend a lot of time coloring pictures. After they understand the notion of *fewest*, coloring can turn into a mathematical activity. Ask your students to color a simple picture or map so that any two regions that share a border are different colors. Then give them another copy of the picture or map, and ask them to color it with as few colors as possible. Start with pictures that have fewer than four regions and build up to pictures that are more complex, showing twelve to fifteen regions. Such activities help introduce students to geometric ideas, including *next to*, *border*, *region*, and *inside* (that is, the space to color). These activities also introduce students to the mathematical notion of minimization (that is, the use of the fewest), a concept that is related to the activity in which students find the shortest path.

Chapter 4, "Vertex-Edge Graphs in Grades 3–5," discusses similar but more advanced map-coloring activities and includes activities related to coloring the vertices of vertex-edge graphs. Teachers of prekindergarten–grade 2 should review those activities before introducing age-appropriate ones to their students. A look at the activities in the next chapter can highlight the links between coloring and vertex-edge graphs.

With assistance, even students who are quite young can work with the applet Graph Creator to build and manipulate vertex-edge graphs. They can use the vertex button to draw vertices and the edge button to draw edges. Once they have constructed a graph, they can color its vertices, or they can use the arrow button to move them so that they can obtain a different drawing of the same graph or determine whether this graph is the same as or different from another graph.

From Here to There

The investigation From Here to There consists of four activities that introduce the properties and characteristics of vertex-edge graphs to students in prekindergarten–grade 2. You can use this sequence of activities to acquaint your students with a variety of ideas associated with vertex-edge graphs. You can also alter each activity slightly so that it becomes simpler or more complex to suit the needs of specific groups of students. Suggestions in the text help you adapt each activity to your students.

Goals

- Build and explore vertex-edge graphs by using concrete materials
- Explore simple properties of graphs, such as the numbers of vertices and edges
- Use graphs to solve problems related to paths, circuits, and networks in concrete settings
- Follow and create simple sets of directions related to building and using graphs
- Informally explore the notion of "the best," in the context of finding the shortest path

Materials and Equipment

Activity 1—Islands and Bridges

For demonstration—

- Four paper plates, each with a picture of a different fruit (an apple, a banana, a cherry, or a date) drawn or pasted on it
- Five hand-drawn paper or poster board "bridges" to connect the plates together, as shown in figure 3.2 (or strips of plain paper or poster board)

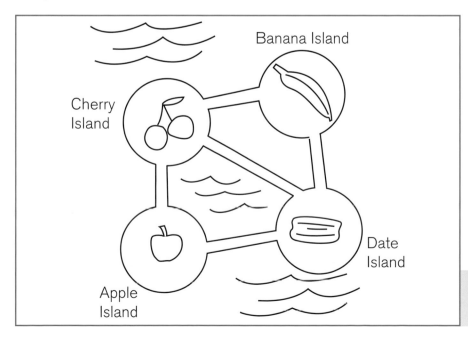

In the imaginary world of activity 1, the islands are named for fruits—Apple Island, Banana Island, Cherry Island, and Date Island. The alphabetical names facilitate consideration of vertices A, B, C, and D later. However, if your students are unfamiliar with dates, select another fruit.

Fig. **3.2.**

Five bridges connecting four islands

For each team of three or four students—

- Five paper plates (different colors—red, green, white, blue, and yellow—or white plates colored with crayons to give these colors), with the outside edges removed to let them lie flat, or five circles cut from construction paper in the different colors
- Eight four-foot lengths of string
- Colored chips or cubes to use as markers

Activity 2—Let Me Count the Paths

pp. 174–75

The text discusses a graph whose vertices are a school, a playground, a water park, a roller-skating rink, and a tire park, and the blackline master "Graphics for Five Sites" includes sample pictures for these sites. However, using familiar local sites can increase your students' interest in the activity.

For demonstration—

- A sheet of easel paper, labeled "Paths from School to _____," with the blank filled in with the name of a familiar after-school play site (or simply "Playground")

For each group of students—

- Five paper plates, each showing the name (or a picture) of one of five sites—your school plus four different play sites where your students might want to go after school (or the sites pictured on the blackline master "Graphics for Five Sites")
- A roll of masking tape
- Three sheets of easel paper, each labeled "Paths from School to _____," with the blank filled in with the name of a different play site (or "Water Park," "Roller-Skating Rink," or "Tire Park")

Activity 3—The Best Paths for After-School Fun

pp. 176, 177

For each group of students—

- A plastic bag containing thirty-three "traffic lights" (each should be 1 1/2 inches by 3 inches and can be made from a green, a yellow, and a red linking cube or three small circles of those colors pasted on a white rectangle)
- A copy of the blackline master "How to Place the Traffic Lights on Your Graph"
- Four large arrows, each made from one rectangular piece of 4-by-22-inch poster board and one triangular piece of poster board large enough to serve as an arrowhead

For each student—

- Four copies of the activity sheet "Paths from School to _____," each with the blank filled in with the name of a different familiar play site (or "Playground," "Water Park," "Roller-Skating Rink," or "Tire Park")

Activity 4—Having All the Fun after School

p. 178

For each student—

- One copy of the activity sheet "Circuits That Visit All the Play Sites"

Prior Knowledge

Students should be able to—

- distinguish and count objects;
- determine the number of objects in a set of up to twenty-five objects by counting the objects one at a time; and
- compare and order whole numbers to determine, for example, whether one number is less than or greater than another.

Activities

In the four activities in the investigation, the students work in groups and discover ideas associated with vertex-edge graphs. In activity 1, Islands and Bridges, they make large vertex-edge graphs on the floor and explore simple properties of the graphs, such as the number of edges, the number of vertices, and the number of ways to travel from a vertex (that is, the degree of a vertex). In activity 2, Let Me Count the Paths, the students enumerate the number of different ways to travel between two locations. In activity 3, The Best Paths for After-School Fun, they determine which of the possible paths that they found in the previous activity provides the "best" path from school to a play site. Finally, in activity 4, Having All the Fun after School, they find the best route that starts at school, visits all the play sites, and then returns to the school. The investigation From Here to There is intended to give young students a first exposure to ideas of vertex-edge graphs, so no preliminary activities are necessary as preparation for these activities.

Activity 1—Islands and Bridges

In this activity, students build vertex-edge graphs and explore their properties. The activity does not introduce the terms *vertex* and *edge* immediately but prepares students to encounter them a little later.

Begin by displaying on the floor four "islands," as shown in figure 3.2, separated by about three feet and connected by five "bridges," as shown in the figure. Make the islands from paper plates, and on each, draw or paste a picture of a different fruit (apple, banana, cherry, or date). Hand-draw bridges on paper or poster board, or use blank strips of one or the other to represent bridges. Your display can be fanciful, perhaps with bridges like that in the margin, or it can be plain and simple.

Ask the students to imagine that the classroom floor is a big lake with four islands and that the only way to travel from one island to another island is to walk across one or more bridges. Ask for a volunteer to show the class how to proceed from Apple Island (the plate with the picture of an apple) to Banana Island (the plate with the picture of a banana). Ask for another volunteer who can show a different way of getting from Apple Island to Banana Island. If the students are eager to give more answers, you can allow four students to provide different routes from Apple Island to Banana Island.

First, have the students walk through their routes themselves, and then ask for a volunteer to provide directions from Apple Island to Banana Island for another student to follow. For example, the student offering directions might say, "Start at Apple Island, then walk to

A kindergarten student walks along the bridge from Apple Island to Banana Island.

Photo by Colette DeLeo; all rights reserved

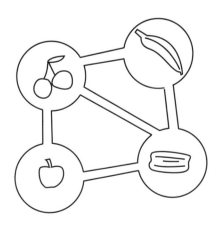

Cherry Island, then to Date Island, and then to Banana Island." Ask the student to pause after each instruction until the student who is following directions has carried it out.

Next, ask the students whether anyone can find a route that goes from Apple Island to all the other islands and then back to Apple Island. Many routes are possible, so you may be able to invite each student in your class to show his or her route or to provide directions for another student to carry out. You can allow students to give duplicate solutions.

Explain to the students that they may use the same bridge twice. However, if you are teaching second graders, wait until all the students have presented their routes, and then ask whether any routes take someone from Apple Island to all the other islands and then back to Apple Island without crossing any bridge more than once. Two such routes exist—Apple Island to Cherry Island to Banana Island to Date Island to Apple Island and Apple Island to Date Island to Banana Island to Cherry Island to Apple Island—and the second of these routes is just the reverse of the first. Second graders may be able to reason that there are no other routes by recognizing, for example, that if they go from Apple to Cherry to Date (instead of Banana), and then to Banana, they have to repeat at least one bridge to return to Apple Island.

Divide the class into groups of three or four students, and announce that each group will now build its own make-believe world of islands and bridges. Give every group five paper plates in red, green, white, blue, and yellow (or five circles cut from construction paper in five colors) to represent the islands. Also give each group eight pieces of string, each about four feet long, to represent bridges. Assign each group a section of floor space, and ask the students to arrange all their islands on the floor (not too close together) and insert some or all of their bridges to connect them. Tell the students that they must connect all the islands so that they can walk across bridges from any island to any

Photo by Colette DeLeo; all rights reserved

A group of kindergarten students builds a make-believe world of islands and bridges, with long strips of construction paper representing the bridges.

other island. However, they can do this by creating as many bridges as they want—they do not have to use all the pieces of string. The only restriction is that the bridges must not cross one another.

After all the groups have completed this task, have the entire class visit each group's display. Ask one student from each group to talk about its make-believe island world and the number of bridges that the group used. Have a group member walk through a route that begins at one island, visits each of the other islands, and returns to the original island. Alternatively, for some groups, ask a group member to provide directions to someone who is not in that group and let him or her walk the route.

Can the students always begin at one island, visit all other islands, and return to the first island? If the group members have followed the instruction that they must connect all the islands, the answer to that question is yes. Later in the chapter, "The Mathematics in the Investigation" discusses what happens if a teacher does not give that instruction or the students ignore it.

This later section also addresses the question, Can students always begin at one island, visit all other islands, and return to the first island without crossing any bridge twice? Not necessarily. However, if students ask the question or announce that they have already crossed a particular bridge, you can tell them that completing the route without crossing a bridge a second time is sometimes impossible.

If you do this activity with a larger number of islands and bridges—perhaps as a follow-up activity or with older students—it may be difficult for students to keep track of the sites that they have already visited. You can, however, provide the students with colored chips or cubes that they can leave on each island as they visit it so that they can keep track of where they have been.

Next, ask each student to stand on an island and count the number of different bridges that he or she can choose to walk over to leave the island and reach another island. Ask each student to report his or her answer in turn by saying, "My island has __ bridges" and then counting out the bridges from that island. Ask all students whose islands have one bridge to raise a hand, then all whose islands have two bridges, then all whose islands have three bridges, then all whose islands have four bridges, and so on. While each student is raising his or her hand, count the number of students—or have a student count them—and announce, for example, "There are five students whose islands have four bridges."

At this point, you can introduce the mathematical terminology *vertex* and *edge*. Explain that mathematicians have to deal with connections all the time—sometimes bridges connect islands, wires connect computers, streets connect buildings, highways connect cities. In fact, mathematicians deal with connections whenever they have a collection of objects that they want to link together. Mathematicians have created a model that they can use to describe all these situations. The special name for this model is *vertex-edge graph*. A vertex-edge graph consists of two different kinds of objects—vertices and edges. Just as the bridges connect the islands, the edges connect the vertices. Little circles can represent vertices, just as this activity uses round paper plates to represent islands. Lines represent edges, just as this activity uses string (or strips of paper or whatever) to represent bridges. The edges do not have to be straight lines; they can be curved or wiggly, just like the string bridges in the activity.

Draw the graph in figure 3.3 for your students to see, and explain that it shows one possible way of drawing a vertex-edge graph to represent the islands and bridges that they worked with originally. Sketch the network shown in figure 3.2. Explain that when mathematicians want to talk about a specific vertex, they often use a capital letter of the alphabet. Point out that in the vertex-edge graph, each letter stands for the name of an island—*A* stands for Apple Island, *B* stands for Banana Island, *C* stands for Cherry Island, and *D* stands for Date Island. Also point out that the vertex-edge graph looks similar to the pattern of islands and bridges in your sketch. For each island, a vertex appears in the graph, which also has a corresponding edge for each bridge. You can say, for example, "An edge joins vertices *A* and *D* just as a bridge joins Apple Island and Date Island." Also note that no bridge joins Apple Island to Banana Island, and no edge connects vertices *A* and *B* in the vertex-edge graph.

Mathematicians have a special name for two vertices that are connected by an edge—they call them *neighbors*. In the make-believe island worlds, two islands are neighbors if a bridge joins them. To illustrate this relationship, select one group and ask each member to stand on a different vertex. Have all your students gather around the graph and elicit other volunteers to stand on each unoccupied vertex until every vertex has someone standing on it. Ask one of these students to shake hands with each of his or her neighbors and say, "Hi, neighbor." As the handshakes take place, have the rest of the class count this student's total number of handshakes aloud. After the student has finished shaking hands with all his or her neighbors, ask how many neighbors he or she has. Repeat this process for each student who is standing on a vertex of the graph.

Next, ask each student to count the number of bridges that his or her island has and tell the class that number. Ask the students what they

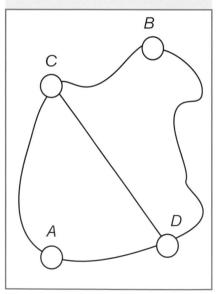

Fig. **3.3.**

A graph that represents figure 3.2. Vertex *A* and vertex *C* are neighbors. What other vertices are neighbors of *A*?

Navigating through Discrete Mathematics in Pre-K–Grade 5

Photo by Colette DeLeo; all rights reserved

Each student standing on a vertex is holding hands (or touching feet) with all of his or her neighbors.

notice about the number of neighbors and the number of bridges. Some students will say that for their island, the number of neighbors is the same as the number of bridges, and some students will report that their islands have more bridges than neighbors. First, ask students to explain why they have the same number of neighbors as bridges. They will say that each bridge goes to a different neighbor, so the number of bridges is the same as the number of neighbors.

All your students may have an equal number of bridges and neighbors; however, if a group connects two islands with more than one bridge, the number of neighbors of each of those islands is less than the number of bridges leaving those islands. In figure 3.4, a graph that could represent your students' islands and bridges, two edges connect vertex A to vertex B. As a result, the number of neighbors of vertex A (three) is smaller than the number of its edges, which is four. However, if only one edge may connect two vertices in a graph, then the number of edges coming out of any vertex is the same as the number of its neighbors.

In a second-grade class, you may want to introduce the term *degree*, a special name for the number of bridges coming out of an island—or the

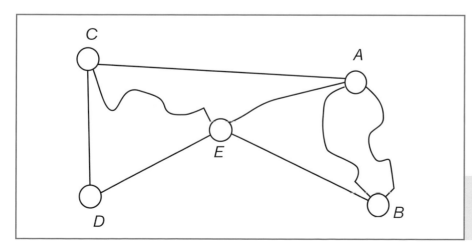

Fig. **3.4.**

Vertex A has three four edges but only three neighbors, B, C, and E.

Working with vertex-edge graphs supports learning related to Curriculum Focal Points for pre-K–grade 2. Young students develop an understanding of whole numbers, counting, and comparison while they design and build vertex-edge graphs, count the numbers of vertices and edges, tell how many neighbors the vertices have, and compare the numbers of neighbors for all the vertices.

number of edges coming out of a vertex. Then the students can raise their hands to indicate their responses to questions similar to the following:

- "Whose island has degree 3?"
- "Whose island has degree 4?"
- "How many islands have degree 2?"

Activity 1 is appropriate for any grade level from prekindergarten through second grade. In addition, you can use it as an initial activity for students in higher grades. You can ask younger students to replicate the graph in figure 3.2 before asking them to make their own graphs. You can also repeat the first part of this activity by using other simple graphs. Examples include removing the bridge joining Cherry Island and Date Island or replacing that bridge with one joining Apple Island and Banana Island. You can ask older students to build graphs that use a larger number of vertices and edges.

Activity 2—Let Me Count the Paths

Before beginning activity 2, students should be familiar with the graph properties discussed in activity 1. In activity 2, they work in groups with the vertex-edge graph shown in figure 3.5 or one like it but with vertices representing different sites. You can vary the names of the sites to include local sites that your students know well. Make one large copy of the graph on the floor for each group of four students. Use paper plates as vertices and strips of masking tape as edges. Label the plates with appropriate sites, or use pictures if your students cannot yet read; figure 3.6 shows a graph with pictorial icons.

Fig. **3.5.**

Use paper plates and masking tape to create the graph on the floor.

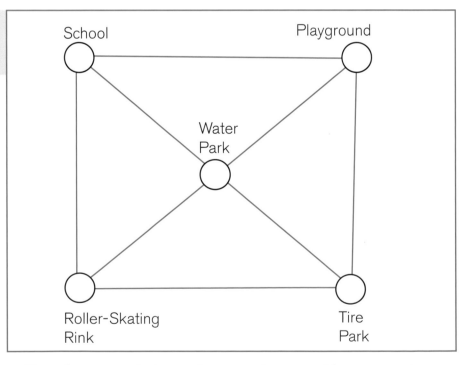

If you have enough time and your students are able, you can give them the materials and ask them to work together in groups to build the graph themselves. Although students can connect the sites by using the pieces of string from activity 1, masking tape allows them to make

Navigating through Discrete Mathematics in Pre-K–Grade 5

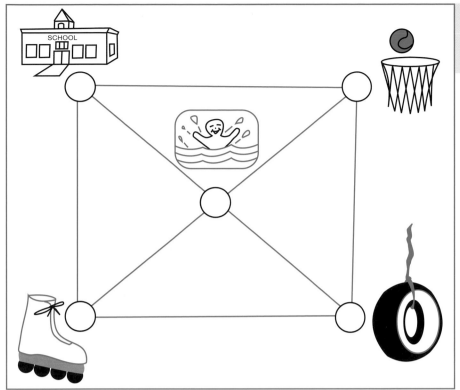

Fig. **3.6.**

Students who do not read can use a pictorial version of the graph.

the straight, flat edges that they need for activity 3. The graphs should be large enough for the students to walk through, so they should place the vertices on the floor first. After you verify that the vertices are far enough apart, have the students insert the edges by placing the tape on the floor from vertex to vertex.

Gather your students around one of the graphs. Review a few properties of graphs by asking how many vertices and edges are in the graph. The students should respond that it includes five vertices and eight edges. Have a student stand on the vertex labeled "School," and ask questions such as the following, which name the play sites identified in figure 3.5:

- "In how many different ways can a person leave the vertex labeled 'School'?" (Three)
- "What is the degree of vertex labeled 'School'?" (degree 3)
- "In how many different ways can a person leave the vertex labeled 'Water Park'?" (Four)
- "What is the degree of that vertex?" (degree 4)
- "In how many different ways can a person leave the vertex labeled 'Playground'?" (Three)
- "What is the degree of that vertex?" (degree 3)

Explain the scenario for this activity: The students can choose from the four play sites the one where they wish to play after school. (With younger children, you can start with a simpler situation. For example, instead of using the graph in figure 3.6, you can use the graph in figure 3.3, with the school at C, for example, and play sites at A, D, and B.)

Tell the students that a different bus will leave the school and go to each play site, where the students' parents will pick them up at five

The graphs should be large enough for the students to walk through, so they should place the vertices on the floor first.

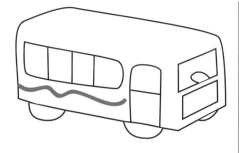

o'clock. In figure 3.5, for example, what routes can the bus driver use when driving from the school to the playground? In vertex-edge graph terminology, this question becomes, "What paths in the graph start at the vertex labeled 'School' and end at the vertex labeled 'Playground'?"

Work with the entire class to find as many different ways as possible to go from the school to the play site whose location in your graph corresponds to the vertex labeled "Playground" in figure 3.5. Ask a number of students to walk through the graph while they suggest different paths, or have them provide directions while other students walk through the graph. As the students make suggestions, post a list of all paths that they find—even those that repeat a previous suggestion—on the sheet of easel paper that you have headed "Paths from School to _____," with the name of the play site filling the blank. The bold edges in figure 3.7 show one possible path for the graph in figure 3.5. Depending on the reading level of your students, you may wish to post these paths by using pictures instead of words or by using a capital letter to represent each word, such as *S* for "school," *P* for "playground," and so on. Figure 3.7 shows three ways to describe the path shown in bold.

Fig. **3.7.**

Three ways to describe the path shown in bold from the school

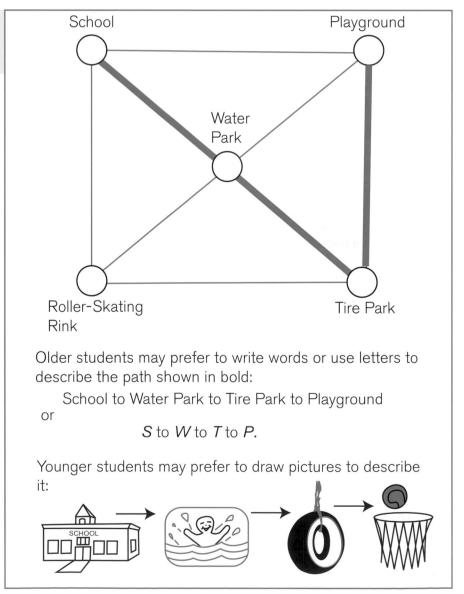

Older students may prefer to write words or use letters to describe the path shown in bold:

School to Water Park to Tire Park to Playground
or
S to *W* to *T* to *P*.

Younger students may prefer to draw pictures to describe it:

The students should make progress toward listing all the possible paths that proceed from one location to another, although doing so should certainly not be the focus of the lesson. Nor should teachers expect young students to find all the paths. Whenever the students think that they have found all the paths, ask them whether any two paths on the list are the same. Then eliminate duplicate paths so that only one statement of each path remains on the list. Ask the students whether they can find any other paths that are not on the list. Add their suggestions. When you have removed all duplicate paths and inserted any additional ones, explain that this list shows all the different possible routes that the class could find from the school to the site in question. For the graph in figure 3.5, the eight different routes from the school to the playground are as follows:

- School to playground

- School to water park to playground

- School to water park to tire park to playground

- School to water park to roller-skating rink to tire park to playground

- School to roller-skating rink to water park to playground

- School to roller-skating rink to tire park to playground

- School to roller-skating rink to water park to tire park to playground

- School to roller-skating rink to tire park to water park to playground

Students working with this graph might also suggest the following route: school to water park to tire park to water park to playground. If so, take the opportunity to ask the students to consider whether they should count that route. A student in second grade (or even first grade) might say that a route like that one would be foolish—the bus driver would be wasting time going back over a section of road that he or she had already traveled. In fact, if the students counted this route, then they could also count routes in which the driver went back and forth twice between the water park and the tire park, routes in which the driver went back and forth three times, or even routes in which the driver went back and forth ten times. There would then be infinitely many routes from school to playground, just as there are infinitely many whole numbers.

Divide the students into three groups, and ask each group to move to one of the graphs in the room. Assign each group a play site other than the one that the students have just investigated, and provide each group with a sheet of easel paper labeled "Paths from School to _____," with the name of the new play site filled in (or the name of one of the other play sites in fig. 3.5: "Water Park," "Roller-Skating Rink" or "Tire Park").

Ask the students in each group to work together to find all possible paths from the school to their assigned play site. After all the groups have completed their work, review each list with the entire class. You can ask such questions as the following:

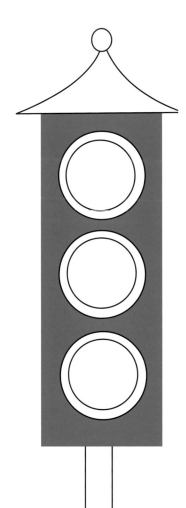

- "Are any paths repeated?"
- "Can anyone add a different path to the list?"
- "How many different routes did you find?"
- "How do you know that you have found all routes?"

(In a graph labeled as in fig. 3.5, seven routes are possible from the school to the water park, eight routes are possible from the school to the roller-skating rink, and nine routes are possible from the school to the tire park.)

Save these lists. In activity 3, the students will use them to determine the path that provides the best route to each location.

Activity 3—The Best Paths for After-School Fun

Finding the best path in a graph depends on what the word *best* means in a particular context. For example, the best path can be the route that provides the quickest travel time, the most interesting scenery, the shortest distance, the smallest amount of traffic, or the fewest traffic lights. This activity defines the *best path* as the one with the fewest traffic lights.

In activity 3, the students work again with the graphs from activity 2 after placing traffic lights on each strip of masking tape representing an edge. Then they walk through each path on their group's graph, counting the traffic lights.

To prepare for the activity, you should make "traffic lights" from linking cubes or colored paper, as described in the materials list. Make enough for each group of students to have at least as many traffic lights as you decide to draw on the blackline master "How to Place the Traffic Lights on Your Graph." The blackline master includes instructions for teachers, and figure 3.8 shows an arrangement of thirty-two lights—an appropriate number for students in grade 2. You will probably decide to draw fewer lights on "maps" for younger students. Make one copy of your map for each group, and place it in a plastic bag along with the group's traffic lights. In addition, for each student, prepare a four-page set of activity sheets from the blackline master "Paths from School to _____," with the name of a different play site (or "Playground," "Water Park," "Roller-Skating Rink," or "Tire Park") filled in on each sheet.

To get the students started on the activity, post the chart that you created on easel paper in activity 2—"Paths from School to _____" (with the blank showing the name of whatever site you used). Give each student a copy of the activity sheet "Paths from School to _____" for this site. The sheet includes a table for the students to complete. Ask each student to copy all the paths listed on the easel paper onto the activity sheet. Assign the students to groups to work on the graphs on the floor and ask them to bring their copies of the activity sheet with them.

Provide each group with a plastic bag of traffic lights and the map showing the placement of the lights that you have determined in advance. Ask students to place the traffic lights on their graphs according to the picture that they see. Have students count out loud the number of traffic lights on each edge in their map and then count out loud again while they place each traffic light along an edge of the graph on

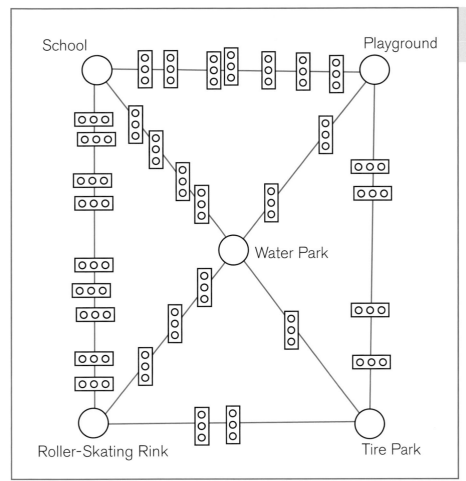

Fig. **3.8.**

Traffic lights along the edges of the graph

the floor. This process will help them place the correct number of traffic lights on each edge.

Explain that the graph now shows the number of traffic lights that a bus driver must pass through to travel from one location to the next. For example, figure 3.8 shows seven traffic lights along the edge from the school to the playground. Notice that four traffic lights are along the edge that joins the playground and the tire park. Thus, if a bus driver wants to go from the school to the tire park by using the route that passes the playground, he or she needs to pass through 7 + 4, or a total of 11, traffic lights. If students working with the graph in figure 3.8 are asked how many traffic lights are on the route from the roller-skating rink to the water park, they should respond that three traffic lights are along that route.

Tell the students that bus drivers like to avoid stopping at a lot of traffic lights and that the students' task is to help the drivers find the best route to take. The first bus driver whom they will help is the one whose route goes from the school to the play site named on the easel paper. Work with the entire class to find the number of traffic lights along the first path listed on the paper. Ask the students to find the total number of traffic lights at which the bus driver may have to stop if the bus travels that route. Have a student from each group walk along each edge of this path on the group's graph and count out all the traffic lights that he or she passes along the way. For example, suppose that a student is traveling on the path from the school to the water park to the

Bus drivers like to avoid stopping at a lot of traffic lights, so the students' task is to help the drivers find the best route to take.

The direct route is not always the best route, depending on what best means in the situation.

playground in the graph in figure 3.8. The student would count four traffic lights along the edge from the school to the water park, and then two more traffic lights along the edge from the water park to the playground, for a total of six traffic lights. Have your students write their counts in the corresponding space on the activity sheet. Ask each group of students to work together to discover how many traffic lights are along each path on their lists and then decide which of these paths is the best one.

While the students are working on paths to the first site, give four large arrows to each group. After each group decides which path is the best, a student should place an arrow on top of each edge that belongs to this path. For example, in figure 3.8, the best route from the school to the playground passes through the water park. This route has six traffic lights, which is the smallest number for any route from the school to the playground, so the bus driver should take it to get to the playground.

When all the groups have finished, ask the students to look at each group's graph and review the work. Discuss the similarities and differences among the graphs. Did each group identify the same path as the best? If necessary, explain that students can find the best path by adding the number of traffic lights on each edge in that path. Repeat this activity to find the best path from the school to each of the other play sites, giving the students the appropriate activity sheet for each one.

Students inspecting a graph with the traffic lights and vertices shown in figure 3.8 might observe that the best route from the school to the water park is the direct route. Although they would be correct in this example, the direct route is not always the best one. For instance, the direct route from the school to the playground in the figure is not as effective in minimizing traffic lights as the route that passes by the water park. If the students had to explain why the best route from the school to the water park is the direct route, they might say that any other route from the school to the water park must go first to the playground, which involves seven traffic lights, or it must go first to the roller-skating rink, which involves nine traffic lights, so such paths would not be better than the direct route, which involves only four traffic lights.

No matter how the students allocated the traffic lights, the direct route would in fact be best for at least one of the three sites to which there is a direct route from the school. In this situation, the direct route to the water park is the best route, but the direct route to a different site could have been best. Another possibility is that the best route to every one of those three sites is the direct route—for example, if each of those edges has the same number of traffic lights.

To extend your students' work in activity 3, you might ask each team to reallocate its traffic lights among the different edges and repeat the problem. Or you might ask each team to design and build its own graph, pose its own best-path problems, and then give the problems to the other teams to solve.

You can make this lesson easier for prekindergarten students by creating a simpler graph (that is, a graph that has a smaller number of vertices or a smaller number of edges), as well as by using a smaller number of traffic lights on each edge for the children to count. Creating a more complicated graph that includes more vertices or edges can make the activity more difficult for older students.

This activity is appropriate for students who can count but who are not yet able to add single-digit numbers. You can make the lesson more difficult for students who can add by increasing the number of traffic lights on the edges, by assigning to the edges numbers that are larger whole numbers, or by moving from the traffic-light model to one in which the number on the edge represents the distance traveled or the time taken. The numbers on the edges then do not need to be whole numbers. In such situations, the numbers assigned to the edges are called *weights*, a neutral term that in various circumstances can represent time, distance, cost, or another quantity.

Activity 4—Having All the Fun after School

Suppose that in the scenario some students want to visit all four play sites and then return to the school. What would be the best way for them to travel to all those sites? In activity 4, your students investigate that question by returning to the graphs with traffic lights on the edges that they created in activity 3. This time they need to determine all the possible routes that start at the school, visit each of the four play sites, and return to the school. Again, they are looking for the best path, defined as the path with the fewest traffic lights, but now they are looking for a specific type of path—one that begins and ends at the same location. Mathematicians use the term *circuit* for a path that begins and ends at the same vertex.

Give each student a copy of the activity sheet "Circuits That Visit All the Play Sites." This activity sheet includes a table for students to complete while they look for the best circuit that starts and ends at the school. For each route, the students determine the total number of traffic lights. Finally, they compare the numbers of lights for all the possible circuits to determine the circuit that has the minimum number of traffic lights.

The Mathematics in the Investigation

This investigation introduces young students to the basic concepts and properties of vertex-edge graphs and some of their elementary applications. The students first encounter vertex-edge graphs as a make-believe world of islands and bridges that they can walk across to travel from one island to another. In the course of the investigation, they learn basic terminology—*vertex, edge, neighbor, degree of a vertex, path,* and *circuit*—and they try to find all paths that take them from one vertex to a specified second vertex without revisiting any vertex between the two.

The investigation introduces the notion of a best path between two vertices by assigning a weight to each edge—the number of traffic lights—and by defining the best path as the one with the smallest weight—that is, the minimum number of traffic lights. Students who may not yet be able to add can find the best route by counting the traffic lights while they traverse each path. The number of routes is small, so students can do an exhaustive search and compare numbers. They also find the best route that starts at a given vertex, visits all the other vertices, and returns to the initial vertex.

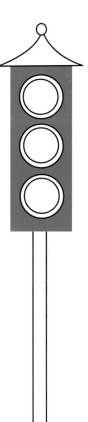

Activity 3, The Best Paths for After-School Fun, introduces students at an elementary level to the shortest-path problem. As the students work on activity 4, Having All the Fun after School, they encounter the traveling salesman problem in the simplified context of visiting a number of sites before returning to school. This problem arises in many contexts but takes its name from the context in which a sales representative has to visit a number of sites before returning to the company's office. At the time when the problem received its name, all traveling sales representatives were male.

The problems discussed in this investigation link to real-life examples. People deal with a shortest-path problem each time that they have to travel from one site to another, and parents deal with a traveling salesperson problem each time that they organize a car pool. The answer to the traveling salesperson problem can determine the best way for the host to drop off five children at their homes after a birthday party and then return home.

Working on the investigation may also prompt a discussion of *connected graphs* and *disconnected graphs*. In activity 1, some students may create a network of islands and bridges that is not connected. For example, students who use only three bridges may create a graph that looks like the one in figure 3.9. Students who use four bridges may create a graph that looks like that in figure 3.10. Even though you ask the students to be sure to connect all the islands, they may ignore that instruction and arrive at something that looks like figure 3.9, or they may create a situation like the one in figure 3.10 and claim that they have indeed followed the instructions since bridges connect each island in figure 3.10 to another island.

In such a case, you can introduce the notion of *connectedness*. Even if the question does not arise, you may want to discuss the notion during the investigation. The basic idea is that in a connected graph, every two vertices are connected by a path. More formally, a graph is connected if a path exists from each vertex to every other vertex. In a connected graph, someone can travel from any vertex to any other vertex. Figures 3.9 and 3.10 are examples of graphs that are disconnected. Some disconnected graphs have a vertex of degree 0—that means, of course, that

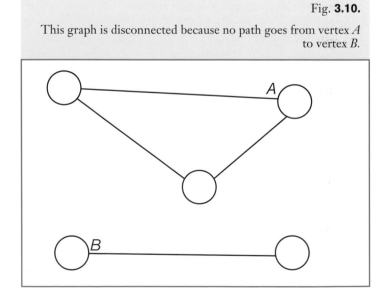

Fig. 3.9.

One vertex is not connected to the others.

Fig. 3.10.

This graph is disconnected because no path goes from vertex *A* to vertex *B*.

72

Navigating through Discrete Mathematics in Pre-K–Grade 5

no bridge leads out of the island, as in figure 3.9. In figure 3.10, no vertex has degree 0. However, the graph is still disconnected, since no path connects vertex A to vertex B.

Sometimes students may have difficulty determining whether a graph is connected or disconnected. For example, the graph in figure 3.11 is connected; a path leads from any of the five vertices of this five-pointed star to any other vertex. However, the graph in figure 3.12 is disconnected; despite appearances, no path exists from vertex A to vertex B. This graph has only six vertices; there are no vertices where the lines cross.

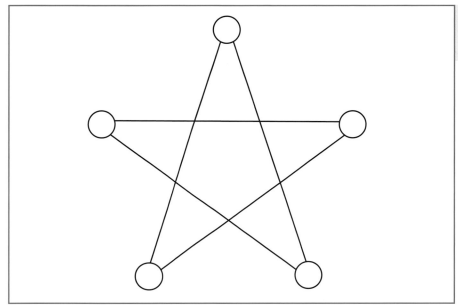

Fig. **3.11.**

A connected graph

Of course, it is possible to add a vertex at each crossing, but the result would be a different graph, one with twelve vertices. You can visualize the graph in figure 3.12 as one triangle on top of another. Chapter 4, "Vertex-Edge Graphs in Grades 3–5," explores these ideas further.

A student who asks during activity 1 whether it is possible to visit all the islands without repeating any bridges is raising another kind of connectedness issue. Consider, for example, the graph in figure 3.13. Suppose that this graph represents two groups of islands, East Islandia (consisting of the vertex A and the vertices and edges to its right) and West Islandia (consisting of vertex B and the vertices and edges to its left). The only way of getting from one group of islands to the other is to use the bridge that connects vertex A with vertex B. Someone who starts in one island group and uses that bridge to go to the other island group has no way to return to the

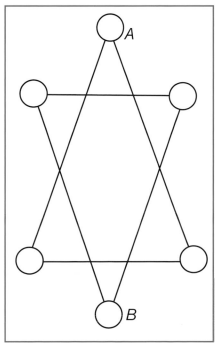

Fig. **3.12.**

The graph is disconnected because no path goes from vertex A to vertex B.

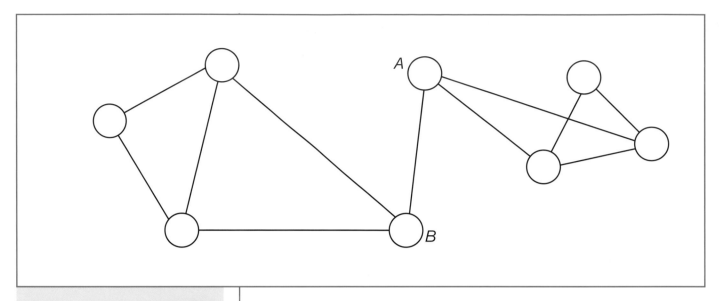

Fig. **3.13.**

Removing the edge that joins vertex
A to vertex *B* makes the graph
disconnected.

first island group except by crossing that bridge a second time. Likewise, the make-believe islands that the students construct may have a bridge that is the only link between two portions of a graph. A vertex-edge graph that has no such edge is *strongly connected*. Removing the edge joining *A* and *B* in figure 3.13 results in a disconnected graph. This property makes it an important edge. However, in a strongly connected graph, removing any edge will yield a new graph that is still connected. Students can have fun determining whether such an edge exists in a graph. If your class is ready for such an exploration, see activity 1 in chapter 4. The elementary concepts introduced in the activities in this chapter's investigation lay a foundation for the more advanced ideas in the next chapter.

NAVIGATING *through* DISCRETE MATHEMATICS

Chapter 4
Vertex-Edge Graphs in Grades 3–5

All students in grades 3–5 should—

- *draw vertex-edge graphs to represent concrete situations;*

- *investigate simple properties and features of graphs, such as vertex degrees and edge weights, and explore ways to manipulate two graphs physically to determine whether they are the "same";*

- *use graphs to solve problems related to paths, circuits, and networks in concrete and abstract settings;*

- *color maps and color the vertices of a graph by using the minimum number of colors, as an introduction to the general problem of avoiding conflicts;*

- *follow, devise, and describe step-by-step procedures related to working with graphs;*

- *analyze graph-related problems to find the "best" solution.*

Students in grades 3–5 should extend their earlier explorations with vertex-edge graphs to learn that they can model many real-life situations by using vertex-edge graphs. They should begin to understand that a vertex-edge graph can be an appropriate mathematical model in situations in which they want to focus on the relationships among a set of objects.

If your students have not previously encountered vertex-edge graphs, you may want to review the activities introduced in chapter 3 and adjust them for a more advanced grade level. Before presenting the activities in chapter 4, allow your students opportunities to build vertex-edge graphs, to count their numbers of vertices and edges, to explore their simple properties (for example, identifying the number of neighbors at a vertex), and to solve simple problems (for instance, finding the shortest path between two vertices in a small graph). These early experiences can help reinforce basic skills such as counting, learning addition facts, and following directions and can also help students develop combinatorial thinking while they try to find all the different paths from one vertex to another. The activities in chapter 4 focus on modeling and solving problems in grades 3–5 by using two main features of graphs—coloring and paths.

Vertex coloring, often referred to simply as *coloring*, assigns colors to the vertices of the graph, with the property that adjacent, or neighboring, vertices—that is, two vertices that are connected by an edge—are different colors. Vertex coloring can model many ordinary situations and help solve a variety of real-world problems.

For example, a planner can simplify the problem of scheduling meeting times for several committees by creating and then coloring a graph whose vertices represent the different committees. The planner draws an edge to join two committees if they have a member in common. A coloring of the graph assigns different colors to adjacent vertices or, in this case, to two committees that have a member in common. Assigning different colors to these committees means that they must meet at different times. The coloring allows the planner to create a schedule that indicates when the committees can meet. A planner who wants each of the committees to meet in the morning or afternoon of a two-day period—that is, in one of four time slots—is essentially asking whether a coloring that uses no more than four colors is possible.

Other real-life situations that can be analyzed by using graph coloring include—

- installing lights at traffic intersections, with the vertices representing streams of traffic and the edges representing conflicts between streams;

- setting up fish tanks, with the vertices representing species of fish and the edges representing conflicts among species;

- designing maps, with the vertices representing regions (for example, states, countries, or counties) and the edges representing common borders.

Finding paths through vertex-edge graphs can model many other everyday situations—situations in which the goal is to identify a route that achieves a particular purpose. Problems that students can analyze by using paths in graphs include the following:

- Can a newspaper carrier find a route that travels along each road within a certain territory exactly once? If not, what route will involve the fewest repetitions of roads?

- Can a traffic-light inspector find a route that visits each traffic light within a certain territory exactly once? If not, what route involves the fewest repetitions of lights?

- Can a school bus driver find the shortest way to go to pick up a number of children and deliver them safely to the school. (Chapter 3 discusses this question at the pre-K–grade 2 level, and chapters 3 and 4 of the companion volume [Hart et al. 2008] discuss the topic at the middle school and high school levels.)

One recommendation related to vertex-edge graphs for students in grades 3–5 that this chapter does not address at length is that students investigate simple concepts involving graphs—such as degrees of vertices, subgraphs, and weights of edges. To implement this recommendation, you can begin by having your students complete activity 3, The Best Path for After-School Fun, in chapter 3. That activity uses a graph to model play sites that students might visit after school. Each vertex represents a location, and each edge represents a road that they can use for traveling between locations. The activity adds weights—in this case, traffic lights—on the edges of the graph. Figure 3.8 shows the weighted graph that the activity uses to introduce young students to the concept of a *weighted graph*—that is, a graph in which a number,

For more ideas about vertex coloring, see "Graphs, Colors, and Chromatic Numbers" (Hamberg 1998; available on the CD-ROM).

called its *weight*, appears on each edge. When students understand how to add whole numbers, you can place any whole number (or fraction or decimal number) on each edge in a graph to represent the weight of that edge. This weight may represent many things, including the length of the road, the time needed to travel the road, or the cost to repave the road. Figure 4.1 shows the same weighted graph but uses numbers to represent the weights. This more abstract version of the graph is appropriate for students who are more mature mathematically.

You can also ask students in grades 3–5 to find different ways to connect all the vertices by using the minimum number of edges (for one example, see the bold edges of the graph in figure 4.2). There are many ways to select four edges that link all the vertices together in a network. Have your students explore all the possible ways of making such connections in a graph, and ask them to verify the number of traffic lights along all the roads in each of these possible networks (in this example, 4 + 7 + 4 + 2 = 17). Ask your students to find a network for which the total weight is as small as possible. This network consists of the bold edges in the graph in figure 4.3, and these edges have a total weight of 4 + 2 + 1 + 2 = 9. Such problems furnish a wonderful way of having your students work on their addition facts. Simply change the graph and the types of numbers on the edges to reinforce the type of addition facts that the class is learning.

You can also build students' skills by inviting them to play informal games. One possibility might be a little game called "Guess My Graph," in which you have one student privately construct a graph on a sheet of paper and then describe a step-by-step procedure that will enable another student to draw the same graph. You might stipulate one catch: the person who designed the graph is the only one who can talk, and he or she cannot look at his or her partner's graph until the student has finished drawing.

Vertex-edge graphs support Curriculum Focal Points for grades 3–5. Students can apply their understanding of whole numbers, fractions, and decimals by working with numerical weights in a graph and using them to find the shortest route.

Fig. **4.1.**

A weighted graph. The number on each edge represents the number of traffic lights along the corresponding edge in figure 3.8.

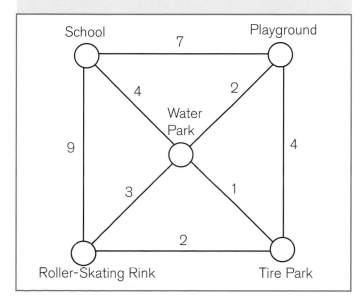

Fig. **4.2.**

The bold edges show one way of connecting all the vertices by using the minimum number of edges.

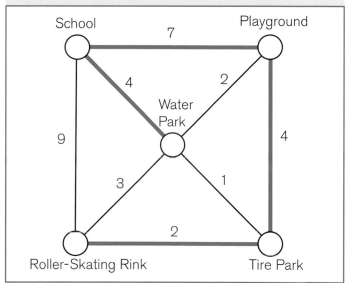

Fig. **4.3.**

The bold edges show the network with the minimum total weight.

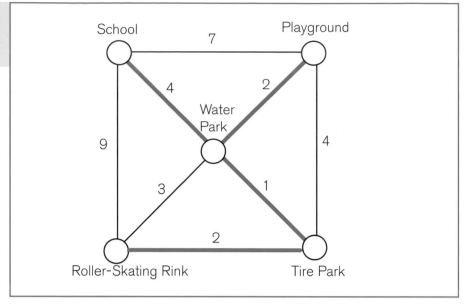

Students can explore vertex-edge graphs by using the applet Graph Creator on the CD-ROM.

Like their younger counterparts, students in grades 3–5 can also work with the applet Graph Creator to build and manipulate vertex-edge graphs. They can use the vertex button to draw vertices and the edge button to draw edges. Once they have constructed a graph, they can color its vertices, or they can use the arrow button to move them so that they can obtain a different drawing of the same graph or determine whether this graph is the same as or different from another graph.

For more information about vertex-edge graphs in grades 3–5, see "Math according to Mooch" (Kritzer and Pagliaro 2003) and "Connecting the Dots: Network Problems That Foster Mathematical Reasoning" (McGivney-Burelle 2005) on the CD-ROM.

Graphs for the Discrete Explorer

The investigation Graphs for the Discrete Explorer presents a sequence of five activities designed to enable students in grades 3–5 who have had some previous experience with vertex-edge graphs to continue their explorations.

Goals

- Color maps and color the vertices of a graph by using the minimum number of colors, as an introduction to the general problem of avoiding potential conflicts
- Draw vertex-edge graphs to represent concrete situations
- Use graphs to solve problems related to paths, circuits, and networks in concrete and abstract settings
- Follow, devise, and describe step-by-step procedures related to working with graphs
- Analyze graph-related problems to find the "best" solution

Materials and Equipment

Activity 1—Coloring Maps

For demonstration—

- (Optional) Suitable props for the teacher to use in assuming the role of Seymour Territory, president and CEO of Beautiful Borders, a company that makes maps for the classroom

For each student—

- A copy of each of the following activity sheets
  - "Coloring Maps—South America"
  - "Coloring Maps—States West of the Mississippi River"
  - "Coloring Maps—Africa"
- Crayons, colored pencils, or markers in at least eight different colors

For each group of three or four students—

- An additional copy of the following activity sheets
  - "Coloring Maps—South America"
  - "Coloring Maps—States West of the Mississippi River"

pp.179, 180, 181

Activity 2—From Maps to Vertex-Edge Graphs

For demonstration—

- A transparency of each of the following blackline masters:
  - "The Western United States"
  - "Twenty-Two Vertices"
- A blank overhead transparency

pp.182, 183, 184, 185, 186, 187, 188

- Two transparencies of the blackline master "Vertex-Edge Graph of the Western United States" (one as is and one colored in four colors [see fig. 4.10])
- Transparency markers
- Maps of South America and Africa that are large enough for the entire class to see

For each student—

- One sheet of tracing paper
- Four paper clips
- A copy of the each of the following activity sheets:
  ○ "Vertex Coloring—Cycles"
  ○ "Vertex Coloring—Wheels"
  ○ "Vertex Coloring—Guess and Check"
  ○ "Additional Practice with Vertex Coloring"
- Crayons, colored pencils, or markers in at least eight different colors

Activity 3—No More Conflicts!

For demonstration —

- A transparency of the blackline master "Using A Tree Diagram to Assign Charlie's Workers to Crews"

pp. 189, 190, 191

For each student—

- A copy of each of the following activity sheets:
  ○ "Charlie the Contractor's Problem—Part 1"
  ○ "Charlie the Contractor's Problem—Part 2"

Activity 4—Visiting Vertices

For demonstration—

- A copy of the graph on the activity sheet "Advertising for a Garage Sale—Part 3"
- A two-foot-long piece of yarn
- Pushpins

pp. 192, 193, 194

For each student—

- A copy of each of the following activity sheets:
  ○ "Advertising for a Garage Sale—Part 1"
  ○ "Advertising for a Garage Sale—Part 2"
  ○ "Advertising for a Garage Sale—Part 3"

Activity 5—Traveling Edges

For demonstration—

- A transparency of the blackline master "Streets in the Neighborhood"

pp. 195, 196, 197, 198, 199

For each student—

- A copy of each of the following activity sheets
  ○ "Efficient Newspaper Routes—Part 1"
  ○ "Efficient Newspaper Routes—Part 2"

Prior Knowledge

Students should be able to—

- understand the following terms: *vertex-edge graph*, *vertex*, *edge*, *neighboring vertex*, *degree of a vertex*, and *path*;
- count the number of vertices and edges in a graph;
- identify the degree of a vertex and identify when two vertices share an edge; and
- determine whether a number is even or odd.

Preliminary Activities

This chapter's investigation is a second-level exposure to ideas of vertex-edge graphs. Preliminary activities will be like those in chapter 3, which actively engage students in constructing and analyzing simple vertex-edge graphs.

Activities

The investigation includes a sequence of five activities. Students find the minimum number of colors needed to color three different maps in activity 1, Coloring Maps. They create vertex-edge graphs from maps in activity 2, From Maps to Vertex-Edge Graphs. In this activity, they learn that coloring the vertices in the graphs can represent coloring regions in the maps. They take their discoveries in a slightly different direction in activity 3, No More Conflicts! Here they use vertex-edge graphs and vertex coloring to defuse potential conflicts in a variety of situations. In activity 4, Visiting Vertices, the students explore traveling through vertex-edge graphs by visiting every vertex exactly once. In activity 5, Traveling Edges, they traverse vertex-edge graphs by traveling along every edge exactly once.

Activity 1—Coloring Maps

To engage your students in this activity, assume the role of Seymour Territory, president and CEO of Beautiful Borders, a company that makes maps for use in elementary school classrooms. You may want to gather suitable props to help you play your part convincingly. Your students will act as mapmakers in the company. Working individually and in small groups, they will determine how to save money in the production of three different maps—of South America, the states west of the Mississippi River, and Africa.

Give a copy of the activity sheet "Coloring Maps—South America" and crayons, colored pencils, or markers in at least eight colors to each student. Then step into your role as CEO of Beautiful Borders and address your mapmakers:

> As you know, I am Seymour Territory, president and CEO of Beautiful Borders. For years, our great company has made maps for schools. Today I have called you—my most trusted employees—together because we have a problem to solve. The Rainbow School has ordered a map of South America for each of its twenty-six classrooms. You have a draft of this map in front of you. The Rainbow

School has asked us to color this map so that whenever two countries share a border—say, Argentina and Chile, for example [*point to the two countries and their common border*]—we show them in different colors to make it easier to see where the borders are. We could use a different color for every single country, but if we did, our production costs would go through the roof. It costs a lot of money to put lots of different colors on the press! So I need you to color this map by using as few colors as possible.

Have the students color their own maps. After they have completed the task, assign them to groups of six to compare their work and reach a consensus on the minimum number of colors needed to show South America with no two adjacent countries in the same color. Ask the members of each group to discuss whether they could color the map by using one color fewer. Why, or why not? Then, continuing in your role as Seymour Territory, give your employees their next assignment:

Now I would like to hear a proposal from one representative from each group. I need to know three things:

1. What is the minimum number of colors needed to color the map?

2. How can you color the map by using that many colors?

3. Why can't you color the map by using one color fewer?

Allow each representative to present the findings of his or her group. By the end of the class discussion, the students should agree that they can color the map of South America by using four colors but no fewer. Some of the groups are likely to have discovered that four colors are necessary because Paraguay, Brazil, Bolivia, and Argentina each share a border with each of the other three countries in the group. The color of each has to differ from the color of the other three countries, resulting in a minimum of four colors.

Speaking as Seymour Territory, wrap up the discussion of the map of South America:

Congratulations. I am convinced that my trusted employees have solved the problem. We will go to production and use only four colors! [*Pretend that a phone rings and you answer it.*] Hello? Yes, you have reached Beautiful Borders. Seymour Territory here; how can I help you? [*Pause as though listening.*] Oh, hello, Mr. Biv. We're ready to go to production with your South America maps. I estimate that we can have them for you in a few days. [*Pause again.*] You also want what? [*Pause.*] Yes, I'm sure that we can make those maps too. Thank you for calling. [*Hang up the phone.*]

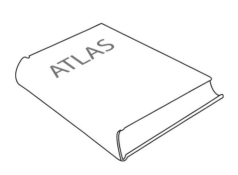

Tell your employees that that was Roy G. Biv, the principal of Rainbow Elementary School, and he wants to order an additional map for each classroom in his school—a map of the states west of the Mississippi River. Say that fortunately Beautiful Borders has some draft copies of this map as well, so work can begin right away. Distribute copies of the activity sheet "Coloring Maps—States West of the Mississippi River." Give each student a copy of the sheet, and provide each group with an extra copy for a presentation. Ask the students to generate their own solutions by coloring the map with the fewest colors and then discuss their solutions with the other members of their groups. Ask each group to arrive at a consensus on the minimum number of colors required to color the map and discuss why they cannot use one color fewer to color their map.

After all the groups have completed their work, select a few students to explain how they solved the problem and to defend their solutions to the other members of the class. Do all mapmakers agree that the number of colors proposed is indeed the least? Why, or why not? Also ask the groups to justify why they cannot color the map by using one color fewer.

The area known as the "Four Corners" (the point at which Utah, Colorado, Arizona, and New Mexico all meet) is often a trouble spot for students in map coloring. Some students are likely to think that they need four colors to color these states. Others will be comfortable in using two colors that alternate around the Four Corners, with Utah and New Mexico appearing in one color and Colorado and Arizona appearing in another. The deciding factor here is the definition of *border*. If two states share a border, the students must use different colors for them. The coloring rule indicates that neighboring states or countries must be different colors; otherwise, the two pieces of land blend together, and deciding where one state ends and the next one begins is not easy. Students who are trying to color this map therefore need to decide whether they should consider a point to be a border.

Is a point a border? Answering yes means using four colors to color this portion of the map; answering no permits using two colors. Hence, if the goal is to minimize the number of colors, it is better not to consider a point to be a border. Two states that meet at a point can still be distinguished easily on a map even if they are the same color, so mapmakers have no need to use different colors to color them. Students should come to this conclusion by discussing—or arguing about—the matter in their groups. If you tell the students at the outset that Arizona and Colorado can be the same color, they lose an opportunity to develop their reasoning skills. "Doing mathematics" sometimes calls for creating definitions. This activity gives students an opportunity to consider what is important in defining the idea of *sharing a border*.

When all the groups have completed their work on the map, help them reach an agreement about what is possible and what is not. All should agree that they can color the map of the states west of the Mississippi River by using four colors but not three. However, students will probably be unable to provide a full explanation. Unlike the map of South America, the map of the states west of the Mississippi River does not include four states each of which borders all the others. Students can probably identify another trouble spot—Nevada and its neighboring states—where they find it difficult to use only three colors. At this point, however, they are unlikely to be able to explain why using three colors to color this map is not possible. They will discover the complete explanation in activity 2, From Maps to Vertex-Edge Graphs.

Collect the maps of the states west of the Mississippi River so that you can use them in the next activity. If you wish to spend more time on this topic, you can use the activity sheet "Coloring Maps—Africa." Alternatively, you can assign this map for homework or as a problem of the week. Ask students to color the map of Africa by using the minimum number of colors, and ask them to articulate why that number of

The Four Corners

Nevada and Its Neighbors

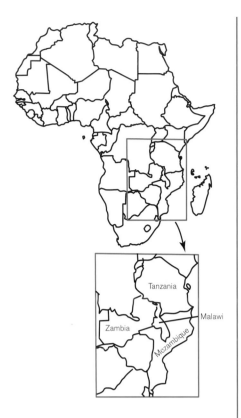

colors is necessary. Like the map of South America, the map of Africa requires at least four colors because Africa includes a group of four countries each of which borders the other three: Zambia, Tanzania, Mozambique, and Malawi (see the margin). However, your students cannot convincingly claim that they can color the map of Africa by using four colors until they have actually produced such a coloring. They should not find this task to be too difficult.

Activity 2—From Maps to Vertex-Edge Graphs

Before beginning this activity, students should be familiar with the ideas presented in activity 1. If your students have had previous experiences with coloring maps but have not colored the map of the states west of the Mississippi River, distribute the activity sheet "Coloring Maps—States West of the Mississippi River" and have them determine the minimum number of colors required to color this map. As discussed earlier, they will probably discover that they need four colors but be unable to give a full explanation of why they cannot use just three.

Begin probing why the map of the states west of the Mississippi River requires four colors. Because three states share a border in several areas, the map obviously needs at least three colors just to color those states. One example of three such states is Washington, Oregon, and Idaho; another example is North Dakota, South Dakota, and Minnesota; and yet another is Colorado, Kansas, and Oklahoma—and there are more. Take a moment to verify this fact with your students. Each state in the three tristate areas in figure 4.4 borders the other two neighboring states—even if the shared border is short, as in the case of the border between Oklahoma and Colorado.

Although these examples demonstrate that *at least three* colors are necessary to color the map of the states west of the Mississippi River, they do not show conclusively that three colors are sufficient to color it. The phrase *at least three* indicates that three, four, five, or more colors may be necessary to color the map. From their work, the students already know that four colors are enough for this map. But how can

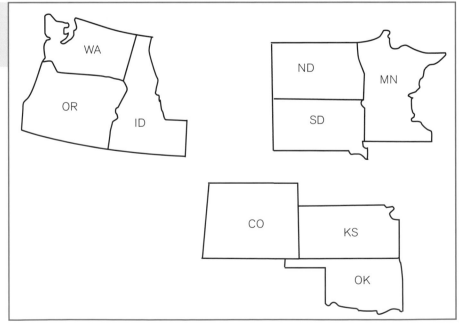

they know definitely that it requires four colors? By the end of this activity, they will be able to answer this question.

This situation can be modeled mathematically by placing a small circle inside each state and drawing an edge to connect the circles of any two states that share a common border, as in the map in figure 4.5. An edge joins the circles inside Washington and Oregon, since those two states share a common border. Another edge joins the circles inside Washington and Idaho, because those states also share a common border. A third edge joins the circles inside Oregon and Idaho, which share a common border, too.

This mathematical model of the "sharing a common border" relationship among states has a name. The model is called a *vertex-edge graph* because it is a graph that consists of vertices and edges. Figure 4.5 shows such a graph with three vertices (small circles) and three edges (lines that connect two circles). The vertex-edge graph forms a triangular arrangement, as would graphs for each of the other examples in figure 4.4. However, the same technique can be used to model the bordering relationship in more complicated maps, like that in figure 4.6, which results from adding Iowa and Nebraska to the map of North Dakota, South Dakota, and Minnesota shown in figure 4.4. Because North Dakota, South Dakota, and Minnesota each border the other two states, the model includes an edge that joins them in a triangular arrangement. Minnesota also borders Iowa, so an edge joins those two states. South Dakota also borders both Iowa and Nebraska, so edges join South Dakota to both of those states. Finally, Iowa and Nebraska share a border, so an edge joins them. Notice that no edge connects Minnesota to Nebraska. Nor does an edge connect North Dakota to either Iowa or Nebraska, because those states do not border each other.

Removing the map from figure 4.6 leaves a freestanding vertex-edge graph, as shown in figure 4.7. By itself, this vertex-edge graph can serve as a mathematical model of the border relationships of these five states. It includes the essential information about the map—specifically, the number of states, or *regions*, of the map (where a vertex represents each state) and the way that these states share borders with neighboring regions (an edge connecting two vertices represents each border).

Someone who is investigating the number of colors necessary to color a map need not color the actual map but can instead simply color the spaces inside each of the vertices. If an edge joins two vertices, the vertices share a border and must be different colors.

Draw the graph in figure 4.7 on the board or a sheet of easel paper, and color it with the whole class. Figure 4.8 shows a possible coloring. Explain that you have to begin somewhere, so you will just pick any vertex and color it—say, North Dakota. In figure 4.8, the North Dakota vertex is aqua. Because an edge joins this vertex to the vertex for Minnesota, the Minnesota vertex cannot be the same color. In figure 4.8, it is gray. Edges join both the North Dakota and the Minnesota vertices to the South Dakota vertex, so the South Dakota vertex cannot be the same color as either the vertex for North Dakota or the vertex for Minnesota. It requires a third color, and in figure 4.8 it is black.

Point out to your students that each of these three states shares a border with the other two, so the result is a triangular arrangement, requiring three colors in the graph. Make sure that the students

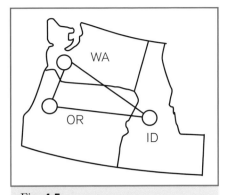

Fig. **4.5.**

Small circles represent states, and lines joining these circles represent common borders.

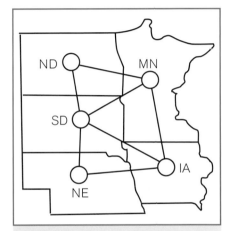

Fig. **4.6.**

Modeling the bordering relationship of five states by superimposing a vertex-edge graph on the map of the states

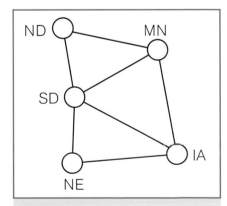

Fig. **4.7.**

A vertex-edge graph modeling the border relationship of the five states

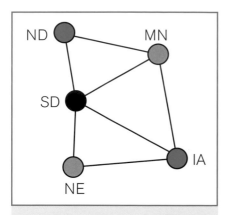

Fig. 4.8.

The vertex coloring of the graph uses three colors.

understand that because this small portion of the graph requires three colors, the entire graph needs at least three colors. Emphasize that knowing that a graph requires at least three colors does not, however, permit concluding that it requires *only* three colors.

The students can be sure that they can color the graph by using three colors only after they have actually used three colors to color it. Say, "Can you complete the coloring of this graph without using any additional colors?" Point out that an edge joins the Iowa vertex to the Minnesota and the South Dakota vertices, so the Iowa vertex cannot be either of the colors of those vertices. However, it can be the same color as the North Dakota vertex, since no edge joins Iowa and North Dakota. In figure 4.8, the Iowa vertex cannot be gray or black, but it can be aqua. Likewise, because an edge joins the Nebraska vertex to the vertices for South Dakota and Iowa, the Nebraska vertex cannot be the color of either of those vertices. However, it can be the same color as the Minnesota vertex, since no edge joins the vertices for Minnesota and Nebraska. In figure 4.8, the Nebraska vertex cannot be black or aqua, but it can be gray. The students can now be sure that they can color the graph in figure 4.7 by using three colors, since they have actually completed the coloring.

Distribute the colored maps of the western United States that students made in activity 1, and give each student one piece of tracing paper and four paper clips. Explain that, as in the previous examples, they are going to construct a vertex-edge graph that is a mathematical model of their map. Ask each student to place a piece of tracing paper on top of his or her map of the western United States and clip them together at the four corners of the page.

To demonstrate the first step in the process of creating this model, place a transparency of the blackline "The Western United States" on an overhead projector, and lay a blank transparency on top of this map. Show the students how you want them to place a vertex inside each state. If your students have learned or are learning the state capitals, you can have them place each vertex roughly at the location of the state's capital. Ask the students to make each vertex an open circle, roughly the size of a pea, so that they can color the region inside the circle later. Place transparency of the blackline "Twenty-Two Vertices" on top of the transparency "The Western United States," and ask the students to be sure that they have twenty-two vertices on their sheets of tracing paper in approximately the same places as on the transparency.

The next step is to draw an edge between every two vertices representing states that share a border. Draw one or two sample edges on the transparency, and then allow students to create their graphs. After some time, remove the transparency "Twenty-Two Vertices" and place a transparency of the blackline "Vertex-Edge Graph of the Western United States" on top of the transparency "The Western United States." Ask students to work with a partner to verify that their graphs are the same as the graph on the transparency and that they correspond to the map. As a review, ask students the following questions about simple properties of this graph:

- "How many vertices does the graph have?" (Twenty-two)
- "How many edges does it have?" (Forty-nine)

Beginning to make a vertex-edge graph by placing a vertex in each state

Navigating through Discrete Mathematics in Pre-K–Grade 5

Remove the transparency "The Western United States" from the overhead projector so that students see just the vertex-edge graph. Ask students to separate the tracing paper sheets from their maps and set the maps aside—they will need them later but not now.

Select a few different vertices, and describe what each one represents and what each edge coming out of that vertex represents. For example, if you choose the vertex at the top left of the graph, you can explain that this vertex represents a state that borders two other states, since two edges come out of this vertex. Say, "Unless you remember the map of the states or you labeled each vertex, just looking at the vertex-edge graph isn't going to tell you which state this vertex represents. But you do know how this state relates to those around it—specifically, you know that this state borders two other states."

Explore other properties of graphs by pointing to a number of vertices and asking students the degree of that vertex. After students are able to answer such questions, ask questions similar to the following:

- "How many vertices have degree 2?" (Two)
- "How many vertices have degree 3?" (Three)
- "What other degrees do vertices in this graph have?" (4, 5, and 6)
- "How many vertices are there of each degree?" (Two vertices of degree 2, three of degree 3, eight of degree 4, three of degree 5, and six of degree 6.)
- "How many vertices in this graph have odd degree?" (Six)
- "How many vertices in this graph have even degree?" (Sixteen)

Explain to the students that they are next going to color graphs. They will soon color the graph that they have built for the western United States, but they will first color some smaller graphs and look for patterns. Give each student a copy of the activity sheet "Vertex Coloring—Cycles." Point out that in the left column are four different graphs, each of which is a *cycle*—a graph in which the vertices and edges are connected so that they look like beads on a necklace. The more vertices and edges that a cycle has, the longer the necklace.

Work through the first example (see the margin) with your students. Remind the students that when they color vertex-edge graphs, they color the small region inside each vertex and assign two vertices different colors if an edge joins them. This rule is similar to the map-coloring rule that assigns different colors to two states if they share a border. What is the minimum number of colors needed for this graph?

Show your students that they can color a vertex-edge graph by coloring one vertex at a time. In the first example, with three vertices, pick an arbitrary vertex and color it any color—say, red. Pick a second vertex. Ask, "Can I use the same color that I used for the first vertex? Remember, I want to use the smallest number of colors that I can in the entire graph." The students should see, however, that you must use a second color—say, blue—for the second vertex, since both remaining vertices connect with the first vertex that you selected. One uncolored vertex remains. Say, "Notice that an edge joins this vertex to the red vertex and another edge joins it to the blue vertex." The students should recognize that you must use a third color—say, green—to color

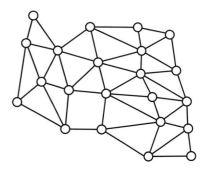

A vertex-edge graph of the western United States

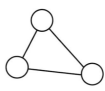

A cycle is a graph in which the vertices and edges are connected so that they look like beads on a necklace. The more vertices and edges that a cycle has, the longer the necklace.

1. How many colors do you need to color a cycle with 10 vertices?

2. How many colors do you need to color a cycle with 35 vertices?

3. Can you write a rule that describes how to find the smallest number of colors needed for any cycle?

that vertex. Thus, the minimum number of colors needed for this graph is three.

Summarize with your students that whenever they find a triangular arrangement in a graph, they know that at least three colors are necessary to color the entire graph, since a small portion of the graph (that is, the triangular arrangement) requires three colors. Explain that this kind of coloring is called a *vertex coloring*. In this particular example, they have found a coloring of the cycle that uses three colors, so they can actually color this graph by using three colors.

After working through the first example together, ask your students to complete the chart on the activity sheet individually, finding the number of vertices, the number of edges, and the minimum number of colors for each graph. Have them verify their solutions with a partner and work on the three questions at the bottom of the page (see the margin). After they have finished, ask them to discuss the patterns that they found in each column. The students should easily find all the patterns in the activity sheet. Although they may not describe their conclusion in this way, they should discover that a cycle with an odd number of vertices requires three colors, though a cycle with an even number of vertices requires only two colors.

Moreover, students will certainly discover that an appropriate way of coloring a cycle with an even number of vertices is to alternate colors—for example, coloring the first vertex that they select red, then a neighboring vertex blue, then a neighboring vertex red, and so on, with the final vertex colored blue. If, however, the cycle has an odd number of vertices and they attempt to use only two colors after beginning in the same way, with red, then when they arrive at the final vertex and prepare to color it red, they will discover that it cannot be red, because it is adjacent to the initial vertex, which also is red. Hence, the final vertex requires a third color.

The next activity sheet introduces another type of graph—a *wheel*. A wheel consists of a cycle and an additional vertex that is joined by an edge to every other vertex in the cycle. The additional vertex is called the *hub* of the wheel, and the edges coming out of the hub are called the *spokes* of the wheel. Draw on the board a wheel like that in figure 4.9 and explain the terms *wheel*, *hub*, and *spoke*.

Distribute the activity sheet "Vertex Coloring—Wheels." A column of cycles appears next to a column of wheels, allowing students to describe similarities and differences in the two types of graphs. Ask your students to complete the next two columns in the chart. From the activity sheet "Vertex Coloring—Cycles," they already know that a cycle with an even number of vertices requires two colors and that a cycle with an odd number of vertices requires three colors. They should quickly realize that they need to insert that information in the column labeled "Minimum Number of Colors—Cycles." Have students individually find the minimum number of colors for each of the four wheels and then verify their solutions with a partner.

Finally, after partners agree, they should work together to solve the problems at the bottom of the page. They should be able to explain the relationship between the evenness (or oddness) of the number of vertices and the number of colors needed to color the cycle that surrounds the hub of the wheel in their answers to the questions posed in step 2:

Fig. **4.9.**

A wheel with five spokes

- How many colors do you need to color a wheel if 50 vertices surround the hub?
- How many colors do you need if 35 vertices surround the hub?

In the first situation, students can reason, for example, that 50 is an even number and that these vertices are in a cycle that is on the outside of the wheel. Therefore, they need two colors to color all 50 vertices. But a wheel also has one vertex located at the hub, and this vertex connects to each vertex along the cycle. Therefore, the hub needs a third color. Hence, a wheel with 50 surrounding vertices requires three colors.

In the second situation, students can reason similarly: 35 is an odd number, and these vertices are in a cycle on the outside of the wheel, so three colors are necessary to color all 35 vertices. But a wheel also has one vertex located at the hub, and this vertex connects to each vertex along the cycle; therefore, the hub needs a fourth color. Hence, a wheel with 35 surrounding vertices requires four colors.

Wheels with an even number of vertices surrounding a hub vertex are called *even wheels*. *Odd wheels* are graphs with an odd number of surrounding vertices. Even wheels require three colors, and odd wheels require four colors.

After your students complete the activity sheets "Vertex Coloring—Cycles" and "Vertex Coloring—Wheels," assign the activity sheet "Vertex Coloring—Guess and Check" for homework. The vertex-edge graph that appears on this sheet is the same as the one that your students drew on tracing paper from the map of the states west of the Mississippi—but do not tell them yet! Step 2 directs them to color this graph by using the minimum number of colors—but first, in step 1, they must make a conjecture about the number of colors that they will need to color it. Be sure that they give their reasons.

When you review the homework with your students the next day, make the connection between their coloring of this vertex-edge graph and their earlier coloring of the map of the states west of the Mississippi River. Figure 4.10 shows a coloring of the graph superimposed on the map. Use four colors to color a transparency of the blackline "Vertex-Edge Graph of the Western United States" and superimpose the result, as in the figure, on top of the transparency "The Western United States." Emphasize that the coloring of the graph can become a coloring of the map if the students color each state in the map with the color of the corresponding vertex in the graph. Point out that the reverse is also true: any coloring of the map can become a coloring of the graph. Reinforce the idea that each vertex represents a state and that an edge joins two vertices when those two states share a border.

To help your students discover why the map of the states west of the Mississippi River requires four colors, direct them to look for a state surrounded by an odd number of states with each one sharing a border with two others. This configuration corresponds to finding an odd wheel in the graph on the activity sheet "Vertex Coloring—Guess and Check." If the students find such a state, then they know not only that the odd wheel requires four colors but also that the entire graph that contains the odd wheel requires at least four colors. After they actually color the graph by using that number of colors, they know that they have found the minimum number of colors needed.

A wheel consists of a cycle and an additional vertex that is joined by an edge to every other vertex in the cycle. The additional vertex is called the hub *of the wheel, and the edges coming out of the hub are called the* spokes.

Fig. **4.10.**

The map requires four colors.

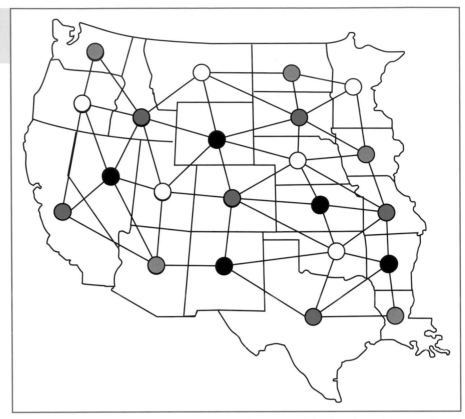

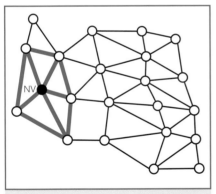

Fig. **4.11.**

Nevada (NV) is the hub of an odd wheel.

Ask the students whether they can find an odd wheel in this graph. There is only one, and it has the vertex representing Nevada as its hub. The Nevada vertex is a neighbor to five other vertices that are arranged in a cycle around the hub (see fig. 4.11.) The students then know that the wheel whose hub is Nevada requires four colors.

"What about Utah?" some students might ask. "Isn't it the hub of an odd wheel, too?" Ask the students to find the Utah vertex on one of the graphs on the activity sheet "Vertex Coloring—Guess and Check." Utah does have exactly five neighbors. It has five edges coming out of its vertex. Have your students draw a red line on top of each of these edges so that they can see the spokes clearly. Next, ask them to identify the edges along the cycle part of this wheel by drawing a blue line on top of these edges. They should have marked six blue edges and five red edges. Do these red and blue edges form a wheel? They should see that a spoke is missing from the wheel because Utah and New Mexico, as previously discussed, do not share a border (except at the Four Corners). The dashed edge in figure 4.12 shows the missing spoke. But remember that a wheel, by definition, is a graph that has spokes going from its hub to every vertex in the surrounding cycle. Hence, this part of the graph is not a wheel.

You can also ask students to find all even wheels in the graph. Five vertices are hubs of even wheels. Four of these hubs have degree 6—at Nebraska, Oklahoma, South Dakota, and Wyoming—and one hub has degree 4—at Kansas. The activity sheet "Additional Practice with Vertex Coloring" provides reinforcement for students' understanding.

Activity 3—No More Conflicts!

Graph coloring is a tool for defusing potential conflicts in many situations. In a schedule assigning teachers to after-school committees, two committees that meet at the same time are in conflict if a teacher is slated to participate on both. Scheduling the committees at different times resolves the conflict. In a pet store where the owner wants to place fish in tanks, two fish are in conflict if one is likely to attack the other. Placing the fish in different tanks defuses the situation. On a map, two states that share a border can be thought of as in conflict if they appear in the same color. Assigning the states different colors resolves the conflict by preserving the boundaries of each. Graph coloring can resolve all these conflicts and more. In this activity, students learn how to solve problems by constructing vertex-edge graphs and using vertex coloring to defuse the pontential conflicts.

Distribute the activity sheet "Charlie the Contractor's Problem— Part 1," and explain to the students that they need to help Charlie assign his six workers to crews that have no two members with the same skill. His workers are electricians, plumbers, carpenters, and masons. Five of them are skilled in not just one but two trades; the sixth is a skilled mason but has no other trade:

- Elizabeth, Nathan, and Hope are all electricians, so they have to be on different crews.

- Mary, Nathan, and Ryan are all carpenters, so they have to be on different crews.

- Mary and Zachary are both masons, so they have to be on different crews.

- Elizabeth, Ryan, and Hope are all plumbers, so they have to be on different crews.

Charlie's crews can have as many or as few workers as necessary to assign all six workers to crews with no two members having the same skill. Charlie could, of course, create six crews, with each crew consisting of one worker.

The first problem on the activity sheet asks the students to assign the six workers to crews to meet Charlie's requirement. The second problem then calls on them to try to determine the *minimum number* of crews that Charlie can create and still be sure that no crew has two people with the same skill. This situation is similar to the one in which the students colored regions of a map. In the map situation, the goal was to use as few colors as possible. In the contractor situation, the goal is to create as few crews as possible.

Do not expect your students to give complete solutions to the problems on the sheet. They should merely begin to discuss how to solve them, and the answers that they find will vary. Their explanations of how they know that they have found the minimum number of crews will almost certainly be incomplete. In subsequent work together as a class, the students will answer these questions more fully, and they will then see all the possible solutions.

Allow each student to work with a partner to try to create crews for Charlie. The student pairs should reason their way through the problem to see whether they can come up with a solution. Many students will discover through trial and error that Charlie needs four crews. Do not tell your students whether their solutions are correct. The next activity sheet will help them make this discovery on their own.

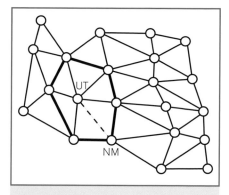

Fig. **4.12.**

Although Utah is surrounded by a cycle (bold edges), Utah and its neighbors do not form a wheel, since Utah does not share a border with New Mexico. The dashed edge shows the missing spoke.

Step 1: Decide what the vertices, edges, and colors will represent.

Step 2: Create a vertex-edge graph that models the situation.

Step 3: Use the minimum number of colors to color the vertices of the graph.

Step 4: Write a few sentences that tell how your solution resolves the conflicts and how you know that you have found the minimum number of possible solutions.

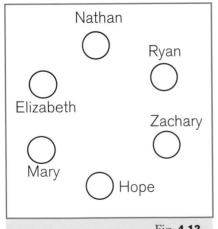

Fig. 4.13.

Arrange all the vertices in a circle as a first step in creating a conflict graph.

One way to assign the six workers to four crews so that no crew has two people with the same skill is to assign the workers as follows:

- Crew 1: Nathan
- Crew 2: Ryan and Zachary
- Crew 3: Hope and Mary
- Crew 4: Elizabeth

However, solving problems like this one without using vertex-edge graphs does not provide an easy answer to the question, "How do you know that you have the minimum number of crews?" Students need to look for another way to solve the problem so that they can be certain that they have formed the minimum number of crews.

Distribute the activity sheet "Charlie the Contractor's Problem—Part 2." This activity sheet outlines a general four-step process for students to follow while they learn how to use vertex-edge coloring to help solve the problems involving potential conflicts. Review with the students the map coloring that they did in activity 1. Remind them that they could not use the same color for two countries with a common border. In the situation in activity 3, they cannot assign two workers with the same skill to the same crew.

The situations are likely to strike the students as somewhat similar, so you can introduce the term *conflict* to describe both. Point out that in the map-coloring situation, two states are potentially in conflict if they share a border, and in "Charlie the Contractor's Problem—Part 1," two workers are in conflict if they share a skill. The mapmaker's goals are similar to Charlie's—to defuse potential conflicts. The mapmaker does this by assigning different colors to states with shared borders, and the contractor does this by giving different crew assignments to workers with the same skills.

Explain that vertex coloring can help solve many problems that involve potential conflicts and that the four steps outlined on the activity sheet "Charlie the Contractor's Problem—Part 2" show how to proceed. Use these steps to work through the problems on the activity sheet "Charlie the Contractor's Problem—Part 1" together with your class. Step 1 calls on the students to decide what the vertices, edges, and colors will represent in this problem. Emphasize that this first step is essential, since it will organize the students' thinking and determine how they construct the graph in step 2.

Because the workers are in conflict if they have the same skill, each vertex in the graph represents a worker, and students draw an edge between two vertices if those two workers are in conflict. To defuse the conflict, students assign colors to workers; in this situation, the colors represent different crews. In the map-coloring problem, students try to find the minimum number of colors, and in the new situation, they seek the minimum number of crews.

Show the students how to create this conflict graph by first arranging all the vertices in a circle, as shown in figure 4.13. Next, begin inserting edges on the basis of the information in "Charlie the Contractor's Problem—Part 1." Figure 4.14 shows how students use the first piece of information: Elizabeth, Nathan, and Hope are all electricians, so each one is in conflict with the others. Students therefore join the vertices labeled Elizabeth and Nathan with an edge, the vertices labeled

Elizabeth and Hope with a second edge, and the vertices labeled Nathan and Hope with a third edge. Most students will recognize the first two conflicts by joining Elizabeth first with Nathan and then with Hope, but some may forget the last edge, which joins Nathan and Hope.

The second piece of information is that Mary, Nathan, and Ryan are all carpenters, so they have to be in different crews. Ask your students who is in conflict here. The students should conclude that they need to draw edges between Mary and Nathan, between Mary and Ryan, and between Nathan and Ryan—the three edges shown in aqua in figure 4.15.

Finally, ask your students to insert the remaining edges in the graph on the basis of the third and fourth pieces of information. Mary and Zachary are both masons, so they have to be on different crews, as depicted by the aqua edge in figure 4.16. Elizabeth, Ryan, and Hope are all plumbers, so they have to be on different crews, as depicted by the three aqua edges in figure 4.17. The students have now created a vertex-edge graph that models the potential conflicts in Charlie's situation. Step 2 of the activity sheet "Charlie the Contractor's Problem— Part 2" is now complete.

The students next need to color this graph by using the minimum number of colors, as outlined in step 3. Allow time for the students to color the graph individually and review their work with their partners. By the end of their discussions, all students should recognize that the minimum number of colors needed to color this graph is four.

Step 4 directs the students to reflect on, interpret, and summarize their work. Whole-group discussions should help them understand that the minimum number of crews that Charlie can create so that no crew has two workers with the same skill is four. Charlie can create four crews in many ways, and students will subsequently return to that problem.

How can the students be sure that Charlie cannot create three crews? To answer this question, they need to reason and reflect on the structure of their graph and how they colored it. They should observe that edges connect each vertex representing Ryan, Nathan, Hope, or

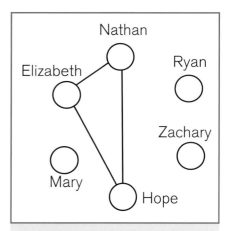

Fig. 4.14.
Because Elizabeth, Nathan, and Hope are all electricians, each of them is in conflict with the others.

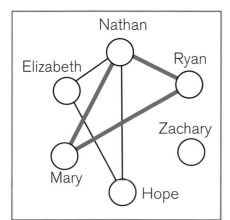

Fig. **4.15.**
Mary, Nathan, and Ryan must be on different crews, so an edge joins each pair.

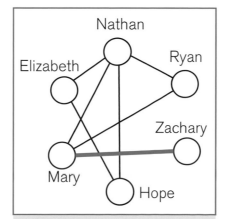

Fig. **4.16.**
Mary and Zachary must be on different crews, so there is an edge between them.

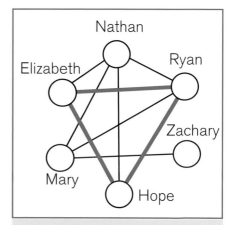

Fig. **4.17.**
The graph reflects all the information about which pairs of workers cannot be on the same crew.

Elizabeth to all three of the other vertices. Figure 4.18*a* uses bold aqua lines for these edges. This portion of the graph is similar to the portion of the map of South America that shows Paraguay, Brazil, Bolivia, and Argentina, with any two of the four countries sharing a common border, as illustrated in figure 4.18*b*. Just as in the situation of the map, in the graph of the workers, the minimum number of colors needed is four because each vertex in a group of four vertices (or workers) is in conflict with the other three. Hence, the entire graph requires at least four colors.

If the students can actually color the graph by using four colors, then they know that they have used the minimum number of colors. This last statement is important, since knowing that *at least four* colors are needed leaves open the possibility that five—or an even larger number—may be needed. But if the students have found a coloring that uses four colors, then they know that four is in fact the minimum. And indeed, your students already produced colorings of the graph that use four colors. Thus, they should now understand that four is actually the minimum number of colors (or crews).

As in many real-life problems, Charlie can assign his six workers to four crews in more than one way. The chart in figure 4.19 shows six possible ways of assigning the workers. Why are exactly six crew assignments possible, and how can your students find them? To answer these questions, begin with what the students already know. They have

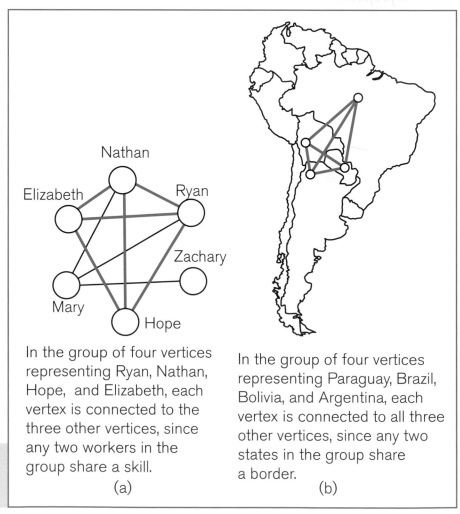

In the group of four vertices representing Ryan, Nathan, Hope, and Elizabeth, each vertex is connected to the three other vertices, since any two workers in the group share a skill.

(a)

In the group of four vertices representing Paraguay, Brazil, Bolivia, and Argentina, each vertex is connected to all three other vertices, since any two states in the group share a border.

(b)

Fig. **4.18.**

Bold edges mark similar configurations in graphs (*a*) and (*b*).

	Assignment A	Assignment B	Assignment C	Assignment D	Assignment E	Assignment F
Crew 1	Nathan Zachary	Nathan	Nathan	Nathan Zachary	Nathan	Nathan
Crew 2	Ryan	Ryan Zachary	Ryan	Ryan	Ryan Zachary	Ryan
Crew 3	Hope Mary	Hope Mary	Hope Mary	Hope	Hope	Hope Zachary
Crew 4	Elizabeth	Elizabeth Zachary	Elizabeth Zachary	Elizabeth Mary	Elizabeth Mary	Elizabeth Mary

determined that they need four crews because the four vertices labeled Nathan, Ryan, Hope, and Elizabeth all connect to one another, as shown in figure 4.18a. Thus, students must color these four workers by using four different colors—that is, these workers must be on four different crews.

Figure 4.20 illustrates the use of a tree diagram to complete the crew assignments after arriving at this point. Tree diagrams are a special kind of vertex-edge graph (chapter 2 discusses them). The diagram in the figure also appears on the blackline "Using a Tree Diagram to Assign Charlie's Workers Crews." Place a transparency of the blackline on the overhead projector and show the top row to your students. This row

Fig. 4.19.

Columns A–F record the six ways of assigning employees to four crews.

Fig. 4.20.

Using a tree diagram to assign Charlie's workers to crews

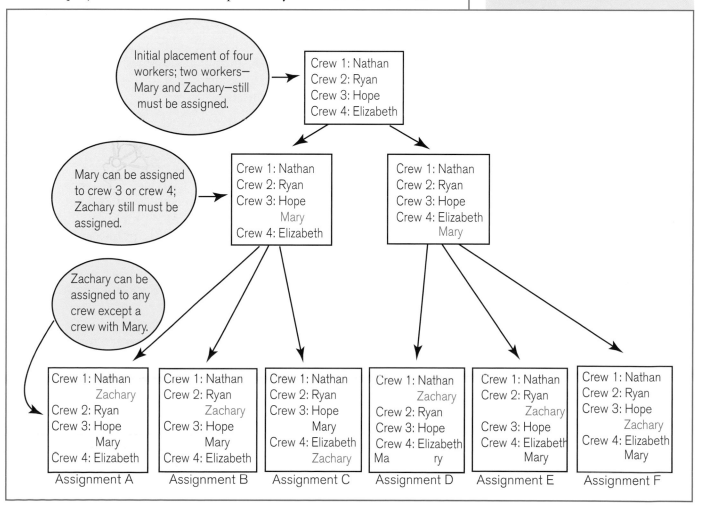

shows the naming of the four crews—crew 1, crew 2, crew 3, and crew 4—and the assigning of Nathan, Ryan, Hope, and Elizabeth to different crews.

To what crews can Mary and Zachary belong? Direct your students' attention to the middle row of the tree diagram. This row identifies possible assignments for Mary. Mary is in conflict with Nathan and Ryan, whom the top row assigns to crews 1 and 2, respectively, so Mary can be on only crew 3 or crew 4. The middle row displays these two possibilities—in the left box, Mary is in crew 3, and in the right box, Mary is in crew 4.

Only Zachary now remains unassigned. Zachary is in conflict only with Mary, so he can belong to any crew that does not have Mary. The bottom row of the tree diagram shows six possible assignments for Zachary. Thus, there are six crew assignments (A–F) altogether.

Students can also use the multiplication principle of counting in this situation. After they have assigned Nathan, Ryan, Hope, and Elizabeth to four different crews, they have two choices for Mary's assignment, since she is in conflict with Nathan and Ryan. Then they have three choices for Zachary, because he is in conflict with Mary. Thus, the number of possible assignments is 2×3, or 6. The tree diagram provides a visual representation of this multiplication; the top box branches out to two boxes, and then each of those two boxes branches out to three boxes. Use the overhead transparency to point out these connections to your students.

Your students might suggest that they could find additional ways to assign workers to crews if instead of placing Nathan in crew 1 and Ryan in crew 2, they switched them, assigning Nathan to crew 2 and Ryan to crew 1, and then working out all the crew assignments as they did before. In that case, one of the resulting crew assignments would be assignment G, shown above assignment A in figure 4.21. Are these two crew assignments the same or different? Why? Allow your students to discuss these questions with a partner. (The crew assignments are the same—in both, one crew consists of Nathan and Zachary, one consists of Ryan alone, one consists of Hope and Mary, and one crew consists of Elizabeth alone. Only the names of the crews are different.)

Because your students now have some experience in solving conflict problems by using vertex coloring, you can extend their knowledge by giving them more complex problems and problems in other contexts. For example, tell your students that you are going to buy a number of particular species of fish and you might not be able to buy just one tank and put all the fish together because some of the fish are likely to eat others. Ask them whether they think that graph coloring can help them determine the minimum number of tanks.

What would the vertices, edges, and colors represent in this situation? Give the students time to offer their suggestions. Start with the edges. They would represent conflicts, so an edge between two fish would mean that one might eat the other. So the vertices would be fish, and the colors would be the different tanks that would be necessary to resolve the conflicts.

Assign the students to groups and ask each one to create a conflict problem for another group to solve. Have each group research and select ten different species of fish, some of which present threats to others, and pose a problem about the minimum number of tanks needed to

A tree diagram is a special kind of vertex-edge graph.

Crew 1	Ryan
Crew 2	Nathan
	Zachary
Crew 3	Hope
	Mary
Crew 4	Elizabeth

Assignment G

Crew 1	Nathan
	Zachary
Crew 2	Ryan
Crew 3	Hope
	Mary
Crew 4	Elizabeth

Assignment A

Fig. **4.21.**

Are these crew assignments the same or different? Why?

hold the fish. Have each group use graph coloring to come up with a solution for its problem and place it in a sealed envelope. The next day, have groups of students solve one another's problems.

Activity 4—Visiting Vertices

In this activity, students work individually and in groups on two types of problems involving graphs. Problems of the first type involve starting at a selected vertex of a graph, visiting each vertex, and returning to the first vertex. Problems of the second type involve traveling along each edge of a graph.

The activity sheet "Advertising for a Garage Sale—Part 1" presents a problem of the first type. Each student supposes that his or her family is having a garage sale, and the student's job is to put up an advertising poster at each intersection of streets in the neighborhood. A vertex-edge graph on the activity sheet represents the network of intersecting streets. To complete the task as quickly as possible, the student must choose a route that begins at the family's house, visits each vertex exactly once, and returns home.

The graph in figure 4.22 represents the neighborhood. The edges represent streets, and the vertices represent intersections. The letter labels for the intersections give an easy way of identifying each street—for example, street *AB* is the edge between intersection *A* and intersection *B*. (*BA* is another name for the same street.) The family's house is at the intersection marked *H*.

To prepare your students for this activity, you might ask them to count the number of vertices—nine in all—in the graph. Can the students explain why the route has to cover at least nine streets? The reason is that to put up posters at all the intersections, someone must travel on at least eight streets and then on at least one more street to return home. He or she might be able to put up all the posters without revisiting any intersection that already has a poster, but another possibility is that he or she might need to pass through one or more intersections again to reach the next intersection on the route.

Also be sure that your students understand that they need to travel on a sequence of streets in visiting the vertices—that is, they must travel on one street, then another, and so on. They also need to understand that when they travel on a given street, the next street on which they travel has to start where the first street ends. If, for example, one of the streets is *AB*, then the name of the next street on the list has to include *A* or *B*.

Whether you explain all the preceding points at the beginning of the activity or let the students discover them in their groups depends on the ages and abilities of the students. Another alternative is to give the students a few minutes to discuss the problem in their groups and then encourage them to articulate their ideas about the problem. Distribute the activity sheet "Advertising for a Garage Sale—Part 1" to your students and assign them to groups, but ask them to work individually on the problems before checking their solutions with the other group members.

The students should find that accomplishing the task of displaying posters at each intersection and returning home without visiting any intersection more than once is indeed possible and that they can accomplish it in exactly four ways. One route is *H* to *G* to *I* to *F* to *E* to

Fig. **4.22.**

A vertex-edge graph representing the neighborhood

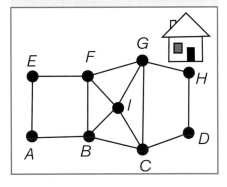

A to *B* to *C* to *D* to *H*, a second is *H* to *G* to *F* to *E* to *A* to *B* to *I* to *C* to *D* to *H*, and the third and fourth routes are just the reverse of those two routes.

Distribute the activity sheet "Advertising for a Garage Sale—Part 2." The problem that this sheet presents varies the first situation slightly. A developer has added new streets to the neighborhood, as shown in figure 4.23. A modified vertex-edge graph represents the new situation. Each student again supposes that he or she is a member of the family living at *H*. Can the student still find a route that allows him or her to begin at home, pass through each intersection exactly once, and return home? This variation on the problem has only two solutions: One such route travels from *H* to *G* to *L* to *K* to *F* to *E* to *A* to *B* to *I* to *C* to *D* to *H*, and the other is the reverse.

Fig. **4.23.**

A developer has added new streets, shown as edges *FK*, *KL*, and *LG* in the vertex-edge graph of the neighborhood.

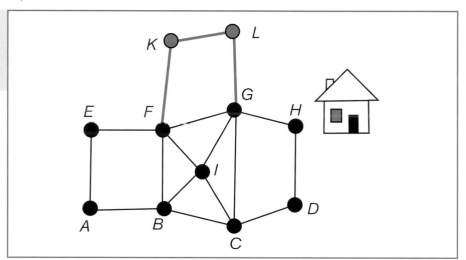

Distribute the activity sheet "Advertising for a Garage Sale—Part 3." The problem on this sheet varies the situation again. A developer has added yet more streets, this time on the other side of the neighborhood, as depicted in figure 4.24. Can someone living at *H* still find a route that begins at home, travels through each intersection, and returns home?

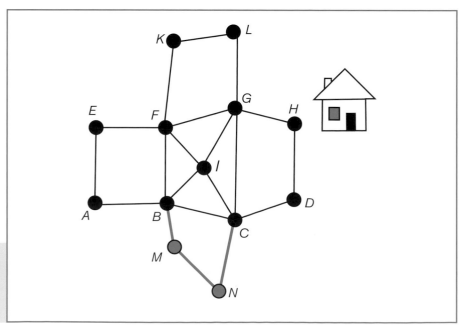

Fig. **4.24.**

A developer has added more new streets, shown as edges *BM*, *MN*, and *NC* in the vertex-edge graph of the neighborhood.

A path that visits each vertex exactly once and returns to the starting point is a *Hamilton circuit*, named for the Irish mathematician William Rowan Hamilton. A Hamilton circuit is sometimes called a *Hamilton cycle*. Recall that a graph that is a cycle is like a beaded necklace. Each bead of the necklace represents a vertex, and each length of string between consecutive beads represents an edge joining the two vertices. The aqua edges in figure 4.25 depict the Hamilton circuit in the graph on the activity sheet "Advertising for a Garage Sale—Part 2."

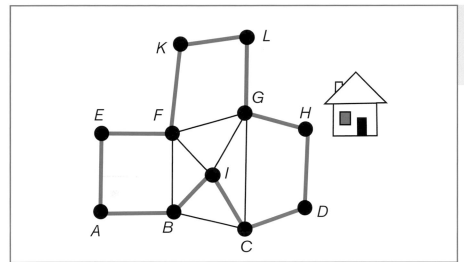

Fig. **4.25.**

A path that starts at a vertex, visits every other vertex once, and returns to the initial vertex is called a *Hamilton circuit*.

Not every graph has a Hamilton circuit. Determining whether a graph has one may be difficult, and finding one in a graph that has one may also be challenging. Your students are likely to find a Hamilton circuit quickly in the graphs in the activity sheets "Advertising for a Garage Sale—Part 1" and "Advertising for a Garage Sale—Part 2." However, the graph in "Advertising for a Garage Sale—Part 3," shown in figure 4.24, does not have a Hamilton circuit. Students need to realize that some graphs simply do not have Hamilton circuits.

To help your students conclude that the graph in "Advertising for a Garage Sale—Part 3" does not have a Hamilton circuit, post the graph on a bulletin board, with a pushpin at each vertex. Using a two-foot strand of yarn, create a path through the graph. Begin at one vertex and use the pushpin to anchor an end of the yarn. Stretch the yarn to another vertex and encircle its pushpin, moving in this way from vertex to vertex along the edges of the graph. After you are unable to encircle each vertex just once and return to the initial vertex, invite your students to try. Ask them to explain the difficulties that they experience, allowing their unsuccessful attempts to shape their reasoning about why the task is impossible.

In the case of the graph in figure 4.24, one explanation involves observing that for a Hamilton circuit to include the vertices *E* and *A*, it must include the edges marked *FE, EA,* and *AB,* which are aqua in figure 4.26. Similarly, if the Hamilton circuit includes the vertices *M* and *N*, it must include the edges marked *BM, MN,* and *NC,* and if it includes the vertices *K* and *L*, it must include the edges marked *GL, LK,* and *KF.* Figure 4.27 adds aqua lines for these edges. For the Hamilton circuit to include the vertices *H* and *D*, it must include the edges marked *GH, HD,* and *DC,* which figure 4.28 makes aqua also. But those

Many puzzles on restaurant placemats involve finding a Hamilton circuit.

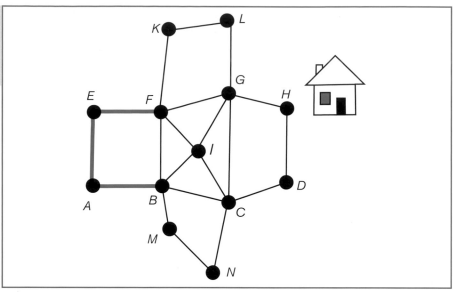

Fig. 4.26.

Including vertices *E* and *A* in a Hamilton circuit involves traveling on edges *FE*, *EA*, and *AB*, shown in aqua.

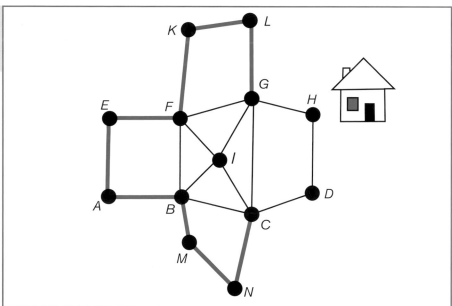

Fig. 4.27.

A Hamilton circuit in the graph must include all the edges shown in aqua.

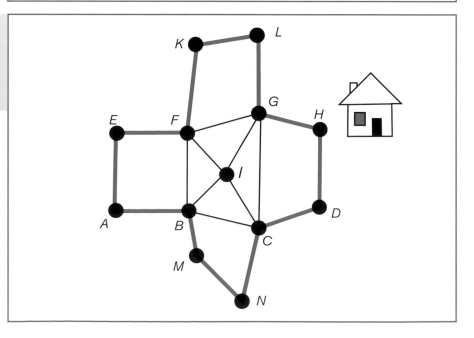

Fig. 4.28.

A Hamilton circuit must include all the edges shown in aqua, but the result is a circuit that does not include vertex *I*. The graph therefore has no Hamilton circuit.

edges together form a cycle, so there is no way to include vertex I as well without making a detour from one of the vertices *B*, *C*, *G*, or *F* to *I* and then back. However, such a detour would involve visiting that vertex twice. Therefore, no Hamilton circuit can exist in this graph. Explaining why a graph does not have a Hamilton circuit is not easy, but it can provide students with an opportunity to develop and present their mathematical reasoning.

Activity 5—Traveling Edges

Visiting vertices in a graph involves starting at a vertex in a graph, traveling to all the other vertices exactly once, and then returning to the initial vertex. A different type of journey through a graph involves starting at a vertex, traveling along every edge exactly once, and returning to the initial vertex. For a given vertex-edge graph, the traveling-edges problem involves finding whether the graph has such a path.

The statements of the visiting-vertices and the traveling-edges problems may sound similar, but the problems are actually different. Because the similarity in the statements can confuse students, wait until they understand the visiting-vertices problem and have practiced finding solutions in the context of several different neighborhoods before you introduce the traveling-edges problem.

When your students are ready, distribute the activity sheet "Efficient Newspaper Routes—Part 1," which presents a traveling-edges scenario. Each student supposes that he or she delivers newspapers each day after school to houses on every street in the neighborhood represented in the vertex-edge graph in figure 4.22. The student rides a bike and throws papers skillfully to houses on either side of the street. The student's own house is at the intersection marked *H*, and he or she wants to find an efficient route that starts and ends at home and travels on every street in the neighborhood just once.

Before the students work on the problem in their groups, you might read the problem and instructions aloud, checking to be sure that each student understands the situation. Do the students realize, for example, that because they can deliver papers to houses on both sides of a street as they ride, they do not need to travel in both directions on any street? Do they understand that they must deliver the papers along every street? You might ask them to count the streets—fourteen in all—and explain why the route has to travel on every one at least once. Do they realize that they may be able to deliver all their papers without repeating any streets, or they may have to repeat one or more streets?

In this problem, students can create a paper route that does not repeat any street—that is, a paper route that begins and ends at home (vertex *H*) and travels along all fourteen streets exactly once. Moreover, *many* routes that travel along the fourteen streets exactly once are possible. Thus, although this problem is complicated, every group of students is likely to come up with an answer, and different groups may arrive at different answers.

After each group has had an opportunity to find a solution, you can ask the groups to mark their paper routes on a transparency of the blackline "Streets in the Neighborhood." Ask your students to use colored pens to mark their routes, with different groups using different colors. One solution is shown in figure 4.29. Although the graph here is the same as the graph in figure 4.22, figure 4.29 displays a number on

Fig. **4.29.**

A newspaper carrier whose route from
home (vertex *H*) follows the order of the
numbers travels along each street exactly
once. The route forms an *Euler circuit* that
begins and ends at home.

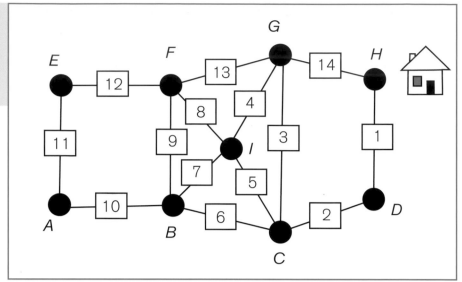

each edge. A person who travels the streets in the order of the numbers
will find that he or she has traveled along each street exactly once, fin-
ishing at home. (Note that the numbers are not weights but are just
labels that indicate an order in which the streets can be traveled.)

After you have congratulated the students on finding a solution, distribute copies of the activity sheet "Efficient Newspaper Routes—Part
2," which presents the same problem but with a slightly different map,
with two additional vertices and three additional streets, for a total of
seventeen streets (the graph is the same as in fig. 4.24). Try as they
might, your students will not be able to find a paper route that does not
repeat streets in this map. The best that they will be able to do is to find
a route that repeats just one street—*FG*. If they do not repeat that particular street, then their route will repeat more than one street.

Why were the students able to find efficient solutions in the graph of
neighborhood streets shown on "Efficient Newspaper Routes—Part 1"
but not in this one? The difficulty arises because vertices *F* and *G* in the
second graph have odd degree. Why is that a problem? In the first map,
F has degree 4. A newspaper carrier can ride his or her bicycle down
one street to *F* and then leave by a second street. Later, the carrier can
ride down a third street to *F* and then leave by a fourth street. In the
second map, however, a carrier who rides a bicycle down the fifth, or
last, untraveled street to *F*, must leave *F* by a route that he or she has
already traveled.

Whenever a graph has a vertex of odd degree, finding a path that
starts at a given vertex, travels on each edge exactly once, and then
returns to the initial vertex is impossible. However, if all the vertices
have even degree, a route that starts and ends at the same place and
covers each edge exactly once is possible. A Swiss mathematician,
Leonhard Euler, made these discoveries in the eighteenth century. An
Euler circuit is a route that travels along each edge of a graph exactly
once and returns to its starting point. Note that although an Euler circuit traverses each edge only once, it can visit a vertex any number of
times. The solution in figure 4.29, for example, visits vertex *F* twice—
once from vertex *I*, in traveling along edge 8, and then again from vertex *E*, in traveling along edge 12.

As a culminating experience with vertex-edge graphs, you might ask your students whether the graphs in the activity sheets "Visiting Vertices or Traveling Edges?—Part 1" and "Visiting Vertices or Traveling Edges?—Part 2" have Hamilton or Euler circuits. What are the most efficient ways of traveling along all the edges and visiting all the vertices in each of the graphs?

"Does this graph have an Euler circuit?" and "Does this graph have a Hamilton circuit?" may sound like similar questions, but they can have very different answers. Some graphs have both kinds of circuits, and some have neither. Some have one kind of circuit but not the other. It is sometimes difficult to tell whether a graph has a Hamilton circuit—or to find one that is known to exist. However, a graph with a vertex of odd degree definitely does not have an Euler circuit.

The Mathematics in the Investigation

This investigation begins with map coloring—an activity that calls for showing two regions on a map in different colors if they share a border. Using the same color would make determining where one region ends and the other begins difficult. The challenge in map coloring is to use as few colors as possible. When a map contains four regions and each of them borders each of the others, each region requires a different color. Concluding that four colors are sufficient for the whole map, however, requires an actual coloring in four colors.

Even if a map contains no group of four regions each of which borders the other three, it still may require four colors, as in the map of the twenty-two states west of the Mississippi. To demonstrate why four colors are necessary for that map, this chapter introduces vertex-edge graphs and models each map by using a vertex-edge graph whose vertices correspond to the regions in the map and whose edges join pairs of vertices associated with regions that share a border. After exploring vertex-edge graphs and their colorings, the chapter notes that an odd wheel—that is, a graph with an odd number of vertices that form a cycle and a vertex that serves as a "hub," with links to each vertex in the cycle—also requires four colors. In the map of the western United States, Nevada is the hub of an odd wheel, and consequently, four colors are necessary to color the twenty-two western states. Actually coloring the map by using four colors proves that four colors are sufficient.

In fact, four colors are sufficient for coloring any map drawn on a plane (or a sphere). Although this statement was thought to be true for more than a hundred years, no proof existed until 1976, when two American mathematicians at the University of Illinois, Wolfgang Haken and Kenneth Appel, successfully demonstrated it. Their conclusion is known as the *four-color theorem.*

Although four colors are sufficient for coloring any map, simply referring to the theorem when someone asks for a map coloring is not enough; producing an appropriate coloring is necessary. The theorem asserts that a coloring exists but does not provide it.

The chapter also discusses paths in vertex-edge graphs, particularly Hamilton circuits and Euler circuits. A Hamilton circuit passes through each vertex exactly once and then returns to the initial vertex. An Euler circuit travels along each edge exactly once and then returns to

Four colors are sufficient for coloring any planar map. More than four colors are required for other maps, such as those on the surface of a torus ("doughnut"), which can require as many as seven colors.

*The four-color theorem,
proved successfully in 1976,
states that coloring any
planar map requires no
more than four colors.*

the initial vertex. The task of posting notices efficiently at each intersection of streets in a neighborhood involves looking for a Hamilton circuit. The task of delivering newspapers efficiently along each street in a neighborhood involves looking for an Euler circuit. Not every graph has an Euler circuit or a Hamilton circuit. For example, a graph in which some vertices have odd degree does not have an Euler circuit. Students explore these ideas in more detail in grades 6–8.

The activities in this chapter implicitly address the recommendations to find the "best" solution and to follow, devise, and describe step-by-step procedures related to working with graphs. In the coloring activities, the best solution refers to a coloring that involves the minimum number of colors; and in the path activities, the best solution refers to a circuit that involves no repeated edges (for an Euler circuit) or no repeated vertices (for a Hamilton circuit). This chapter's path activities call for following, devising, and describing paths and circuits through given neighborhoods. Students in grades 3–5 who encounter these activities or others like them will be prepared to tackle more challenging problems involving vertex-edge graphs in grades 6–8.

NAVIGATING *through* DISCRETE MATHEMATICS

Chapter 5
Iteration and Recursion in Pre-K–Grade 2

All students in pre-K–grade 2 should—

- *describe, analyze, and create a variety of simple sequential patterns in diverse concrete settings;*

- *explore sequential patterns by using physical, auditory, and pictorial representations;*

- *use sequential patterns and iterative procedures to model and solve simple concrete problems;*

- *explore simple iterative procedures in concrete settings by using technology, such as Logo-like environments and calculators.*

This chapter's investigation, Picture after Picture, introduces students in prekindergarten through grade 2 to the topic of *iteration*—a term that the dictionary defines simply as *repetition*. To repeat a procedure, process, or rule over and over is to perform an iteration. People tend to become tired of doing the same thing again and again, but computers and robots are extremely good at iterating for long periods of time. Nonetheless, people must understand what iteration is because sometimes they must use an iterative process or direct a computer or a robot to perform one for them. One way in which young children can learn about this process is through work with sequential patterns.

In Picture after Picture, students develop sequential thinking by identifying, describing, and creating patterns for sequences of pictures. The focus is on two types of sequential patterns: repeating patterns and growing patterns. An example of a repeating pattern is a pattern of pictures in which a picture of a frog and a picture of a lion alternate; an example of a growing pattern is a pattern of pictures showing first one frog, then one lion, then two frogs, then one lion, then three frogs, then one lion, and so on. Growing patterns like this one, in which the next group of frogs has one more frog than the current group, also help prepare students for the NEXT-NOW activities that they encounter in subsequent grades. The rule NEXT = NOW + 1, which describes this situation, is called a *recursion*, since it captures the recurring aspect of the growth of the groups of frogs.

The early activities in this investigation reinforce two major attributes of sequences: *directionality* and *ordinal position*. The students must recognize that five pictures in a row progress from left to right, with the left-

*Navigating through
Algebra in
Prekindergarten–Grade 2
(Greenes et al. 2001)
presents initial pattern
activities. For example,
Clown Line-Up helps
prekindergarten and
kindergarten students
identify, extend, and create
repeating patterns; Snakes
and More Snakes guides
them in exploring growing
patterns; and Footprints lets
them create and analyze
their own patterns. How
Does It Grow? presents
first and second graders
with growing patterns
composed of squares and
triangles.*

*"Children identify,
duplicate, and extend
simple number patterns
and sequential and growing
patterns (e.g., patterns
made with shapes) as
preparation for creating
rules that describe
relationships." (NCTM
2006, p. 12)*

most picture in the first position, the next picture in the second position, the next picture in the third position, and so on. In the investigation's later activities, students describe and continue the pattern in various sequences and find multiple ways of continuing the same sequence.

The students in your class have probably already encountered repetition, sequencing, and patterns. Young children play and learn through repetitious activity; they love to have adults read them the same story or sing the same song over and over. Prekindergarten children learn to repeat a given act in response to a verbal command. Games like "Simon Says," "Mother, May I?" and "Duck, Duck, Goose" help develop the essential aspects of repetition that coordinate listening and fine motor skills.

Your students are also likely to have encountered sequencing. Young students' initial experiences with sequencing often occur in subject areas outside mathematics—for example, in language arts or science settings. In language arts, the teacher may give students a group of pictures to arrange in sequence to reflect the order of the events in a story. Students who are not yet reading may put four pictures in sequence to make a book; older students can work with a larger number of pictures. In science settings, the teacher may present the life cycle of a butterfly in four stages: the egg, the caterpillar, the chrysalis, and the butterfly. Activities like these can introduce or reinforce sequential thinking, particularly if they use numbers—either cardinal (one, two, three, and so on) or ordinal (first, second, third, and so on)—to refer to the items arranged in order.

Parents and teachers should engage prekindergarten children in identifying patterns in many different contexts so that by the time the children enter kindergarten, they can begin to think about sequential patterns. This chapter's investigation assumes that students have had initial experiences with repetition, sequencing, and patterns. Chapter 1 of *Navigating through Algebra in Prekindergarten–Grade 2* (Greenes et al. 2001) provides a sampling of such early pattern activities.

Picture after Picture

The investigation Picture after Picture consists of a sequence of four mathematical activities designed for children in prekindergarten through grade 2 who have already had some experience with repetition, sequencing, and patterns.

Goals

- Describe, analyze, and create a variety of simple sequential patterns
- Explore sequential patterns by using pictorial representations

Materials

The investigation calls for showing students a sequence of pictures one at a time while permitting them to see all the previous pictures in order. One method is to stand the pictures in the tray below a chalkboard; other methods can accomplish the same goal.

Blackline masters include drawings of four animals—a lion, a bird, a frog, and a donkey. Reproducing these on card stock (8 1/2 inches × 11 inches) will give serviceable placards for classroom display. The materials list indicates minimum numbers of placards for each activity, but creating a few extra cards showing each animal will allow flexibility in answering students' questions. Also, in activities 2 and 3, the specified numbers permit modeling all the sequences in the activity; smaller quantities may be suitable for classes working with only a portion of the activity.

To have enough animal placards for all the activities, you will need fourteen lions, sixteen birds, eleven frogs, and ten donkeys. Several extra cards of each will give you flexibility in answering students' questions.

Activity 1—Repeating Picture Patterns

For demonstration—

- Four lion placards
- Six bird placards
- Eight frog placards

For each student—

- A copy of the blackline master "Cards for 'Guess My Pattern'"
- A pair of scissors
- A plastic snack bag
- (Optional) A copy of the activity sheet "Repeating Patterns in Number Sequences"

pp. 200, 201, 202, 204, 205

Activity 2—Growing Picture Patterns

For demonstration—

- Eight lion placards
- Sixteen bird placards
- Ten frog placards
- Ten donkey placards

For each student—

- A copy of the blackline master "Cards for 'Guess My Pattern'"

pp. 200, 201, 202, 203, 204, 206, 208, 209, 210, 211

- A copy of each of the follow activity sheets:
  - "Guess How I Continue—Part 1"
  - "Guess How I Continue—Part 2"
  - "Guess How I Continue—Part 3"
  - "Guess How I Continue—Part 4"
  - "Guess How I Continue—Part 5"
  - "Guess How I Continue—Part 6"
- A plastic bag containing the student's game cards from activity 1
- Five strips of white paper, approximately 3 inches × 7 inches

Activity 3—What Sequence Starts with …?

For demonstration—

- Fourteen lion placards
- Ten bird placards
- Eleven frog placards
- Three donkey placards
- A sheet of card stock (8 1/2 inches × 11 inches) to represent a blank placard

For each student—

- A copy of each of the following activity sheets:
  - "What Sequence Starts with …?—Part 1"
  - "What Sequence Starts with …?—Part 2"
  - "What Sequence Starts with …?—Part 3"
  - "What Is the Missing Term?"—Part 1"
  - "What Is the Missing Term?"—Part 2"
- A plastic bag containing the student's game cards from activities 1 and 2

Activity 4—What's Our Pattern?

For one team of students (half of the class)—

- Eight frog placards
- Eight bird placards

For another team of students (the other half of the class)

- Eight lion placards
- Eight donkey placards

To divide between the two teams—

- Sixteen sheets of white card stock (8 1/2 inches × 11 inches)

Prior Knowledge

Students should be able to—

- identify pictures of four different animals—lion, bird, donkey, and frog;
- use positional words, such as *right*, *left*, *before*, *after*, *next*, and *between*;

pp. 200, 201, 202, 203, 212, 213, 214, 215, 216

pp. 200, 201, 202, 203

- understand and use ordinal numbers to identify the positions of elements in a sequence (first through twentieth);
- compare quantities to tell how many more one quantity is than another; and
- identify the next item in an alternating sequence.

Preliminary Activities

Before encountering the activities in this chapter's investigation, your students should have had initial experiences with sequencing and sequential patterns. To provide such experiences, you can do the following:

- Give the students a sheet of paper with four pictures on it. Ask them to cut out the pictures, color them, and order them from left to right so that they tell a story. Allow them to create a storybook by gluing the four pictures onto construction paper in the proper sequence.

- Order the stages of development in a life cycle for your students. For example, show the first stage, second stage, third stage, and fourth stage in the life of a butterfly (egg, caterpillar, chrysalis, butterfly).

- Read your students a story that includes a sequence of events, and have them create a picture book with a page for each event, in the proper order. To prepare students for recursion in later grades, you might read stories in which the last event links back to the first event. Stories by Laura Numeroff—*If You Give a Mouse a Cookie* (1985), *If You Give a Pig a Pancake* (1998), *If You Give a Moose a Muffin* (1991), *If You Take a Mouse to the Movies* (2000), and *If You Take a Mouse to School* (2002)—are good examples.

- Review the days of the week in order with your students, associating a number with each day: Sunday is the first day of the week, Monday is the second, and so on, ending with Saturday is the seventh day. What is the twelfth day if the students continue, considering Sunday as the eighth day? Likewise, recite the months of the year, associating a number with each month: January is the first month, February is the second, and so on, ending with December is the twelfth month. What is the fifteenth month if the students continue, considering January to be the thirteenth month?

- Give your students a list of objects, such as the following:
  Circle, square, circle, square, ____, ____, ____
  Monkey, lion, monkey, lion, ____, ____, ____
  Girl, boy, girl, boy, ____, ____, ____ .

  Examples should have alternating patterns consisting of shapes, pictures, or even actual students. Ask the students to identify the pattern and extend the list by naming the next few items.

- Have your students work through activities in chapter 1 of *Navigating through Algebra in Prekindergarten–Grade 2* (Greenes et al. 2001).

All of these preliminary activities introduce young children to the ideas that one thing can happen after (or before) another and that a sequence of events sometimes exhibits a pattern that continues. However, these first exposures are limited because they do not model several important aspects of sequences:

- A pattern may generate an infinite number of terms in the sequence (that is, sequences may continue forever).
- Descriptions of sequences often call for specialized terminology.
- A pattern in a sequence may be complicated and difficult to detect.
- A sequence may contain more than one pattern, so it can continue in more than one way.

The investigation Picture after Picture addresses each of these aspects of sequences and expands young children's initial experiences, preparing them to analyze, describe, and create simple sequential patterns.

Activities

This investigation presents a sequence of four activities. In activity 1, Repeating Picture Patterns, students examine sequences that exhibit repeating patterns and learn terminology for describing sequences. In activity 2, Growing Picture Patterns, they examine sequences that reflect growing patterns and analyze these sequences by grouping the terms in various ways. In activity 3, they learn that many answers may be possible to the question in the activity's title—What Sequence Starts with …? They also learn that their answer is valid if they can provide a justification for their method of continuing a given sequence. Groups of students work to create sequences with patterns that challenge their classmates in activity 4, What's Our Pattern?

Activity 1—Repeating Picture Patterns

Tell your students that they are going to play a little game called "Guess My Pattern." Give each student a copy of the blackline master for cards for the game. Point out that the sheet shows sixteen game cards—four copies of cards showing four different animals—lion, frog, bird, and donkey. Ask the students to cut out all the game cards and place them face up on their desks in no particular order. (The students do not use the cards that show donkeys until activity 2.)

The next step is for you to show several sequences of cards with various pictures and ask your students to find a pattern in each sequence. Of course, not all sequences have patterns—some are random. However, all the sequences that you display will have repeating patterns. Each will consist of the first two cards (or three cards, or four cards, and so on) repeated over and over.

Begin with a sequence that alternates between two objects. Facing the chalkboard, place a lion card on the left end of the chalk tray, then place a frog card to the right of the lion, then another lion card to the right of the frog card, and so on. Continue in this way until you have displayed the first eight cards of the sequence, as shown in figure 5.1.

It is important to introduce the use of the counting numbers to name the items in a sequence. Thus, as you place the initial lion card, say, "This is the first card." When you place a frog card beside it, say, "This is the second card." When you place another lion card beside the frog

A second grader cuts out game cards for "Guess My Pattern."

Photo by Colette DeLeo; all rights reserved

Navigating through Discrete Mathematics in Pre-K–Grade 5

Fig. **5.1.**

A sequence generated by a repeating
lion-frog pattern

card, say, "This is the third card." Continue in this fashion until you say, "This is the eighth card."

Also, remember that some students may not initially grasp the *directionality* of sequences—that is, they may not be acquainted with the convention that sequences start at the left and continue to the right. Thus, as you place the cards, you may want to emphasize that you begin on the left with a lion card and continue by placing a frog card to the right of the first card, and so on.

After placing the eight cards, invite your students to use their game cards to play "Guess My Pattern." Ask, "What group of animals repeats?" After the students determine the repeating group, they should select game cards and display those animals—one lion and one frog—in the correct order, from left to right, on their desks.

Pose the following questions:

- "Can you explain why the pattern of this sequence is that one lion and one frog repeat?"
- "How many times does the pattern of one lion and one frog repeat in my sequence of cards?" (Four times)
- Could the pattern of this sequence be one lion repeating? (No, because the sequence also has frogs in it)

Ask each student to discuss the following question with a partner: "Does the pattern of this sequence consist of one lion, one frog, and one lion repeating?" The students should conclude that it does not, because then the sequence would have to be lion, frog, lion; then lion, frog, lion; then lion, frog, lion; and so on. Two lions would sometimes appear next to each other, but the sequence has no consecutive lions.

Point to your first four placards, and pose the following question for the students to discuss with their partners: "Does the pattern consist of one lion, one frog, one lion, and one frog repeating?" The students should conclude that this description of the pattern is also correct, since it also generates the given sequence.

However, when mathematicians refer to a repeating pattern, they usually identify the smallest group of repeating objects that they can use to build the sequence. Thus, the repeating pattern in this example is one lion and one frog, although saying that the repeating pattern is one lion, one frog, one lion, and one frog is not incorrect.

This chapter follows a convention of using commas to separate consecutive objects in a sequence that employs words or numbers, and thus the text represents the sequence pictured in figure 5.1 as "lion, frog, lion, frog, lion, frog, lion, frog." However, when the text refers to a *pattern* in the sequence, it separates consecutive objects by hyphens. Thus, a repeating lion-frog pattern generates the sequence in figure 5.1. A repeating lion-frog-lion-frog pattern, as previously described, also generates this sequence. The hyphen notation provides a compact

When mathematicians refer to a repeating pattern, they usually identify the smallest group of repeating objects that they can use to build the sequence.

and more visual way of describing the pattern and simplifies the discussion of patterns.

A student may suggest that the repeating pattern in figure 5.1 is frog-lion. If you ask what has happened to the first lion, he or she might say that this sequence starts with a lion and then frog-lion repeats forever. This answer is not wrong, but it is more complicated and therefore less desirable than the simpler frog-lion answer. When students reach grade 4 or 5, they may recall these early experiences with repeating patterns as they work with repeating decimals and learn, for example, that they can abbreviate the number 0.24242424… as $0.\overline{24}$ but also as $0.\overline{2424}$ or $0.2\overline{42}$.

Tell your students to get ready for a new sequence in "Guess My Pattern." Remove the first sequence of placards from view and begin building the sequence displayed in figure 5.2. This sequence shows a lion and two frogs, another lion and two more frogs, then a third lion and two more frogs, and finally a fourth lion and two more frogs. As you place each card in the sequence, again say, "This is my first card, this is my second card, this is my third card," and so on, until you have displayed a total of twelve cards.

Fig. 5.2.

A sequence generated by a repeating lion-frog-frog pattern

Ask your students to guess the pattern and display their answers on their desks in the same way as before. After giving them sufficient time to create the lion-frog-frog pattern, explore with them the following questions:

- "What pattern did you find?" (The pattern repeats lion-frog-frog.)
- "How many times does lion-frog-frog repeat?" (Four times; show the repetitions.)
- "Can this sequence continue as long as your cards last, no matter how many cards you have?" (Yes; no matter how many times the group repeats, another repetition of the group can always appear at the end.)
- "Does this pattern have any smaller group that repeats?" (No)
- "Is there another group of cards that repeats?" (The first six cards also repeat—twice—in the given sequence of twelve cards, but lion-frog-frog uses fewer objects to generate the sequence.)

Give special attention to the last two questions. When the students consider whether a smaller group repeats, they may suggest the possibility that lion repeats or that lion-frog repeats. If they don't make these suggestions, elicit them with a question or two. Explain that to be sure that they have found the smallest group of repeating objects, they need to ask themselves whether a smaller group repeats and determine that the answer is no. Thus, a good problem-solving strategy is to ask themselves that question automatically whenever they think that they have found the smallest group that repeats.

When the students consider whether another group of cards repeats in the given sequence, they may point out that the first six cards—lion-

Photo by Colette DeLeo; all rights reserved

A second-grade student continues a repeating lion-frog-frog picture pattern.

frog-frog-lion-frog-frog—also repeat. Separate the first six cards from the final six so that the six-card pattern is evident. Although the question "What cards repeat?" thus has two different answers, remind the students that mathematicians search for patterns that contain the fewest objects, so the group lion-frog-frog is a better way to describe the pattern that generates the sequence than lion-frog-frog-lion-frog-frog.

Remove these cards from view, and create another sequence for "Guess My Pattern." Make the sequence shown in figure 5.3, again saying, "This is the first card in the sequence, this is the second card," and so on. This sequence alternates two lions with three frogs. Ask your students to guess the pattern and use their cards to show their answers as before.

After your students have displayed the lion-lion-frog-frog-frog pattern, ask someone to describe it. Be sure that the student mentions two points: (1) that the lion-lion-frog-frog-frog group is the smallest repeating group that he or she could find, and (2) that it repeats twice.

Continue the process, using the sequences shown in figures 5.4, 5.5, and 5.6. In figure 5.4, the pattern that repeats is frog-lion-bird; in figure 5.5, it is frog-lion-lion-bird-bird-bird; and in figure 5.6, it is frog-lion-frog-bird. In each case, have the students describe the pattern that they find, noting that they cannot represent the pattern in the sequence by any smaller group of repeating objects. Ask them whether each sequence can go on forever, and why, or why not.

When the class discusses whether a sequence continues forever, remind the students of the sequence of counting numbers 1, 2, 3, 4, 5, 6, and so on. Stress the fact that the numbers continue forever. Point out that you have been using the counting numbers to name the position of each card in a sequence, and you could continue those sequences

Fig. 5.3.

A sequence generated by a repeating lion-lion-frog-frog-frog pattern

Fig. 5.4.

A sequence generated by a repeating frog-lion-bird pattern

forever, as well—or at least until you became tired and decided to stop. You could certainly keep going as long as you wanted, using the pattern of each sequence as a guide for continuing it.

You have now introduced two kinds of sequences—sequences of cards and sequences of numbers. Next, introduce your students to terminology that mathematicians use when working with sequences. Each object in a sequence is called a *term*; and every sequence has a first term, a second term, a third term, a fourth term, and so on. Remind the

Fig. 5.5.

A sequence generated by a frog-lion-lion-bird-bird-bird pattern

Photo by Colette DeLeo; all rights reserved

Fig. **5.6.**

A sequence generated by a repeating frog-lion-frog-bird pattern

students that each time you placed a card, you told them what term it was in the sequence (the second card, for example, was the second term). Because the counting numbers go on forever, you can give a name to every term in every sequence.

Point to the sequence in figure 5.6—the last sequence that you displayed. Ask the students what the first term of this sequence is. What is the second term? The third term? And so on. Invite a student to come forward and select the tenth term in the sequence. He or she should choose the lion picture farthest to the right. Reinforce the idea that this is the tenth term by pointing to each picture in turn and saying, "This is the first term, this is the second term," and so on, until you reach the tenth picture. If your students are ready for the question, ask them what picture would appear on the card that represents the twentieth term of this sequence. They should determine that it is a bird.

To conclude the activity, have the students work in pairs to create three different sequences with repeating patterns. After each pair of students has completed this task, have two pairs try to find the repeating patterns in each other's sequences.

When everyone is finished, distribute plastic snack bags, ask the students to put their game cards into them, and collect the bags. The students will use the game cards again in activity 2.

As an extension to activity 1 or as homework to reinforce its ideas, students in grade 2 can complete an additional exercise using numbers instead of pictures. Give each student a copy of the activity sheet "Repeating Patterns in Number Sequences." Explain that the three dots (…) at the end of each sequence are a mathematical way of indicating that the sequence continues forever. Ask your students to find the repeating pattern in each of the sequences on the activity sheet. Once they think they have a pattern, they should verify that it actually does generate the given sequence.

In the first sequence (1, 4, 3, 2, 1, 4, 3, 2, 1, 4, 3, 2 …), the pattern that repeats is 1-4-3-2. This 1-4-3-2 repeat is the smallest group of numbers that repeats, and the given sequence shows three such groups. The next term in the sequence is 1.

A second-grade student creates a repeating lion-frog-bird pattern.

In the second sequence (1, 4, 1, 1, 4, 1, 1, 4, 1, 1, 4, 1, …), the pattern that repeats is 1-4-1. For some students, finding the repeating part of the pattern may be difficult because they need to recognize that the number 1 appears in two different positions— both as the first number and as the last number of the repeating part of the pattern. Young students may suggest that the pattern that repeats is 1-4 because they scan a sequence from left to right until they find a repeat of the first number in the group. If they propose 1-4 as the answer, ask them to verify whether it actually does generate the sequence. They will discover that 1-4 generates the sequence

1, 4, 1, 4, 1, 4, 1, 4, 1, 4, …, which does not match the original sequence since it does not have two 1s next to each other.

The students may find the pattern in the third sequence (3, 1, 1, 1, 3, 3, 1, 1, 1, 3, 3, 1, 1, 1, 3, …) a bit puzzling as well. Those who scan this sequence from left to right until they find a repeat of the first number in the group may suggest that the repeating pattern is 3-1-1-1. Encourage them to verify whether 3-1-1-1 actually does generate the sequence. They will find that 3-1-1-1 generates the sequence 3, 1, 1, 1, 3, 1, 1, 1, 3, 1, 1, 1, …, which does not match the original sequence, since it does not have two 3s next to each other. To find the repeating pattern, the students need to extend 3-1-1-1 by one number, obtaining 3-1-1-1-3, which does generate the third sequence. Because the fifteen terms in the sequence consist of three groups of 3-1-1-1-3, the next term is 3 because it is the first number in the next group.

Ask the students what pattern they can see in the sequence 3, 3, 1, 1, 2, 1, 1, 2, 1, 1, 2, 1, 1, 2, …. It clearly is a repeating sequence, but before the repetition of 1-1-2 begins, the sequence has 3, 3. Next, ask them what pattern they can see in the sequence 1, 2, 1, 1, 2, 1, 1, 2, 1, 1, 2, 1, 1, 2, …. This sequence is the same as the preceding one except that the first two terms are 1, 2 instead of 3, 3, so the answer can be that it has a repeating pattern, but before the repetition of 1-1-2 begins, the sequence has a 1, 2. However, the following reasoning is also correct: The sequence has a repeating pattern, in which 1-2-1 repeats. You can ask the following two questions about these descriptions:

- "Are both of these descriptions correct? Why, or why not?" (Yes, they are both correct because both 1-2-1 and 1-1-2—after the initial 1, 2—generate the given sequence.)
- "Does one of these two describe the pattern more correctly than the other?" (No, they are both mathematically correct.)

However, the second description is preferable. The basis for this statement is, in a sense, aesthetic: A simpler description is preferable to a more complicated one. It is simpler to say, "The sequence involves a repetition of 1-2-1," than it is to say, "The sequence involves a repetition of 1-1-2 after an initial 1, 2." By the same token, identifying the pattern in figure 5.1 as frog-lion after an initial lion is correct, but lion-frog is simpler and so is preferable.

Activity 2—Growing Picture Patterns

Finding the pattern in a sequence can be difficult. In the previous activity, all the sequences had repeating patterns. To find the pattern in such a sequence, someone can go through the terms in order until he or she finds terms that begin repeating the initial terms and continue repeating up to the term that began the repetition. The pattern of the sequence is then that the group of terms repeats. However, if no repeating pattern occurs, someone may have to work like a detective to discern the pattern—if one exists. In this activity, students play "Guess How I Continue"—a game that is similar to "Guess My Pattern" but uses sequences that have growing patterns instead of repeating ones.

Introduce growing patterns by using animal placards to make the sequence shown in figure 5.7. As you display each card, say, "This is the first card, this is the second card," and so on, as you did in activity 1, until you have arranged all nine cards in order. Ask your students

A simpler description is preferable to a more complicated one.

whether they notice anything that repeats in this sequence. They may suggest a possibility or two, and you should discuss their suggestions until all the students agree that no group of cards repeats, so the sequence must not have a repeating pattern. If the students do not make any suggestions, ask them whether, for example, lion-frog or lion-frog-lion repeats.

When the students agree that they cannot find a repeating pattern in the sequence, ask them whether they can see any other kind of pattern. Some students may notice that the figure includes three groups of frogs, with one frog in the first group, two in the second, and three in

Fig. **5.7.**

An example of a growing pattern

Photo by Colette DeLeo; all rights reserved

Two second-grade students successfully transform a repeating lion-frog pattern into a growing pattern in which the number of frogs in each group increases.

the third. If they do not notice this pattern, ask how many groups of frogs they see and how many frogs are in each group. After they notice that there are three groups of frogs and that a lion separates each group of frogs from the next group, they should observe that there is one lion and then one frog, then one lion and two frogs, and then one lion and three frogs. When the students recognize this pattern, ask them how the sequence continues. They should suggest that the sequence continues with one lion and four frogs, followed by one lion and five frogs. Add placards for one lion and four frogs to the placards on display.

Students may propose two methods of grouping the terms in the sequence—groups of frogs separated by single lions or groups that include single lions at the beginning. Figure 5.8 uses brackets to show the two groupings. Discuss these ways of grouping the terms with your students. Emphasize that in each, the next group always has one more frog than the current group. This language is important because it helps prepare students for NEXT-NOW activities in grades 3–5.

The general idea is that this pattern has groups of frogs separated by lions, and the number of frogs in the groups is one, then two, and then three. Some students more naturally recognize the pattern according to the first method shown in figure 5.8, and others more naturally use the second.

Use both methods in discussing each of the remaining sequences in the activity. In each case, help the students focus on two aspects of this new kind of pattern:

- Objects that grow in number and objects that serve to mark and separate the growing groups of objects.
- The actual way in which the growing groups of objects grow.

When the students recognize these two aspects, they will be able to describe growing patterns in general as well as analyze particular examples.

With a repeating pattern, it makes sense to ask what the next term of the sequence is. With a growing pattern, a single "next term" is much less significant than the next group of terms, so you should ask students how the sequence continues. The answer may involve any number of terms. In the example given in figure 5.7, the sequence continues with one lion followed by four frogs, as shown in figure 5.8.

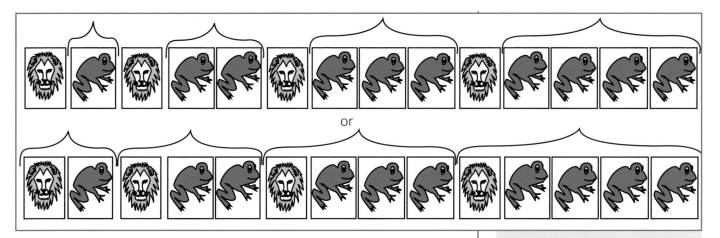

Fig. **5.8.**

Two methods of grouping the terms in the sequence; in both, the number of frogs in the groups increases from left to right.

Give each student a copy of the activity sheet "Guess How I Continue—Part 1" along with a plastic bag of game cards from "Guess My Pattern" in activity 1. Explain that the students will need more game cards for "Guess How I Continue" than they needed for "Guess My Pattern," however. Distribute copies of the blackline master "Cards for 'Guess My Pattern,'" and ask students to cut out the new cards.

Have the students place the activity sheet on their desks and arrange all the game cards face up, in no particular order. Go over the rules of the game: you will display several cards to make a sequence that continues from the students' left to right, and they will use their cards to represent the sequence at their desks. Then they will determine how the sequence continues and use cards to make the next group in the sequence.

Display the sequence of cards in part 1 (the sequence appears two times in fig. 5.9). After the students have created the next group in the sequence, ask them to collaborate again with partners, discussing—

- why their answers are correct;
- what groups of terms in the sequence are growing; and
- what term (or terms) are the markers that separate the growing groups of terms.

After the students have had an opportunity to share their ideas, discuss the results as a class.

In the sequence in part 1, the students should recognize that single lion cards separate consecutive groups of donkeys and that the number

Fig. **5.9.**

Two methods of grouping the terms in the sequence in "Guess How I Continue—Part 1"

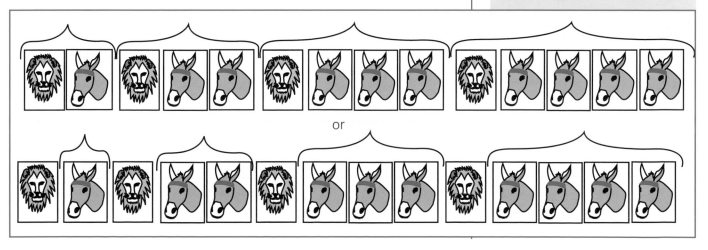

of donkeys in each consecutive group of donkeys increases by one. Students can see the pattern by grouping the cards according to either of the two methods discussed previously. Figure 5.9 illustrates both methods. One recognizes the sequence as groups containing one lion followed by some number of donkeys, with the number of donkeys increasing by one in each consecutive group. The other method recognizes the sequence as groups of donkeys with one lion separating every two consecutive groups.

Distribute the activity sheets for parts 2–5 and go on playing "Guess How I Continue" in the same way. Figure 5.10 shows the sequences in these parts.

Fig. 5.10.

The sequences that the students encounter in parts 2–5 of "Guess How I Continue"

In the sequence in part 2, the students should recognize that the groups of birds are growing, with the next group always including one more bird than the current group. They should also see that the frog cards serve as markers that separate consecutive groups of birds. Alternatively, students can think of the general pattern of this sequence as some number of birds followed by one frog. Specifically, the first group consists of one bird and one frog, the second group consists of two birds and one frog, and the third group consists of three birds and one frog. In response to the question, "How does the sequence continue?" students should place four bird cards followed by one frog card on the activity sheet and then discuss their work with their partners as before.

The sequences in parts 1 and 2 are similar. Each consists of groups of objects whose numbers are growing—donkeys and birds, respectively—separated by a term that serves as a marker—lions and frogs, respectively. However, the sequence in part 1 starts with a marker, and the

Navigating through Discrete Mathematics in Pre-K–Grade 5

sequence in part 2 starts with the first group of objects whose numbers grow. Assist your students in discovering these similarities and differences. Ask them to compare these two sequences to see whether they can identify anything that they have in common, as well as anything that is different. While you review each sequence, help the students note the relationship between NEXT and NOW—the next group in the sequence and the current group.

In part 3, the students should notice that the sequence has two lions—not one—that act as markers between each group of frogs. That is, two lions separate each group of frogs from the next group of frogs. The general pattern is some growing number of frogs followed by two lions. Thus, the sequence continues with four frogs followed by two lions.

The students should realize that the pattern in the sequence in part 4 is very similar to that in the sequence in part 3. In the earlier sequence, the markers—two lions—followed some growing number of frogs. The new sequence simply reverses the order—in part 4, some growing number of frogs follows two lion markers. This time, the markers' position is before each group of a growing number of frogs. Thus, the sequence continues with two lions followed by four frogs.

The general pattern in part 5 is that the frogs are markers that separate the three growing groups of birds. However, in this sequence, the next group always has two more birds than the current group. (In notation that the students will see in subsequent grades, the relationship can be expressed as NEXT = NOW + 2.) Alternatively, the students may see three groups of frogs and birds in the sequence, with the first group containing one frog followed by one bird, the second containing one frog followed by three birds, and the third containing one frog followed by five birds. Here again, the next group always has two more birds than the current group. Thus, to continue this sequence, the students should select one frog followed by seven birds. If the students have explored odd and even numbers, you can help them link the number of birds in the groups with the odd numbers.

You can assign "Guess How I Continue—Part 6" as an extension problem or as homework. The sequence that the activity sheet shows appears in figure 5.11. The pattern is that the numbers of frogs and donkeys are both increasing. Your students can think of the groups of frogs as markers that separate consecutive groups of donkeys, which increase by one donkey from one group to the next. Or they can think of the groups of donkeys as markers that separate consecutive groups of frogs, which are increasing by one frog from one group to the next. Or they may see the sequence as presenting three groups of frogs and donkeys: the first group includes one frog followed by one donkey, the second group includes two frogs followed by two donkeys, and the third group includes three frogs followed by three donkeys.

Figure 5.11 shows these three perspectives. In the first two, the markers do not consist of a fixed number of objects but are also increasing in number, with each marker having one more card than the previous one. In the third perspective, the sequence does not contain markers but simply groups consisting of two growing parts. This example, together with the previous examples, illustrates the variety of growing sequences.

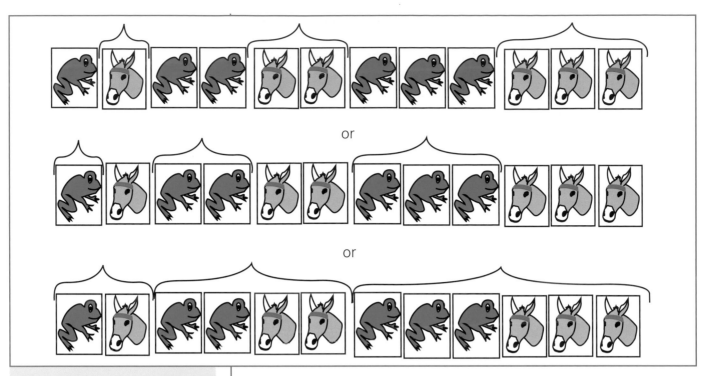

or

or

Fig. **5.11.**

Three different ways of viewing the same growing sequence

Activity 3—What Sequence Starts with …?

In working with a sequence, students often need to detect a pattern (either repeating or growing) and use it to determine either the next term or a missing term. Activity 3 gives students experience with both of these tasks. First, the students consider terms that might come next in given sequences, and then they consider terms that are missing.

The question, "What is the next term in my sequence?" always has more than one answer, because any initial sequence of terms can continue in more than one way. For example, in any sequence of lions and frogs—say, one lion followed by two frogs—the next term may be a gorilla. The gorilla may then be followed by the initial sequence of terms—one lion and two frogs—followed by another gorilla, followed by the initial sequence of terms, and so on. This possibility, though it may seem far-fetched, is one way to continue the sequence.

Because your students know about both repeating sequences and growing sequences, they may devise unexpected ways to continue a sequence. The criterion for whether an unexpected answer is acceptable is whether it is justifiable—that is, whether the explanation that the student provides describes a sequence that is consistent with the initial part of the sequence.

Use placards to display the sequence in figure 5.12. Ask your students what the next term in the sequence is. Most students will probably say frog, which appears to be the most reasonable answer because the pattern seems to be alternating between frog and lion. Ask them what the next ten terms of this sequence are after frog, lion, frog, lion, frog.

Congratulate your students on developing the sequence in which frogs and lions alternate, and then tell them that actually you planned to use a lion for the next term. Display a lion placard as the fifth term in the sequence, as in figure 5.13. Distribute copies of the activity sheet "What Sequence Starts with …?—Part 1," which shows the sequence with a lion as the fifth term instead of a frog. Ask the students to work

in pairs to determine the next term of the sequence, explain the pattern, and identify the next ten terms in the sequence.

Because the students have seen growing patterns, some may conclude that the next term in the sequence is a frog, followed by three lions. However, other students may decide that the sequence has a five-card repeating pattern—frog-lion-frog-lion-lion—and conclude that the next term is a frog, followed by a lion, another frog, and two more lions. Both groups of students conclude that the next term in the sequence is a frog, but they arrive at their conclusions by using different patterns. Still other students might suggest that the next term is a lion if they decide that the sequence consists of one frog and one lion, then one frog and three lions, then one frog and five lions, and so on.

Fig. 5.12.

How might the sequence continue?

Fig. 5.13.

What picture might come next in the sequence? Why?

A small number of initial terms of a sequence can often lead in more than one direction. Students who arrive at different conclusions are correct if they can describe their pattern and convincingly explain how they use it to find the next term in the sequence.

Tell your students that since they have explored what happens when they continue the frog-lion-frog-lion sequence first with a frog, and then with a lion, they will next explore what happens when they continue this sequence with a different card. Remove the last lion placard from your displayed sequence and place a bird placard as the fifth term (after frog, lion, frog, lion). Distribute the activity sheet "What Sequence Starts with …?—Part 2," and ask your students to work in pairs to find the next term in the sequence that starts with these five terms. They should explain their pattern and use their cards to display the first twenty terms of the sequence before recording them on the activity sheet.

The students can develop many possible sequences. If they can justify the sequence, then their answers are correct. You can ask the students in each group to present their sequences and explain their patterns. Write the words "Sequences with Growing Patterns" on the left side of the board and "Sequences with Repeating Patterns" on the right, and ask students to place their sequences under the appropriate heading.

Some ways of continuing the sequence follow:

- It can have a repeating pattern in which frog-lion-frog-lion-bird repeats.

- It can have a growing pattern in which a bird is a marker between increasing numbers of pairs of frogs and lions. (The first group has two pairs, the second group has three pairs, then four pairs, then five pairs, and so on. Alternatively, the second group can have four pairs, then six pairs, then eight pairs, and so on.)

- It can have a growing pattern in which frog-lion-frog-lion is a marker between increasing numbers of birds.

- It can have a growing pattern in which frog-lion is a marker between increasing numbers of birds—and in which zero birds occur after the first marker.

The solutions section (p. 244) shows the first twenty terms of each of the resulting sequences.

To summarize what the students have been doing, tape the first four cards of these sequences—a frog at the left, followed by a lion, a frog, and a lion—to the chalkboard. Next to these cards, draw a blank line, and then ask students how to continue the sequence. Discuss possibilities. Explain that the sequence could continue with a frog (tape a frog card under the blank line on the chalkboard). Or it could continue with a lion (tape a lion card under the frog card). Or it could continue with a bird (tape a bird card under the lion). In other words, a sequence can often continue in many different ways. An answer is correct if it is possible to add a term to a sequence and describe how to continue the sequence with that term.

As the culminating exercise in this part of the activity, distribute the activity sheet "What Sequence Starts with …?—Part 3," which invites students to find two different ways to continue a sequence and then find the first twenty terms in each sequence. Let the students work by themselves to complete the sheet, and then ask each student to share results with a partner, with each pair of students finding as many different ways to continue the sequence as they can.

Next, shift the focus to a missing term in a sequence. Use animal placards to display the sequence in figure 5.14, which consists of a frog, a lion, a frog, a blank space, a frog, a lion, and a frog. Ask what the first term is, the second, the third, and the fourth. The students should recognize that the fourth term is missing from the sequence. Ask the students to pretend to be detectives and try to figure out what the fourth term might be.

In this situation, they will probably quickly decide that the sequence alternates between frogs and lions, and so the fourth term must be a

Fig. 5.14.

What might the fourth term of the sequence be?

Navigating through Discrete Mathematics in Pre-K–Grade 5

lion. Some students, however, may decide that the missing term is a frog or a bird, and they may be able to justify their answers.

Use placards to display the sequence in figure 5.15: frog, lion, bird, frog, blank, bird, frog, lion, bird. The students are again likely to recognize the pattern, even though it includes three objects; and they will probably conclude that a lion belongs in the blank. In this example, students will have more difficulty justifying that a frog, a bird, or a gorilla should fill the blank.

Distribute the activity sheet "What Is the Missing Term?—Part 1," and ask the students to work on it in pairs. First, the students explain why the blank in the sequence frog, lion, frog, lion, lion, frog, lion, blank, lion could be a lion. Then they explain why it could be a frog. Both frog and lion are reasonable answers. The pattern could be growing—one frog, one lion, one frog, two lions, one frog, three lions—so a lion could belong in the blank. However, the pattern could also be repeating—a five-card repeating pattern—frog-lion-frog-lion-lion—so a frog could belong in the blank.

Distribute the activity sheet "What Is the Missing Term?—Part 2," and have students work in groups to fill in the blank for each of the four sequences shown and then find another object that could be the missing term in each case. After the groups have worked on these questions, ask them to present their conclusions. You should anticipate that they will devise some interesting answers.

Many standardized tests include items about sequences like those in these activities, posing such questions as, What is the next term? or What is the missing term? It is sometimes possible to justify more than one of the choices given. However, students should assume that the "correct" answer is likely to be the one based on the simplest pattern.

Activity 4—What's Our Pattern?

Divide the class into two teams and give each team sixteen animal placards. One team should have eight frogs and eight birds, and the other should have eight lions and eight donkeys. You may want to have a few extra placards, depending on how many you have made.

Direct the members of each team to work together to create a pattern and use it to build a sequence of cards. Each team should try to create a pattern that will stump the opposing team, which earns one point if it finds the pattern and can explain how the pattern generates the sequence. Otherwise, it earns no points.

Explain further details: creating a sequence without a pattern will certainly stump the opposing team, but an opposing team that cannot find a pattern can challenge the creating team to describe its pattern. If the creating team is unable to do so, it loses two points, and the challenging team earns two points. If the creating team can describe the pattern, it earns one point, and the challenging team loses one point.

Fig. 5.15.

What might the fifth term of the sequence be?

Tell the students that descriptions such as the following are not acceptable:

- "The sequence is formed by repeating all the terms displayed."
- "The sequence is formed by repeating all but one of the terms displayed"
- "The sequence is formed by repeating all but two of the terms displayed."

After the teams have chosen their patterns, they should build their sequences, with each team member receiving a card for one term in the sequence. When both teams are set, ask them to line up in two rows, opposite each other but far enough apart for every member of one team to see every member of the other team easily. All team members should hold their cards face in so that no one can see them. The team members should not talk while they line up. Designate team captains and ask them to review and verify the order of the team members and terms in the sequences. All the terms should be in order so that when the teams reveal their cards, each team can read the other's sequence from left to right. The captains should then resume their positions in the lines, and you should ask all the students to display their cards simultaneously. Direct the students to stand in silence for two minutes, while they think about possibilities for the opposing team's pattern. Then ask each student to place his or her card on the floor in front of his or her feet. Have the students stand quietly for a few more seconds. Then send the teams to opposite corners of the room to discuss each other's pattern. Permit the students to go back and look at the cards if necessary. Explain that you will be selecting one member of each team to explain the pattern, but because no one knows whom you will choose, everyone on the team needs to understand the other team's pattern and be able to offer a good explanation of it.

When both teams are ready, have them re-form their lines. Choose one team to be first, and call on one of its members to explain the second team's pattern. Ask the second team's captain whether the explanation correctly describes the pattern. Then have the captain give his or her team's explanation of the pattern. Discuss with the class whether the pattern that the first team described is the same as or different from the one that second team had in mind. Even if the second team was thinking of a different pattern, both patterns may be reasonable descriptions of the sequence. For example, the second team might show four frogs and then five birds. The first team's explanation might be that the pattern alternates four frogs and five birds, but the second team might say that after the five birds come six frogs and then seven birds. Both patterns are reasonable descriptions of the sequence.

Next, reverse the roles of the two teams, and ask one member of the second team to explain the first team's pattern. After he or she presents the explanation, ask the first team's captain to say whether he or she agrees with the explanation and to give his or her own explanation of the pattern. Discuss whether the pattern that the second team presented is the same as or different from the one that the first team had in mind.

Assign points to the teams according to the rules previously discussed. Round 1 is now complete. The number of rounds that your class plays will depend on the students and the time available. A class can, for example, play until one team has five points. Each team should use a different sequence in each round.

After the first or second round, you may want to give your students more options in creating sequences. If so, give each team eight white sheets of card stock and tell them that the cards represent polar bears hiding in the snow. Have the students play as before, but require that each team's pattern include all three animals. In the new situation, the teams are more likely to have different explanations for the same pattern.

Your students may come up with interesting patterns, including those that are neither repeating nor growing patterns. This investigation does not cover all types of patterns. For example, the sequence lion, lion, lion, lion, frog, lion, lion, lion, frog, lion, lion, frog, lion, frog is a shrinking pattern. The number of lions in each group becomes smaller and smaller. When the lions disappear, the sequence ends—it is an example of a sequence that terminates. A sequence could, however, grow, then diminish, then grow, then diminish, and so on. An example is lion, frog, lion, frog, frog, lion, frog, frog, frog, lion, frog, frog, lion, frog, lion, frog, frog. This sequence is a combination of a growing pattern, a repeating pattern, and a shrinking pattern. Your students may come up with other interesting patterns, and this activity can be a lot of fun. Just remember that the students have to be able to justify their solutions—in each situation, the pattern must generate the sequence.

The Mathematics in the Investigation

The mathematical focus of this investigation is sequential patterns and sequential thinking. Students who inspect five pictures in a row do not consider them as a sequence unless they recognize two features of a sequence—*directionality* and *ordinal position*—at a conscious level. That is, they must be aware of the order of the pictures from left to right and associate the positions of the pictures in some fashion with the numbers from 1 to 5. Sequential thinking involves looking at, for example, five pictures and being able to see them as consisting of—

- A first picture, which is on the far left;
- A second picture to the right of the first picture;
- A third picture to the right of the second picture;
- A fourth picture to the right of the third picture; and
- A fifth picture to the right of the fourth picture.

The investigation introduces the terminology *term of a sequence*—that is, any sequence has a first term, a second term, and so on. In this investigation, most of the terms of the sequences are pictures of animals, so the activities are appropriate for students in prekindergarten through first grade. Sequences whose terms are numbers are more appropriate for children in grades 2 through 5.

Students in prekindergarten through grade 2 can learn sequential thinking in the context of learning about sequential patterns. A *sequential pattern* is a sequence in which the terms follow a specified pattern. This investigation focuses on two kinds of sequential patterns—repeating patterns and growing patterns. In the first kind of sequence—for example, lion, frog, lion, frog, lion, frog, lion, frog—a

Students who inspect five pictures in a row do not consider them as a sequence unless they recognize two features of a sequence— directionality *and* ordinal position.

group of terms—in the example, lion-frog—repeats over and over. In the second kind of sequence—for example, lion, frog, lion, lion, frog, lion, lion, lion, frog, lion, lion, lion, lion, frog—some of the terms in the sequence function as markers that separate groups of terms, and consecutive groups are growing in number. In this example, the frogs serve as markers and separate groups of lions. The group begins with one lion, then a frog follows, then two lions, then a frog, then three lions, then a frog, and so on.

In this investigation, students examine sequences and try to determine their patterns. They also create sequences and ask other students to discover their patterns. The idea that a sequence can continue forever is another important feature of sequential thinking that students develop as the activities help them use repeating and growing patterns to generate sequences. The investigation also guides students in finding missing terms in a sequence (including the next term) and learning that they can often continue a sequence in more than one way, since more than one pattern may fit the part of a sequence that they are inspecting.

The sequential thinking and familiarity with repeating patterns that students develop in this investigation can help prepare them for work with iteration in grades 3–5, where they will encounter activities that are similar to those in the next chapter. Likewise, their early experiences with growing patterns, in which the next group has one (or two) more members than the present group, can give them a foundation for the NEXT-NOW activities that they will encounter in subsequent grades.

The idea that a sequence can continue forever is another important feature of sequential thinking.

NAVIGATIONS SERIES

PRE-K–GRADE 5

All students in grades 3–5 should—

- *describe, analyze, and create a variety of sequential patterns, including numeric and geometric patterns, such as repeating and growing patterns, tessellations, and fractal designs;*

- *represent sequential patterns by using informal notation and terminology for recursion, such as* NOW, NEXT, *and* PREVIOUS;

- *use sequential patterns, iterative procedures, and informal notation for recursion to model and solve problems, including those in simple real-world contexts, such as growth situations;*

- *describe and create simple iterative procedures by using such technology as Logo-like environments, spreadsheets, and calculators.*

NAVIGATING *through* DISCRETE MATHEMATICS

Chapter 6
Iteration and Recursion in Grades 3–5

To repeat a procedure, process, or rule over and over is to perform an iteration. One way for young children to understand the process of iteration is to work with sequential patterns. As children grow, they need to learn to think analytically about tasks to complete them efficiently themselves or possibly turn them into automated processes.

The investigation in this chapter, Exploring Sequences Step by Step, helps students identify, describe, and create patterns for sequences of numbers and geometric shapes. The goals of the investigation are to develop students' abilities to—

- identify a pattern that describes the relationship between consecutive terms in a sequence;

- use a rule to express that pattern; and

- apply the rule to generate additional terms and extend the sequence.

In later years, when students are familiar with algebraic terminology, they may state the rule *explicitly*, by an equation that expresses the nth term of the sequence as a function of n, such as $f(n) = 2n - 1$. However, students in grades 3–5 more appropriately state the rule *recursively*, by using the previous term to express the next term of the sequence, as in PREVIOUS + 2 = NOW. This *recursive equation*, unlike the *explicit equation* above, focuses on the repetitive, or recurring, aspect of the sequence. *Recursion* is the process of generating each term in a sequence from the previous term. If n is a counting number that is greater than or equal to 1, the explicit equation $f(n) = 2n - 1$ determines the sequence 1, 3, 5, 7,

127

"Students continue identifying, describing, and extending numeric patterns involving all operations and nonnumeric growing or repeating patterns. Through these experiences, they develop an understanding of the use of a rule to describe a sequence of numbers or objects."

(NCTM 2006, p. 16)

"Do It Again, Sam" (Souhrada 2002; available on the CD-ROM) explores other topics in iteration and recursion.

9, 11, …. The recursive formula NOW = PREVIOUS + 2 determines the same sequence for the starting value 1.

If this investigation is your students' first encounter with patterns and sequences, you may want to review by using the activities in the previous chapter, with appropriate adjustments for the students' more advanced grade level. Students in grades 3–5 have learned the basic operations of arithmetic and can recognize patterns in numbers, so they will be prepared for a unit that focuses on such patterns.

The simplest iterative patterns involve beginning with a number—say, 1—and adding a fixed number—say, 2—over and over. Working from the starting point, 1, and applying the rule "add 2," students can generate and explain the sequence that results: 1, 3, 5, 7, 9, …. Students can also begin with 1 and repeatedly multiply by 2, thereby generating the doubling sequence 1, 2, 4, 8, 16, 32, ….

Students in grades 3–5 are also ready to explore number sequences generated by geometric patterns built from squares and triangles. They can explore growth rates by observing that sequences generated by a rule that involves repeated multiplication by a fixed whole number grow much faster than sequences generated by a rule that involves repeated addition of a fixed whole number. This comprehension helps prepare them for later applications of iteration and recursion to models of growth.

Exploring Sequences Step by Step

The investigation Exploring Sequences Step by Step consists of a sequence of five activities designed to allow upper elementary school students to continue the exploration of iteration and recursion that they began in earlier years, when they usually worked with sequences of pictures to learn about repeating and growing patterns.

Goals

- Describe, analyze, and create a variety of sequential patterns, including numeric and geometric patterns, such as repeating and growing patterns, tessellations, and fractal designs

- Represent sequential patterns by using informal notation and terminology for recursion, such as NOW, NEXT, and PREVIOUS

- Use sequential patterns, iterative procedures, and informal notation for recursion to model and solve problems, including those in simple real-world contexts, such as growth situations

- Describe and create simple iterative procedures by using technology, such as Logo-like environments, spreadsheets, and calculators

Materials and Equipment

Activity 1—Sequences of Numbers

For each student—

- A sheet of paper

- A copy of each of the following activity sheets:
  - "Creating Number Sequences"
  - "Other Number Sequences"

- A calculator (optional)

Activity 2—Doubling Sequences

For demonstration—

- A chessboard

For each student—

- A copy of each of the following activity sheets:

  - "8 × 8 Grid"
  - "Grids—Part 1"
  - "Grids—Part 2"

- A pair of scissors

- An envelope or small plastic bag

- A calculator

Students can work with the applet Fractal Tool on the CD-ROM to transform shapes and explore the topic of iteration graphically. The INITIAL *button shows them a shape at the first stage, and the* NOW *and* NEXT *buttons show how the figure changes at each step.*

pp. 217, 218

pp. 219, 220, 221

Activity 3—Sequences Involving Squares

pp. 222, 223, 224, 225, 226, 227

For demonstration—

- A transparency of the blackline master "Squares on Squares"

For each group of two students—

- Eighty square pattern blocks (or the small paper squares that the students created in activity 2)

For each student—

- A copy of each of the following activity sheets:
  - "Sequences of Shapes and Numbers"
  - "More Practice with Sequences"
  - "A Sequence of Square Shapes"
  - "Squares and Backward Ls—Part 1"
  - "Squares and Backward Ls—Part 2"

Activity 4—Sequences Involving Triangles

p. 228

For demonstration—

- Fifty triangle pattern blocks
- A blank overhead transparency
- A transparency of the blackline master "Fourth Term of a Sequence of Triangular Shapes"

For each group of two students—

- Fifty triangle pattern blocks
- A sheet of easel paper
- A roll of transparent tape

For each student—

- Three copies of the blackline master "Fourth Term of a Sequence of Triangular Shapes"
- A pair of scissors

Activity 5—Iteration, Counting, and Vertex-Edge Graphs

pp. 229, 230, 231, 232, 233

For demonstration—

- A transparency of the blackline master "From *A* to *P* on a Grid Graph"

For each student—

- A copy of each of the following activity sheets
  - "How Many Paths from *A* to *P*"
  - "Walking on a Grid Graph"
  - "Pumpkin Paths"
  - "Pascal's Triangle"
- A sheet of paper
- Two different colors of crayons, markers, or colored pencils

Navigating through Discrete Mathematics in Pre-K–Grade 5

Prior Knowledge

Students should be able to—

- identify a number as even or odd;
- add and multiply fluently;
- perform simple operations on a calculator.

Preliminary Activities

Before introducing this chapter's investigation to your students, review chapter 5, "Iteration and Recursion in Pre-K–Grade 2." Gauge your students' abilities to perform those activities, and if appropriate, adapt and present them to give your students a firm understanding of the idea of a sequence and the terms of a sequence.

To be ready for the new investigation, your students should have worked with both repeating and growing sequences and should be familiar with sequential patterns and sequential thinking. Students do not recognize five objects in a row as forming a sequence unless they are conscious of two features of a sequence—*directionality* and *ordinal position*. In other words, the students must recognize that the objects are ordered from left to right, and they must associate the objects' positions with the numbers 1 to 5. Sequential thinking involves not only being able to identify the objects in a sequence but also being able to name them as—

- a first object, on the far left;
- a second object, to the immediate right of the first object;
- a third object, to the right of the second object;
- a fourth object, to the right of the third object;
- a fifth object, to the right of the fourth object; and so on.

Students who understand these ideas are ready to generalize their patterns by using NOW, NEXT, and PREVIOUS language, as presented in the activities discussed below.

Activities

The investigation Exploring Sequences Step by Step includes five activities. In the first activity, Sequences of Numbers, the students explore a variety of sequences of numbers, learn to generate sequences, and encounter terminology for describing sequences. The second activity, Doubling Sequences, focuses on sequences of numbers in which each successive term is twice the previous term. In the third and fourth activities, Sequences Involving Squares and Sequences Involving Triangles, the students examine and find patterns in sequences whose terms are geometric objects built from some number of unit squares or triangles. They associate number sequences with the sequences of shapes and identify patterns in the number sequences. In the fifth activity—Iteration, Counting, and Vertex-Edge Graphs—the students explore counting problems in graph contexts and discover that the solutions involve iteration. This activity serves as a culminating exercise in the investigation, bringing together the three major themes of discrete mathematics in *Principles and Standards for School Mathematics* (NCTM

2000). It also introduces students to the recursive construction of Pascal's triangle.

Activity 1—Sequences of Numbers

Tell your students that a number sequence is just a list of numbers that goes on and on according to a fixed rule. Say, for example, "Suppose that you start with the number 2 and add 3, then add 3 again, then add 3 again, then add 3 again, and keep going." Explain that this process generates a sequence that they can write as 2, 5, 8, 11, 14, …. Tell the students that each number in the sequence is a *term*, and the first number—in this case, 2—is the *first term*, or the *initial term*, of the sequence. Emphasize that adding 3 always gives the next term in the sequence, so in the sequence under discussion, 11 is the fourth term: 2 + 3 + 3 + 3.

Also review the convention of showing the terms in a sequence from left to right. Explain that whenever the students write a sequence, they should put a comma after each term and three dots at the end of their list to indicate that the sequence goes on forever. Whenever they list the terms in a sequence aloud, they should end the list by saying "dot, dot, dot." Stress the fact that every sequence has a fixed *starting point* and a fixed *rule*. Elaborate on the roles of these two elements of a sequence: "To generate a sequence, you start with the starting point and then apply the rule to it to generate a new term in the sequence. Then you use the same rule again, this time applying it to the new term to generate the next term. You continue in this way, by applying the rule over and over." Emphasize the idea that the process of applying a rule over and over is called *iteration*.

Ask your students to write the sequence 2, 5, 8, 11, 14, … on a piece of paper and extend it by applying the rule "add 3" until they find a term whose value is greater than 40. They should obtain the following list: 2, 5, 8, 11, 14, 17, 20, 23, 26, 29, 32, 35, 38, 41, …. Ask questions to probe their understanding:

- "Is it possible to continue to add 3 to the terms of this sequence until the end of class?" (Sure) "Until the end of the day?" (Sure) "Until the end of the week?" (Sure)
- "Does the sequence ever end?" (No, and to show that it does not, mathematicians write three dots […] at the end of a list of terms.)
- "Will we ever run out of numbers that continue the sequence?" (No, the sequence given by the rule "add 3" can continue forever.)
- "The leftmost number—2—is the first, or initial, term in the sequence. The second term is 5, and the third term is 8. So what is the eighth term in the sequence?" (23)
- "How many terms did you have to find before reaching a number greater than 40?" (Fourteen)
- "So how could we refer to the term 41 in the sequence?" (As the fourteenth term; one way that mathematicians refer to a term in a sequence is by its position in the list.
- "What is the twelfth term of the sequence?" (35)

Next, ask the students to find the twentieth term. Although it is not on the list that the students originally generated, they can continue their lists and find the term in question: 41 is the fourteenth term, 44 is

Iteration is the process of applying a rule over and over. For example, applying the rule "add 3," over and over, starting with 2, generates the sequence 2, 5, 8, 11, 14, ….

the fifteenth, 47 is the sixteenth, 50 is the seventeenth, 53 is the eighteenth, 56 is the nineteenth, and 59 is the twentieth term.

Ask your students to make up another sequence of numbers. Assign each student a partner so that the students can work in pairs to play a little game called "What's My Sequence?" Explain how the game works: A student gives his or her partner a starting point and a rule, and the partner must generate at least the first five terms in the sequence. For example, one student might say, "My initial term is 0, and my rule is 'add 5.' What's my sequence?" The student's partner should write 0, 5, 10, 15, 20, …, or say, "Your sequence is 0, 5, 10, 15, 20, dot, dot, dot." To be certain that the iterative pattern is evident, each term should have the correct value and be followed by a comma, and the sequence should end with three dots to show that it continues forever.

Some students may become confused when they hear statements like, "The second term is 5," and "The fifth term is 20," since these statements use numbers in two different ways—to describe the position of a term and to indicate the value of a term—and the same number can serve as either a position or a value, as 5 does in the two statements. Make sure that your students understand the two different ways of using numbers in the context of a sequence.

Next, explain that mathematicians like to use a type of shorthand notation to write their rules. State the rule in the example that the students have been considering: "To find the next number in the sequence, take the number that you have and add 3 to it." Give the shorthand notation for the rule: "You can write this rule as 'NOW + 3 = NEXT,' which indicates that you can generate the next number in the list by taking the 'now' number—that is, the current number in the list—and adding 3 to it."

Have your students use the rule NOW + 3 = NEXT to generate a sequence of numbers. Ask for a volunteer to write his or her sequence on the board. Invite several other students who have found different sequences to post theirs on the board as well. Be sure to write "…" after the last term of each example that lacks the three dots. Point out that although all students used the same recursive rule of iteration, their sequences may different because they chose different initial terms. Inspect the initial term of each sequence on the board.

Distribute the activity sheet "Creating Number Sequences," and ask your students to work individually on step 1. Part (*a*) asks them to generate the first fifteen terms in a sequence that follows the rule NOW + 3 = NEXT and starts with 1. Part (*b*) asks them to do the same thing for a sequence that follows this rule but starts with 0. Part (*c*) asks them for the eighteenth term in the sequence in part (*b*). After an appropriate time, ask the students to work in pairs first to check their solutions to step 1and then to complete step 2, which questions them about their work so far.

For step 1(*a*), the sequence that students find by using the rule NOW + 3 = NEXT, starting with 1, is 1, 4, 7, 10, 13, 16, 19, 22, 25, 28, 31, 34, 37, 40, 43, …. Because students start with 1, the number 1 is the first term in the sequence. When they apply the NOW-NEXT rule, they find that the next number in the sequence is the value of the current number (NOW), or 1, plus 3, so the second term in the sequence is 4. When they apply the rule again, the second term, 4, is the NOW

Mathematicians use three dots (…) at the end of a sequence to indicate that it continues forever. In listing the terms of a sequence aloud, students should finish by saying "dot, dot, dot."

A NOW-NEXT *rule expresses the* NEXT *term of a sequence by using the current (*NOW*) term of the sequence; for example,* NOW + 3 = NEXT *indicates that you obtain the next term by adding 3 to the current term.*

number, and the third term is 7. The students continue until they have calculated all fifteen terms in the sequence.

For step 1(*b*), the sequence that the students find by using the iterative rule NOW + 3 = NEXT, starting with 0, is 0, 3, 6, 9, 12, 15, 18, 21, 24, 27, 30, 33, 36, 39, 42, …. This time, the first term in the sequence is 0. When they apply the NOW-NEXT rule, they find that the next number in the sequence—the second term—is 3, the value of the NOW number, or 0, plus 3. When they apply the rule again, the NEXT number—the third term in the sequence—is 6, the value of the NOW number, or 3, plus 3. The students continue in this manner until they have calculated all fifteen terms in the sequence. By extending this sequence for three more terms, they find that the eighteenth term in this sequence is 51.

In addition to the earlier classroom example where the initial term was 2, the students have now generated two sequences by using the rule NOW + 3 = NEXT, with each sequence starting at a different number. Step 2 asks students to explore the relationships among the three sequences. They find that the sequence that starts with 2 includes the number 26, but neither of the other sequences does. The sequence that starts with 0 includes the number 33, but neither of the others does.

The remaining questions in step 2 lead the students to the conclusion that every whole number appears in one, and only one, of these three sequences. How can they justify this conclusion? They can go through all the numbers one by one and verify that each number is in one of the sequences—0 is in the third sequence, 1 is in the second sequence, 2 is in the first sequence, and then keep going until they reach 44. It then appears that every whole number from 0 to 44 is in one of these three sequences, but how can students be sure that all numbers greater than 44 also appear in one of these sequences? Because counting to check all possibilities would take forever, they need to look for a pattern that can convince them that each of the counting numbers appears in exactly one of these three sequences.

Lining up the sequences in three rows with the terms aligned vertically in columns produces the following arrangement:

Each whole number appears in exactly one of the three sequences.

2, 5, 8, 11, 14, 17, 20, 23, 26, 29, 32, 35, 38, 41, 44, …
1, 4, 7, 10, 13, 16, 19, 22, 25, 28, 31, 34, 37, 40, 43, …
0, 3, 6, 9, 12, 15, 18, 21, 24, 27, 30, 33, 36, 39, 42, …

An interesting pattern emerges. If the students start at the number 0 and read up the first column of numbers—that is, all the first terms in the sequences—they read 0, 1, 2. If next they read up the second column, which contains all the second terms, they read the next three numbers in the sequence of whole numbers: 3, 4, 5. And so on. The arrangement gives them visual confirmation that each whole number is a term in just one of these sequences.

If your students know about multiples or are ready to learn about them, you can pursue this topic, providing numerical as well as visual confirmation that each number appears in just one of the three sequences. Begin by asking the students to determine which sequence includes the number 60 and which sequence includes the number 100. Urge them to find their answers by reasoning rather than actually extending the sequences. The students should first notice that the numbers in the bottom sequence are all multiples of 3 (0×3, 1×3, 2×3,

$3 \times 3, 4 \times 3, 5 \times 3, \ldots$) and then recognize that 60 is also a multiple of 3: $60 = 20 \times 3$. So 60 is in the sequence that begins with 0. How can the students describe all the numbers in the middle sequence? They should recognize that these numbers are all 1 more than a multiple of 3, since each is 1 more than the corresponding number in the bottom sequence. Similarly, the students should conclude that the numbers in the top sequence are all 2 more than a multiple of 3, because each is 2 more than the corresponding number in the bottom sequence.

What about 100? Is it a multiple of 3? What numbers near 100 are multiples of 3? The students should determine that 99 is a multiple of 3: $99 = 33 \times 3$. Therefore, 100 is 1 more than a multiple of 3 and is in the sequence that begins with 1. What about 300? Because 300 is a multiple of 3 ($300 = 100 \times 3$), it is in the sequence that begins with 0. What about 500? Students should reason that 500 is in the sequence that begins with 2: $500 = 498 + 2$, and 498 is a multiple of 3 ($498 = 166 \times 3$).

An alternative method that students can use for determining the sequence in which a number belongs is to remove multiples of 3000, 300, and 30 until they obtain a number that is less than 30 and they can easily recognize the sequence in which it appears. Suppose, for example, that they are asked which of the three sequences contains 7195. They can write 7195 as $6000 + 1195$, then write 1195 as $900 + 295$, and then write 295 as $270 + 25$. Altogether,

$$7195 = 6000 + 900 + 270 + 25.$$

Because 6000, 900, and 270 are all multiples of 3, the number 7195 is in the same sequence as 25—the sequence that begins with 1.

If your students have learned division, they can of course determine in which of the three sequences a number appears by dividing the number by 3. For example, if they want to determine which sequence has 100 as a term, they can divide 100 by 3. The remainder is 1, so 100 is in the pattern that begins with 1. However, third and fourth graders who have not yet learned about division can still do the activity.

You can introduce your students to the fact that a number is a multiple of 3 if the sum of its digits is a multiple of 3. For example, 7854 is a multiple of 3 because $7 + 8 + 5 + 4 = 24$, and 24 is a multiple of 3, but 637 is not a multiple of 3 because $6 + 3 + 7 = 16$, and 16 is not a multiple of 3. This fact may seem mysterious, but the explanation is quite straightforward:

You can introduce your students to the seemingly mysterious fact that a number is a multiple of 3 if the sum of its digits is a multiple of 3; 7854 is a multiple of 3 because

$$7 + 8 + 5 + 4 = 24,$$

and 24 is a multiple of 3, but 637 is not a multiple of 3 because

$$6 + 3 + 7 = 16,$$

and 16 is not a multiple of 3.

$$
\begin{aligned}
7854 &= 7 \times 1000 + 8 \times 100 + 5 \times 10 + 4 && \text{(expanded form of numbers)}\\
&= 7 \times (999 + 1) + 8 \times (99 + 1) + 5 \times (9 + 1) + 4 && \text{(equivalent forms of 1000, 100, and 10)}\\
&= (7 \times 999 + 7 \times 1) + (8 \times 99 + 8 \times 1) + (5 \times 9 + 5 \times 1) + 4 && \text{(distributive property of } \times \text{ over +)}\\
&= (7 \times 999 + 8 \times 99 + 5 \times 9) + (7 \times 1 + 8 \times 1 + 5 \times 1) + 4 && \text{(commutative and associative properties of +)}\\
&= (7 \times 999 + 8 \times 99 + 5 \times 9) + (7 + 8 + 5 + 4) && \text{(simplification)}
\end{aligned}
$$

In the last expression, the three summands in the first pair of parentheses are all multiples of 3, since 999, 99, and 9 are multiples of 3. So whether 7854 is a multiple of 3 depends only on whether the four summands in the second pair of parentheses add to a multiple of 3: $7 + 8 + 5 + 4 = 24$; $24 = 8 \times 3$. Because every number can be represented in this way, the question of whether a number is a multiple of 3 always depends on whether the sum of its digits is a multiple of 3.

Your students have been working with a NOW-NEXT recursive rule: NOW + 3 = NEXT . Introduce a recursive rule that looks different: PREVIOUS + 3 = NOW. The NOW-NEXT rule uses the current term (NOW) to generate the term that follows (NEXT). The PREVIOUS-NOW rule instead uses the term that comes before (PREVIOUS) to generate the current term (NOW). Determining the value of the NOW number means adding 3 to the PREVIOUS number. Explain that when the students apply the rule by using 2 as the PREVIOUS number, they determine that the NOW number is 2 + 3, so the second term in this sequence is 5. To find the third term in the sequence, they iterate the rule again, using 5 as the PREVIOUS number, so the NOW number is 5 + 3, or 8.

Ask, "What sequence do you obtain if you use the rule PREVIOUS + 3 = NOW and start with 2?" The students should discover that by continuing in this way, they generate the sequence 2, 5, 8, 11, 14, 17, …. Next, ask, "Does this sequence look familiar?" Indeed, the students should discover that it is the same as the very first sequence. The rule PREVIOUS + 3 = NOW, starting at 2, and the rule NOW + 3 = NEXT, starting at 2, are therefore two different ways to generate the same sequence. Explain that mathematicians sometimes want to have more than one way of describing a situation, like using both NOW-NEXT and PREVIOUS-NOW rules.

Distribute the activity sheet "Other Number Sequences," and have your students work on it in groups. Steps 1–3 ask them to generate sequences by using specified initial terms and NOW-NEXT rules. The students should find that the first sequence is the counting numbers (1, 2, 3, 4, 5, 6, 7, …), the second is the even numbers (0, 2, 4, 6, 8, 10, 12, …), and the third is the odd numbers (1, 3, 5, 7, 9, 11, 13, 15, …).

Some students may assert that 0 is neither even nor odd. They may believe that only counting numbers can be even or odd. A few students may know that 0 is neither positive nor negative and may have that idea in mind when they make this assertion. An even number can be defined as—

- a number that is divisible by 2;
- a number that is some number plus itself;
- a number that ends in 0, 2, 4, 6, or 8.

You may want to leave the question of whether 0 is an even number for another day.

Step 4 on the activity sheet "Other Number Sequences" gives students practice with PREVIOUS-NOW rules by presenting three sequences and asking them to write such rules and specify start values. Students should learn that when they try to find the rule that generates a given sequence, they can choose any term, with the exception of the initial term, to be the now term and use its previous term to generate a PREVIOUS-NOW statement. They then have to verify that the rule works for all other pairs of consecutive terms.

The last step is necessary because the two terms that they initially compare may have more than one relationship, and the first relationship that they discover may not be the one that applies to all consecutive terms. For example, if the first two terms of a sequence are 2 and 5,

Mathematicians sometimes want to have more than one way of describing a situation, like using both NOW-NEXT *and* PREVIOUS-NOW *rules.*

Navigating through Discrete Mathematics in Pre-K–Grade 5

the rule could be "add 3," and that rule works if the sequence is 2, 5, 8, 11, …. However, the rule for another sequence whose first two terms are 2 and 5 is to double the number and add 1. Although that rule does not work for the sequence 2, 5, 8, 11, …, it does work for the sequence 2, 5, 11, 23, ….

The rule for the first sequence in step 4 is PREVIOUS + 1 = NOW with a start value of 1, the rule for the second sequence is PREVIOUS + 2 = NOW with an initial term of 0, and the rule for the third sequence is PREVIOUS + 2 = NOW with the first term being 1. In each example, students can replace PREVIOUS-NOW with NOW-NEXT and obtain an equivalent rule that generates the same sequence. Point out that the phrases *initial term*, *first term*, and *start value* are interchangeable.

You can have students use a calculator at any point during this activity to consolidate their understanding of the iteration process. If students start with 4, for example, and repeatedly push the buttons + and 3, they generate the sequence 4, 7, 10, 13, 16, 19, …. They can also use the calculator to check their results. For example, they can verify that 67 is a term in the sequence that they generate by using the rule that the sequence starts with 3 and is generated by NOW + 4 = NEXT. In addition, you can ask them to use the calculator as an aid in generating sequences that involve larger numbers. If you ask them to find the initial term in the sequence generated by NOW + 14 = NEXT that has a seventh term of 93, for example, they should find that the answer is 9.

Activity 2—Doubling Sequences

Give each student a pair of scissors and the three activity sheets "8 × 8 Grid," "Grids—Part 1," and "Grids—Part 2." Ask the students to cut out the 8 × 8 grid on the outside lines and discard the remaining portion of that sheet.

The activity sheet "Grids—Part 1" directs the students to cut the paper grid repeatedly to double, and continue doubling, the number of pieces, which they then stack in front of them. As they complete each step, they fill in a term of a doubling sequence at the bottom of the page. The students begin with one paper grid and cut it into two, then four, then eight, then sixteen, and finally thirty-two pieces, creating the sequence 1, 2, 4, 8, 16, 32, …..

When your students have completed the process, ask them to state the rule that they have been iterating and give the starting point. Their rule should be similar to the following: "Cut each piece of paper grid in half along one of the lines, and put the pieces in a stack," with the starting point being one paper grid. Ask your students to reflect on the sequence that they have created. What patterns can they describe?

The sequence 1, 2, 4, 8, 16, 32, … is an example of doubling. Point out that the NEXT term is always double the NOW term. Doubling a positive number yields twice the original number. Doubling a dollar gives two dollars; doubling three dollars gives six. Doubling a number is the same as adding a number to itself, giving two of the original number. Doubling 8 gives 8 + 8, or 16. Explain that another way in which mathematicians double is by multiplying by 2, so doubling 8 gives 8 × 2, or 16.

At each step of "Grids—Part 1," the students doubled the number of pieces of paper grid by cutting each grid into two smaller grids. Although the grid pieces became smaller, the number of grid pieces

A fourth-grade student has cut the 8 × 8 grid into 1 × 2 pieces and is completing the activity sheet "Grids—Part 1."

Photo by Colette DeLeo; all rights reserved

actually doubled. At each step, the students may have noticed that they also doubled the height of the stack.

Distribute copies of "Grids—Part 2," and let the students complete step 1, which asks for a rule to describe the pattern in the doubling sequence. Call for volunteers to write their rules on the board, and discuss the different rules that they present—and versions of the rule that they do not present. The students can write the rule for doubling in any of the following ways:

$$\text{NOW} + \text{NOW} = \text{NEXT}$$

$$\text{NOW} \times 2 = \text{NEXT}$$

$$\text{PREVIOUS} + \text{PREVIOUS} = \text{NOW}$$

$$\text{PREVIOUS} \times 2 = \text{NOW}.$$

Let the students work together to complete steps 2 and 3. In step 2, they find the next three terms in the doubling sequence, entering 64, 128, and 256 on their activity sheets. In step 3, they use their calculators to obtain the next six terms of the sequence, extending the sequence by entering the terms 512, 1024, 2048, 4096, 8192, and 16,384.

Direct the students' attention to step 4, which calls for comparing three sequences:

    i.   1, 3, 5, 7, 9, 11, 13, 15, …

    ii.   1, 101, 201, 301, 401, 501, …

    iii.   1, 2, 4, 8, 16, 32, 64 …

Sequence (i) is one of the sequences that the students explored in activity 1. It begins at 1 and generates the next term from the previous term according to the rule "add 2." Obtaining each term in a sequence by adding a fixed quantity to the previous term produces a sequence that grows rather slowly, particularly when compared with the doubling sequence—sequence (iii) in step 4. The tenth term in the doubling sequence 1, 2, 4, 8, 16, 32, 64, … is already 512, but the tenth term in the sequence obtained by starting with 1 and repeatedly adding 2 is only 19. But what happens if a sequence starts with 1 and repeatedly adds a larger number—say, 100? The resulting sequence appears as sequence (ii) in step 4: 1, 101, 201, 301, 401, 501, …. Does this sequence grow faster than the doubling sequence? Or does the doubling sequence eventually catch up with and outstrip it? Step 4 probes these questions.

Table 6.1 lists the first fifteen terms of sequences (ii) and (iii). The table demonstrates that the terms in sequence (ii) are initially much larger than those of sequence (iii), and even its tenth term is a great deal larger than the tenth term in sequence (iii)—901 versus 512. However, the eleventh term of sequence (iii) is larger than the eleventh term of sequence (ii), and by the fifteenth terms, the term in sequence (iii) is much larger than that in sequence (ii).

Students may wonder what would happen if a sequence's initial term is 1 and the sequence generates new terms by repeatedly adding a number that is even larger than 100—say, 1000. If the sequence given by the rule PREVIOUS + 1000 = NOW appeared as sequence (iv) in the last row of table 6.1, the fifteenth term would be 14,001. The first fourteen terms

Table 6.1.
The First Fifteen Terms of Sequence (ii) and Sequence (iii)

Term	1	2	3	4	5	6	7	8	9	10	11	12	13	14	15
Seq. (ii)	1	101	201	301	401	501	601	701	801	901	1001	1101	1201	1301	1401
Seq. (iii)	1	2	4	8	16	32	64	128	256	512	1024	2048	4096	8192	16,384
Seq. (iv)	1														

of this sequence would be larger than the first fourteen terms of sequence (iii), but its fifteenth term—14,001—would still be less than the fifteenth term of sequence (iii)—16,384. If appropriate, have your students construct this sequence (iv) and discuss these growth patterns.

Emphasize to your students that a doubling sequence can start with numbers other than 1. Ask the following questions:

- "What sequence do you obtain if you start with 3 and keep doubling?" (3, 6, 12, 24, 48, 96, 192, …)
- "What sequence do you obtain if you start with 2 and keep doubling?" (2, 4, 8, 16, 32, 64, 128, …)
- "What sequence do you obtain if you start with 0 and keep doubling?" (0, 0, 0, 0, 0, 0, …)

In the last example, iterating the doubling rule over and over again still gives 0, so the terms of the doubling sequence that starts with 0 are all 0. If your students are familiar with negative numbers, you can also ask them what happens if they start with –1 and keep doubling. The sequence is –1, –2, –4, –8, –16, –32, –64, …. Its terms may appear to be growing larger and larger; however, each term is actually less than the previous term on the number line.

Although this activity focuses on doubling sequences, other activities also could explore tripling sequences, in which each term is three times the previous term, or other sequences in which each term is a fixed multiple of the previous term. Activity 4, Sequences Involving Triangles, discusses a tripling sequence.

Sequences in which each term is a fixed multiple of the previous term can model a variety of situations in which growth occurs. The fixed multiple is called the *growth coefficient*, and one such situation is investment. When a person invests money and receives compound interest, the value of the investment at any time is a fixed multiple of the value at the previous time. For example, if the interest rate is 6 percent, then the growth coefficient is 1.06, because the recursive rule is

$$\text{NEXT} = \text{NOW} + (0.06 \times \text{NOW}),$$

which can be written as

$$\text{NEXT} = (1.0 \times \text{NOW}) + (0.06 \times \text{NOW}),$$

which simplifies to

$$\text{NEXT} = (1.0 + 0.06) \times \text{NOW},$$

which in turn simplifies to

$$\text{NEXT} = 1.06 \times \text{NOW}.$$

Similarly, a sequence in which each term is a fixed multiple of the previous term can model the number of fish in a pond.

The CD-ROM that accompanies Navigating through Discrete Mathematics in Grades 6–12 (Hart et al. 2008) includes Trout Pond, an applet-based activity that allows students to investigate the recursive equation

$$\text{NEXT} = r \text{ NOW} + b.$$

The number of grains of rice that the inventor of chess requested, so the story goes, sounded very reasonable—1 grain on the first square of the chessboard, 2 on the second square, 4 on the third square, 8 on the fourth square, and so on, doubling the number each time—yet was more than the output of the entire kingdom.

These applications are more appropriate for middle school students because the growth coefficients are all decimals. However, students in grades 3–5 can appreciate the growth that results when numbers are repeatedly doubled by reenacting the legend of the reward that the inventor of chess supposedly requested from his appreciative royal master: 1 grain of rice on the first square of the chessboard, 2 grains on the second square, 4 grains on the third square, 8 grains on the fourth square, 16 grains on the fifth square, 32 grains on the sixth square, and so on. The king thought that the reward was very reasonable, not realizing that this number of grains of rice would prove to be more than the output of the entire kingdom.

Tell the students the legend and show them a chessboard. Initiate a simulation of the reward by asking the students to cut each of their thirty-two 1×2 grids in half. Each student will then have cut his or her 8×8 grid into sixty-four 1×1 squares. Ask your students to think of each small square as a grain of rice. Call on students in turn to place "grains" on squares of the chessboard:

- Have the first student bring his or her 64 grains of rice forward, place 1 grain on the first square of the chessboard, and leave the remainder beside the chessboard.
- Have the second student take 2 grains of rice from the remainder and stack them on the second square of the chessboard.
- Have the third student take 4 grains from the remainder and stack them on the third square of the chessboard.
- Have the fourth student take 8 grains from the remainder and stack them on the fourth square.
- Have the fifth student take 16 grains from the remainder and stack them on the fifth square.
- Have the sixth student take 32 grains from the remainder and stack them on the sixth square.

At this point, one grain will remain from the initial 64 grains of rice, since the students have placed $1 + 2 + 4 + 8 + 16 + 32$, or 63, grains of rice on the chessboard. Put that grain aside and resume calling on students, as follows:

- Have the seventh student stack all of his or her 64 grains of rice on the seventh square.
- Have the eighth student find a partner and have the two of them merge all their rice to make up 128 grains for the eighth square.
- Have four students combine their 64 grains apiece to make up 256 grains for the ninth square.
- Have eight students pool their 64 grains apiece to make up 512 grains for the tenth square.

If your class has sixteen or more students, then they will have had enough rice to create the stacks of grain on the first ten squares, because the rice from one student covered the first six squares, then one student covered the seventh square with rice, then two students covered the eighth square with rice, then four students covered the ninth square with rice, and then eight students covered the tenth square with rice. Altogether, the first ten squares used the rice from $1 + 1 + 2 + 4 + 8$, or

Navigating through Discrete Mathematics in Pre-K–Grade 5

16, students. If your class has fewer than sixteen students, you may want to have the students cut up additional grids so that you have sixteen stacks altogether, each with 64 grains of rice.

If your class has an additional sixteen students, you can have them take all sixteen of their stacks of rice and stack them neatly on the eleventh square of the chessboard. However, if your class has fewer than thirty-two students, not enough rice will remain to create the stack of 1024 grains needed for the eleventh square. But if you take all the rice on the first ten squares, the number of grains is

$$1 + 2 + 4 + 8 + 16 + 32 + 64 + 128 + 256 + 512 = 1023.$$

You can add one more grain of rice (the one left over from the first stack) so that the class has the 1024 grains needed to cover the eleventh square. This stack of rice will be approximately 4 inches tall. Ask the students to consider the following:

- If they had more rice, they could cover the twelfth square with a stack that would be approximately 8 inches tall.
- If they had more rice, they could cover the thirteenth square with a stack that would be approximately 16 inches tall.
- If they had more rice, they could cover the fourteenth square with a stack that would be approximately 32 inches tall.
- If they had more rice, they could cover the fifteenth square with a stack that would be approximately 64 inches tall.
- If they had more rice, they could cover the sixteenth square with a stack that would be approximately 128 inches tall.

At 128 inches—more than ten feet—the stack of the sixteenth square would probably be higher than the ceiling in the classroom. Did your students imagine that the stack of rice on the sixteenth square would be so tall? And the sixty-fourth square of the chessboard would still be a long way off! The rapid growth of the stacks of rice should help your students understand the connection between doubling sequences and growth.

In the next activity, the students work with square pattern blocks. If you don't have pattern blocks, redistribute all the squares of paper so that each student has approximately sixty-four small squares, as before, and have the students place them in envelopes or small plastic bags for reuse later.

Activity 3—Sequences Involving Squares

Not all sequences consist of numbers. Sequences can also consist of different geometric shapes or copies of a single shape combined in various ways. For example, figure 6.1 shows the first five terms of a sequence of shapes in which the pattern involves three different shapes, and figure 6.2 shows the first five terms of a sequence of shapes each of whose terms is a figure that combines a number of squares.

Distribute the activity sheet "Sequences of Shapes and Numbers," and have pairs of students work together and use pattern blocks to build copies of the first five terms of the sequence of shapes in step 1—the sequence shown in figure 6.2. (If you do not have pattern blocks, instead use the small squares that your students created in activity 2.) Ask the students to complete step 1 by building the next three terms in

You can connect this mathematical activity to study in language arts by using the storybook *A Grain of Rice* (Pittman 1995).

If your students put 1 slip of paper on the first square of a chessboard, 2 on the second square, a stack of 4 on the third square, a stack of 8 on the fourth square, and so on, doubling each time, then their stack on the sixteenth square will be higher than the classroom ceiling.

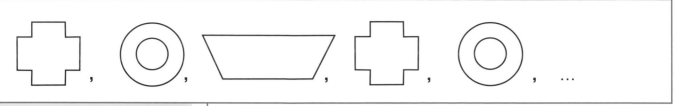

Photo by Colette DeLeo; all rights reserved

Fig. 6.1.

The first five terms of a sequence whose terms are one of three different shapes

the sequence, drawing them, recording the number of squares in each of the first eight terms, and determining how many squares are in the twelfth term.

In reviewing the students' work, you might want to point out that the numbers that the students recorded for the first eight shapes begin

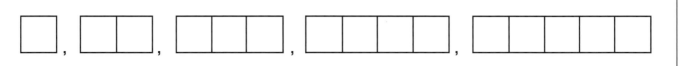

Fig. 6.2.

The first five terms of a sequence of shapes built from squares

a number sequence, 1, 2, 3, 4, …, which describes the number of squares in each of the terms of the sequence of shapes. To determine that the twelfth term has twelve squares, the students might extend either the sequence of shapes or the number sequence for an additional four terms. Before reviewing the solution to this question, ask your students to indicate by a show of hands who used the sequence of shapes to find the answer and who used the number sequence. Select a few students to explain their choice, and help them recognize that they can use either sequence, since both result in the same sequential pattern of numbers.

Ask the students what the NOW-NEXT rule is for the two sequences. For the number sequence, the NOW-NEXT rule is simply NOW + 1 = NEXT. But the NOW-NEXT rule for the sequence of shapes is NEXT = NOW plus one more square on the right or left end.

Figure 6.3 shows the first four terms of the sequence of shapes that appears in step 2 on the activity sheet. Each term after the first is an arrangement of squares in the shape of a backward L. Have your students work in groups and use pattern blocks (or paper squares) to build the next three terms and complete step 2, which asks how many squares are in each of the first seven terms of this sequence of shapes (1, 3, 5, 7, 9, 11, 13) and how many squares are in the twelfth term (twenty-three). Again, be sure that students are able to identify, describe, and extend the pattern in the sequences of shapes, as well as in the number sequences. They should also recognize that although these two sequences look different, the number sequence describes an important feature of the sequence of shapes—namely, the number of squares in each of its terms.

Explain that any sequence of shapes whose terms are an arrangement of squares gives rise to a number sequence that provides the number of squares in each of the terms of the sequence of shapes. In step 1, the number sequence was the sequence of whole numbers, and step 2, it is the sequence of odd numbers.

What is the NOW-NEXT rule for this sequence? The NOW-NEXT rule for the number sequence is NOW + 2 = NEXT. But what is the NOW-NEXT rule for the sequence of shapes? It is NEXT = NOW plus one more square on the top and one more square on the left end.

A fourth-grade student builds the first sequence on the activity sheet "Sequences of Shapes and Numbers."

Navigating through Discrete Mathematics in Pre-K–Grade 5

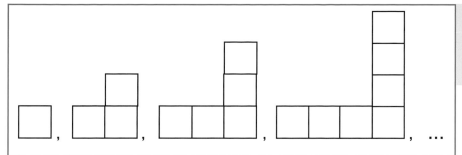

Fig. **6.3.**

After the first term, each term in the sequence of shapes looks like a backward letter L built from squares.

Distribute the activity sheet "More Practice with Sequences," and let your students work individually to arrange squares in yet another sequence of shapes, shown in step 1 and figure 6.4. Direct them to continue work on step 1, completing parts (*a*), (*b*), and (*c*), which ask them to draw the next three terms in the sequence, record the number of squares in each of the first seven terms (1, 4, 7, 10, 13, 16, and 19 terms, respectively), and determine how many terms are in the twelfth term (thirty-four). After completing the previous activity sheet, the students should be able to complete these tasks easily. You can use their work as an assessment tool for determining who understands sequential patterns and who does not.

Parts (*d*) and (*e*) of step 1 ask the students to describe both the sequence of numbers and the sequence of shapes by using NOW-NEXT rules. Depending on your students' skill, you may want to discuss the solutions to these parts as a class so that the students will be more able to create sequences of shapes in step 2 and obtain solutions. The NOW-NEXT rule for the number sequence is NOW + 3 = NEXT, with 1 as the initial term, because the NOW-NEXT rule for the sequence of shapes involves adding one square at the right, one at the left, and one at the bottom. Thus, an informal way of describing this sequence of shapes is NEXT equals NOW plus these three additional squares.

In step 2, each student uses an arrangement of squares to create his or her own sequences of shapes. The student then trades papers with a partner, and the two students analyze each other's sequences. Be sure that the students discuss their sequences and the associated number sequences of the squares.

Next, distribute the activity sheet "A Sequence of Square Shapes," and let your students explore the new sequence that it presents (see fig. 6.5). They may experience some difficulty in discovering the NOW-NEXT rule in this case. The sequence has one square for its first term, four squares arranged in a square for its second term, nine squares arranged in a square for its third term, and so on.

Have your students use pattern blocks (or paper squares) to create the next three terms of this sequence of shapes. Then ask them to

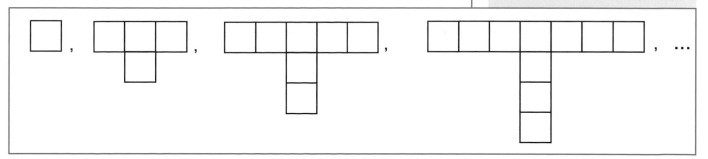

Fig. **6.5.**

What is the next term?

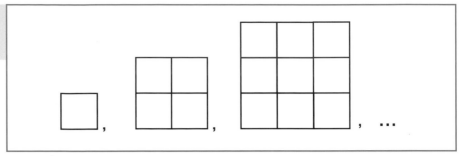

complete steps 1 and 2, which direct them to draw the three new terms and find the number of small squares in each of the first six terms. At first, students may count the small squares one by one. If so, remind them of the array model of multiplication (discussed in chapter 2) to realize that they can determine the number of small squares in each shape by multiplying. That is, they can find the number of small squares in a 5×5 square—with 5 squares on each side—by multiplying 5 times 5 to get 25 small squares. Similarly, 1×1, or 1, small square is in the first shape; 2×2, or 4, small squares are in the second shape; 3×3, or 9, small squares are in the third shape; and so on. The sequence of numbers is thus $1 \times 1, 2 \times 2, 3 \times 3, 4 \times 4, 5 \times 5$, …, which is the same as 1, 4, 9, 16, 25, …. The total number of small squares in an 8×8 square is 8×8, or 64. Remind your students that in activity 2, "Doubling Sequences," they actually cut an 8×8 square into 64 smaller squares.

Explain to your students that the numbers in the sequence 1, 4, 9, 16, 25, … are called *square* numbers because each one gives the number of small squares in a larger square. They also provide the areas of squares of different sizes; if the dimensions of a square are 3 feet by 3 feet, then the area of the square is 3×3, or 9, square feet. To multiply a number by itself is to *square* the number, and the result is the *square* of the number.

Point out that mathematicians use special notation for the square of a number. In multiplying the number 7 by itself—that is, 7×7—mathematicians write 7^2. Explain to your students that they can represent each term in the sequence of square numbers as "some number squared." You can ask your students to convert each term in the sequence into the form (some number)^2 so that they understand that the sequence $1^2, 2^2, 3^2, 4^2, 5^2, 6^2$, … really means the same thing as the sequence 1, 4, 9, 16, 25, 36, …. Representing the terms of the sequence as some number squared explicitly shows students the dimensions of each square in the sequence.

Figure 6.6 shows a 10×10 square with bold segments highlighting a 1×1 square, a 2×2 square, a 3×3 square, a 4×4 square, and so on. The diagram shows very clearly what shape each new square in the sequence adds to the previous square. On an overhead projector display a transparency of the blackline master "Squares on Squares," and discuss the diagram with your students by asking the following questions:

- "What shape do you have to add to the 1×1 square to obtain the 2×2 square?" (The backward L shape that consists of three squares)
- "What shape do you have to add to the 2×2 square to obtain the 3×3 square?" (The backward L shape that consists of five squares)

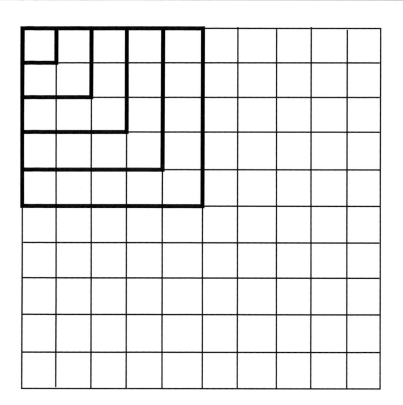

Fig. **6.6.**

The bold segments highlight a 1 × 1
square, a 2 × 2 square, a 3 × 3 square,
a 4 × 4 square, and a 5× 5 square.

- "What shape do you have to add to the 3 × 3 square to obtain the 4 × 4 square?" (The backward L shape with seven squares.)

- "What shape do you have to add to the 9 × 9 square to obtain the 10 × 10 square?" (The backward L shape with nineteen squares)

Remind the students that they investigated this sequence of backward L shapes in step 2 on the activity sheet "Sequences of Shapes and Numbers." Then distribute the activity sheet "Squares and Backward Ls—Part 1," which asks the students to write an equation that expresses the area of each square shown in terms of the area of the previous square and the appropriate backward L. For example, the 2 × 2 square, which has area 4, consists of a 1 × 1 square, which has area 1, and the first backward L, which consists of three small squares, so the equation is 4 = 1 + 3. After the students have completed the new activity sheet, ask them to compare their equations with those of their neighbors. Write the equations on the board, arranged as in figure 6.7 so that the students can see the pattern: each square number is the sum of the previous square number and an odd number, and each equation involves the next larger odd number than the previous equation.

Again display the transparency of "Squares on Squares," and this time point out that the 3 × 3 square consists of a 1 × 1 square and two backward Ls. Draw figure 6.8 on the board to reinforce this observation. Ask the students to write an equation that expresses the area of a 3 × 3 square in terms of the areas of the three pieces and then to check their equation with their partners. Many will find the equation 9 = 1 + 3 + 5.

Distribute the activity sheet "Squares and Backward Ls—Part 2," which asks the students to draw other squares as a 1 × 1 square and a number of backward Ls and to write similar equations for them.

Fig. **6.7.**

Each square number is the sum of
the previous square number and an
odd number, and each equation
involves the next larger odd number
than the previous equation.

4	=	1	+	3
9	=	4	+	5
16	=	9	+	7
25	=	16	+	9
36	=	25	+	11
49	=	36	+	13
64	=	49	+	15
81	=	64	+	17
100	=	81	+	19

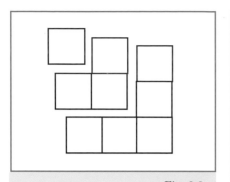

Fig. **6.8.**

The 3 × 3 square consists of a 1× 1 square and two backward Ls.

Arrange the equations as in figure 6.9 so that the students can see the pattern—that each square number is a sum of consecutive odd numbers. Point out that the first square can be said to be the sum of the first one odd number, the second square is the sum of the first two odd numbers, the third square is the sum of the first three odd numbers, and so on. The tenth square, 100, is the sum of the first ten odd numbers,

$$100 = 1 + 3 + 5 + 7 + 9 + 11 + 13 + 15 + 17 + 19.$$

Fig. **6.9.**

Each square number is a sum of consecutive odd numbers.

1	=	1
4	=	1 + 3
9	=	1 + 3 + 5
16	=	1 + 3 + 5 + 7
25	=	1 + 3 + 5 + 7 + 9
36	=	1 + 3 + 5 + 7 + 9 + 11
49	=	1 + 3 + 5 + 7 + 9 + 11 + 13
64	=	1 + 3 + 5 + 7 + 9 + 11 + 13 + 15
81	=	1 + 3 + 5 + 7 + 9 + 11 + 13 + 15 + 17
100	=	1 + 3 + 5 + 7 + 9 + 11 + 13 + 15 + 17 + 19

If your students have already encountered fractions, you can include the following observations in the discussion of area. Remind the students of their work in activity 2, in which they cut an 8 × 8 grid into pieces. Focus on the fact that as the number of pieces of paper increased, the areas of the pieces decreased. Review the process and results:

- The students began with a grid whose area was 64 small grid squares.
- When students cut the original grid in half, each of the two smaller pieces had area 32.
- When students cut those pieces in half, each of the four smaller pieces had area 16.
- When students cut those pieces in half, each of the eight smaller pieces had area 8.
- When students cut those pieces in half, each of the sixteen smaller pieces had area 4.
- When students cut those pieces in half, each of the thirty-two smaller pieces had area 2.
- When students cut those pieces in half, each of the sixty-four smaller pieces had area 1.

The sequence of areas obtained thus far is 64, 32, 16, 8, 4, 2, 1. Each term in this sequence is half the previous term—that is, NEXT = NOW ÷ 2. Continuing this number sequence involves dividing by 2, just as continuing the sequence of shapes involves cutting the area in half. As the pieces become smaller, however, cutting them in half becomes more difficult:

- Cutting the pieces in half again gives 128 pieces, each with area 1/2.
- Cutting the pieces in half again gives 256 pieces, each with area 1/4.
- Cutting the pieces in half again gives 512 pieces, each with area 1/8.
- Cutting the pieces in half again gives 1024 pieces, each with area 1/16.

The resulting sequence is thus

$$64, \ 32, \ 16, \ 8, \ 4, \ 2, \ 1, \ \frac{1}{2}, \ \frac{1}{4}, \ \frac{1}{8}, \ \frac{1}{16}, \ \frac{1}{32}, \ \dots$$

This sequence differs from those that you have looked at previously in that the terms are fractions and the sizes of the terms become smaller and smaller.

If a Logo-like environment is available in your classroom, you can ask students to work in it to generate all the sequences in activity 3, shown in figures 6.2–6.4. For example, when they repeat the instructions "forward 50, right 90" four times, initially moving up (north), they will generate a square. Going forward 50 and then repeating those instructions (forward 50, right 90) results in a second square just above the first square. Going forward 50 again and then repeating those instructions results in the third square just above the second square. Thus, a recursive description of the sequence is that each figure is obtained from the previous one by going forward 50 and then repeating four times the instruction "forward 50, right 90."

Activity 4—Sequences Involving Triangles

Squares are not the only shapes that students can use to create sequences of shapes. Figure 6.10 shows the first four terms in a sequence of triangles. Use pattern blocks to introduce your students to this sequence. On an overhead projector, place triangular pattern blocks on a transparency to model for the students the process of building the first two terms in the sequence shown in the figure. Be sure to leave a small space between the triangles so that your students can see the smaller triangles in the larger one. Ask the students how many small triangles are in the second term of this sequence. Students should respond that there are four small triangles—three triangles pointing up, and one triangle pointing down.

The number of small triangles in each term of the sequence of triangular shapes in figure 6.10 is a square number—a fact that may be quite surprising.

Fig. **6.10.**

Students can use triangular pattern blocks to generate a sequence of shapes.

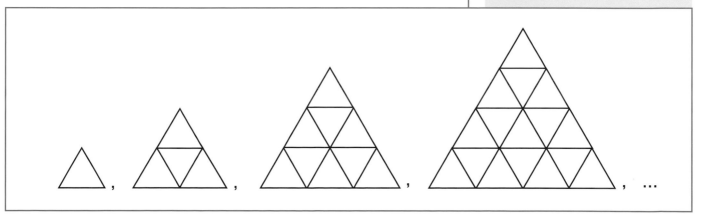

Figure 6.11 shows the first three terms of a different sequence of shapes. Build these three terms for your students with triangular pattern blocks in the same manner as before. The first term consists of a single triangle. The second term consists of three triangles arranged to form a larger triangle with a triangular hole, represented by the white space in the middle of the figure. Explain to your students that the next term in this sequence is built from three copies of the NOW term, arranged to form a larger triangle.

Fig. **6.11.**

The NEXT term consists of three copies of the NOW term, arranged to form a larger triangle.

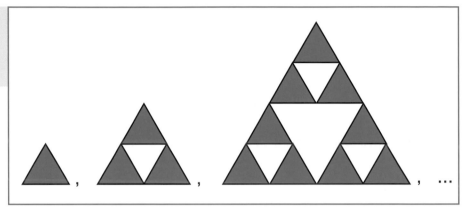

The third term consists of nine triangles arranged around four holes. Ask your students whether they understand how you built this term. They should see that here also the NEXT term consists of three copies of the second term (the NOW term), arranged to form a larger triangle with a triangular hole in the middle. Make sure that your students understand the construction pattern.

Next, show students the fourth term of the sequence (see fig. 6.12) by displaying a transparency of the blackline master "Fourth Term of a Sequence of Triangular Shapes" on the overhead projector. Ask the students how they could build the fourth term from copies of the third term. Again they should see that the fourth term (the NEXT term) consists of three copies of the third term (the NOW term), arranged to form a larger triangle with a triangular hole in the middle.

Fig. **6.12.**

The fourth term of the sequence in figure 6.11

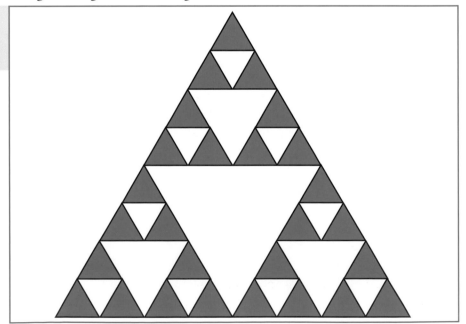

Assign your students to groups of three, and give each group nine paper copies of the blackline master "Fourth Term of a Sequence of Triangular Shapes," with each student receiving three copies. Have each student cut out the large triangle on each copy and connect them carefully with tape (without much overlap) to form the fifth term of the sequence. Remind the students to follow the construction pattern, building the NEXT term from three copies of the NOW term.

When every group has finished, give each one a sheet of easel paper and have the members pool their three copies of the fifth term to assemble the sixth term of the sequence on the easel paper. After the three students have arranged their copies of the fifth term of the sequence on the paper to form the sixth term of the sequence, they should tape the triangles in place.

Next, create larger groups consisting of three groups of students, and send each larger group into a different area of the room. Have each larger group now use the three smaller groups' copies of the sixth term of the sequence to assemble the seventh term. The students may need to cut away pieces of easel paper that get in the way, and then they should tape their copies of the sixth term together to form the seventh term.

If your class has as many as twenty-seven students (nine groups of three), you will now have three copies of the seventh term of the sequence. You can have your students assemble these to form the eighth term of the sequence. If your class has fewer than twenty-seven students, you can use easel paper and prepare in advance as many extra copies of the sixth term as you will need for three copies of the seventh term and ultimately one copy of the eighth.

For example, if you have twenty-one students, you will be able to create seven groups of three and will need to prepare two sheets of easel paper with one copy of the sixth term taped to each sheet. When the class is ready to build the seventh term, you can add your two copies of the sixth term to the seven that the students have created. They will then be able to create three copies of the seventh term and use them to create one copy of the eighth term. Although the activity sounds complicated, it really is not, because it is based on a simple construction rule. Once you and your students begin, you will all discover that it is great fun.

This sequence of triangular shapes, each more detailed than the previous ones, is called *Sierpinski's triangle*. The eighth term of the sequence—the last term that your students have built—is called the *seventh stage* of Sierpinski's triangle, since the first term is stage 0 (see the margin on p. 13). The representation of this term that appears in figure 6.13 is much smaller than the one that your students have built. The fourth term in the blackline master that you copied for your students to work from has a height of approximately four inches. As a result—

- the fifth term that each student built should have a height of approximately 8 inches;
- the sixth term that each group built should have a height of approximately 16 inches;
- the seventh term that each larger group of three groups built should have a height of approximately 32 inches; and
- the eighth term built by the entire class should have a height of approximately 64 inches.

Fig. **6.13.**

The eighth term (seventh stage) of
Sierpinski's triangle

You can display the seventh term (sixth-stage triangle) on your class bulletin board—the height will be about three feet! Or if you build an eighth term (seventh-stage triangle), you can post it in a prominent place in your school—the height will be more than five feet, and your students' work will draw oohs and aahs from others in the school.

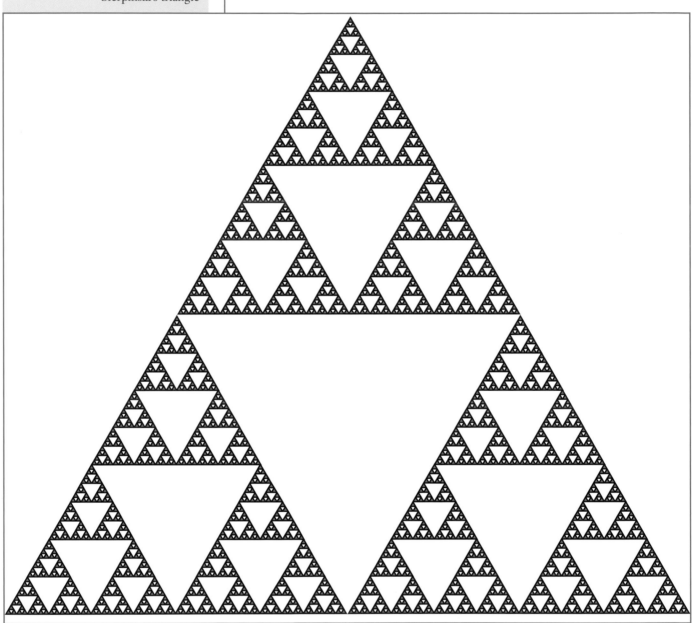

The sequence called Sierpinski's triangle bears the name of the Polish mathematician Waclaw Sierpinski, who lived from 1882 to 1969.

Ask your students how many small triangles are in each term of Sierpinski's triangle. You can write the number of small triangles in each term of the sequence of shapes as a term in the number sequence 1, 3, 9, 27, 81, 243, 729, …. Direct your students to find a rule that describes how to create the next term in the sequence. They should understand that each term of the sequence is exactly three times the preceding term, since they can assemble each shape from three copies of the previous shape. Valid rules for this sequence include NOW × 3 = NEXT and PREVIOUS × 3 = NOW. Students should recognize that these rules both mean the same thing and reflect the fact that the sequence is an example of a tripling sequence.

Activity 5—Iteration, Counting, and Vertex-Edge Graphs

The final activity in this final chapter presents counting problems in graph contexts with solutions involving iteration. This activity serves appropriately as the culminating activity since it brings together the three major themes of discrete mathematics outlined in *Principles and Standards for School Mathematics* (NCTM 2000)—systematic counting, vertex-edge graphs, and iteration and recursion.

Figure 6.14 shows a *grid graph*—that is, a graph in the form of a grid. Ask your students how many vertices and edges this graph has. Both by counting and by multiplying, they should find that it has nine vertices and twelve edges. The graph has three rows and each row has three vertices, so the total number of vertices is 3×3, or 9. Because each row has two edges and there are three rows, the number of horizontal edges is 2×3, or 6. But there are also six vertical edges, so the total number of edges is $6 + 6$, or 12. The letters *A–I* label the vertices in this figure.

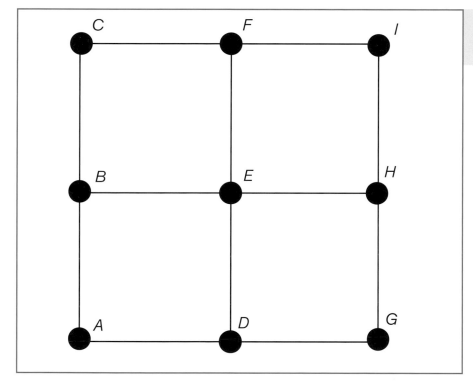

Fig. **6.14.**

How many paths go from *A* to *I*?

Ask your students to imagine that their house is at vertex *A*, their friend's house is at vertex *I*, and their neighborhood is laid out like the graph in figure 6.14, with north pointing upward and east pointing to the right. How many different paths can they take from *A* to *I*? Obviously, they do not want to waste time getting to their friend's house. Consequently, they always travel east or north. To illustrate this fact, say, for example, "Going from *A* to *B* to *E* to *D* is not an efficient way to chart a course from *A* to *I* because you move south when traveling from *E* to *D*." Point out that one acceptable route is *A* to *B* to *E* to *H* to *I*, and explain that an abbreviation for this route is *A-B-E-H-I*.

Give each student a copy of the activity sheet "How Many Paths from *A* to *I*?" Arrange the students in pairs to find as many different routes as possible that start at *A* and end at *I* and travel only east or north. After the students have worked on this problem for a few minutes, have each pair compare notes with another pair to find out how many routes they have created in all. Ask them to make sure that they have not repeated any paths. At this point, each group of four students should have found all six routes marked in figure 6.15. The activity sheet "How Many Paths from *A* to *I*?" provides space for the students to show as many as twelve paths, allowing them to redo work that becomes messy and, more important, keeping them from knowing in advance how many paths they are seeking.

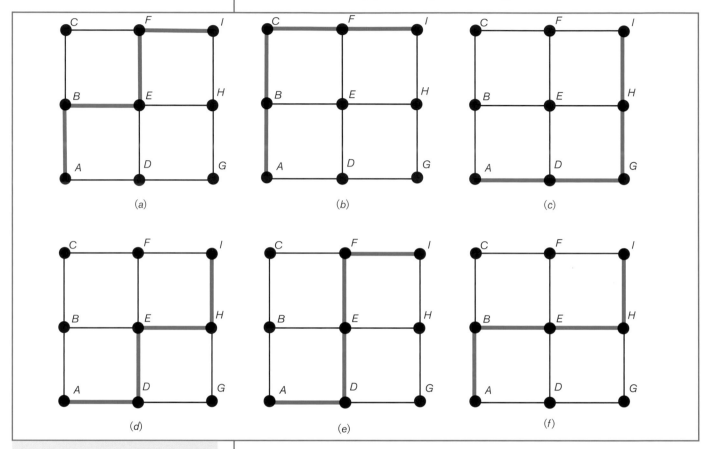

Fig. **6.15.**

Six routes from *A* to *I*

Fig. **6.16.**

Six paths from *A* to *I* with vertices in alphabetical order

- *A-B-C-F-I*   (Fig. 6.15*b*)

- *A-B-E-F-I*   (Fig. 6.15*a*)

- *A-B-E-H-I*   (Fig. 6.15*f*)

- *A-D-E-F-I*   (Fig. 6.15*e*)

- *A-D-E-H-I*   (Fig. 6.15*d*)

Have the groups give each route a name by listing each vertex as they visit it; for example, the name of the first route in figure 6.15 is *A-B-E-F-I*. Ask the groups to put these six routes in alphabetical order, creating the list in figure 6.16. Have each group make a tree diagram that corresponds to the alphabetical list of routes. All the groups should come up with the diagram in figure 6.17.

Next, give each student a copy of the activity sheet "Walking on a Grid Graph." The students suppose that the grid graph on the sheet shows their neighborhood. On a separate sheet of paper, each student creates a tree diagram of all the routes from his or her house, located at vertex *A*, to a friend's house, located at vertex *P*. The student then uses the tree diagram to create an alphabetical list of all the routes.

Using tree diagrams to count all the possibilities takes a lot of time. Is there an easier way? Recursion provides a quicker method. Use a transparency of the blackline master "From *A* to *P* on a Grid Graph" to discuss this method with your students in the context of the problem at hand. Begin by noting that any route from *A* to *P* goes either through *L* or through *O*. If the students find the number of routes from *A* to *L*

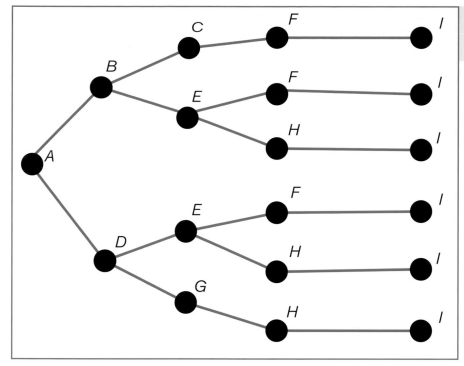

Fig. **6.17.**

A tree diagram of the six routes in figures 6.15 and 6.16

and the number of routes from *A* to *O* and add them together, they will have found the number of routes from *A* to *P*.

How can they find the number of routes from *A* to *L*? Each route from *A* to *L* goes either through *H* or through *K*. So if they find the number of routes from *A* to *H* and the number of routes from *A* to *K* and add them together, they will have found the number of routes from *A* to *L*. Although this process may seem somewhat complex, it makes it possible to find the number of routes from *A* to *P* by first finding the number of routes from *A* to every other vertex in the graph.

Begin with the vertices that are close to *A*. The number of routes from *A* to *B* is 1, and the number of routes from *A* to *E* is 1, so the number of routes from *A* to *F* is 1 + 1, or 2. Place those numbers next to the vertices *B*, *E*, and *F*, as in figure 6.18. In terminology similar to what you have already been using, you can express this situation as

NEW VERTEX = VERTEX AT LEFT AND VERTEX BELOW,

or more simply as

NEW = LEFT + BELOW.

These expressions are similar to the recursive rules discussed earlier in that each term depends on previous terms. However, they differ from the earlier rules in that each term depends on not just one previous term but two. Note that some vertices do not have vertices to the left, and others do not have vertices below them. Therefore, the rule NEW = LEFT + BELOW sometimes needs modification. If a vertex is on the left border of the graph, the rule that applies then is NEW = BELOW, and if a vertex is on the bottom border of the graph, the rule that applies is NEW = LEFT.

Determining the number of paths from *A* to *G* means first finding the number of paths from *A* to *C*. Only one such path exists—from *A* to *B* to *C*. Every path from *A* to *G* goes either through *C* or through *F*, so the number of paths from *A* to *G* (NEW) is the sum of the number of

Fig. **6.18.**

The number on a vertex indicates the number of paths from *A* to that vertex.

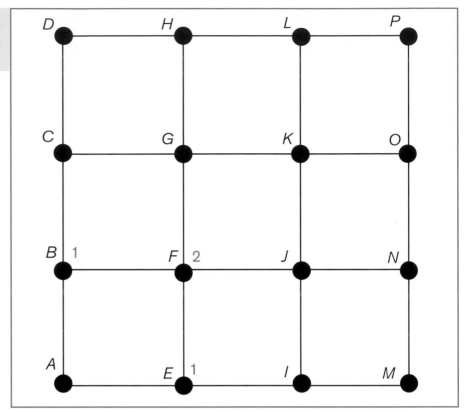

paths from *A* to *C* (LEFT) and the number of paths from *A* to *F* (BELOW)—that is, 1 + 2, or 3. Again,

NEW = LEFT + BELOW.

Figure 6.19 shows the numbers.

Fig. **6.19.**

There are three paths from *A* to *G*.

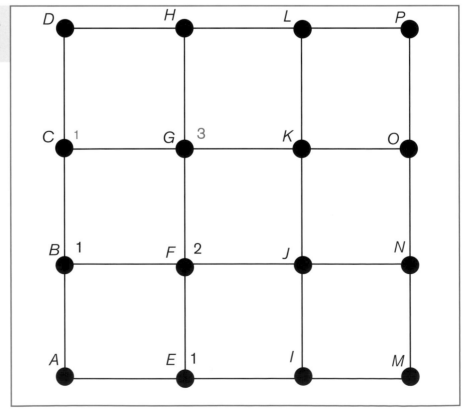

Next, fill in the numbers for *I*, *J*, and *K*. The number of paths from *A* to *I* is just 1—the path from *A* to *E* to *I*. Remind the students that the recursive rule NEW = LEFT + BELOW does not apply to the vertices on the bottom or on the left side of the graph. For vertices on the bottom, like *I*, the rule is NEW = LEFT. The numbers of paths from *A* to *J* and from *A* to *K* are both determined by the rule NEW = LEFT + BELOW; the number of paths from *A* to *J* is 1 + 2, or 3, and the number of paths from *A* to *K* is 3 + 3, or 6.

Continue working with your class until you have labeled every vertex in the graph with the number of paths from *A* to that vertex, as shown in figure 6.20. As you proceed, keep referring to the recursive rule

NEW = LEFT + BELOW.

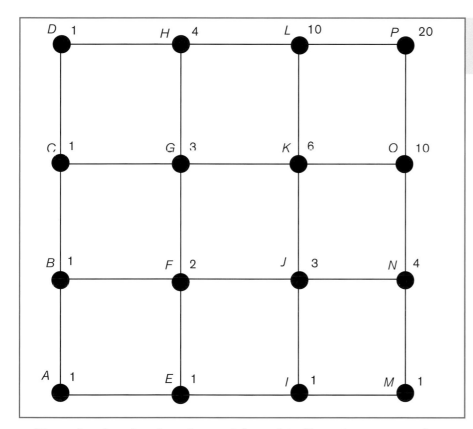

Fig. **6.20.**

There are twenty paths from *A* to *P*.

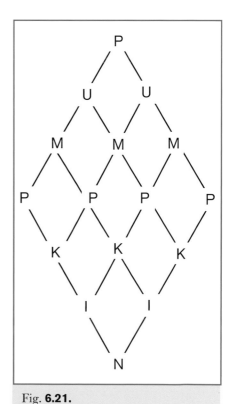

Fig. **6.21.**

How many ways are there to spell *PUMPKIN*?

To apply what they have learned from this discussion, your students can work in pairs on the activity sheet "Pumpkin Paths," which asks them to count the number of paths that they can follow in a given diagram to spell *PUMPKIN*. Figure 6.21 shows the diagram that the students see. They should note that after they use a letter, the next letter has to be just below and to the left or the right of the previous letter.

If students need a hint, ask whether they see any similarities between the paths in the activity sheet "Walking on a Grid Graph" and the ways of spelling *PUMPKIN*. They may observe that the line segments in the activity sheet "Pumpkin Paths" are like the edges in the activity sheet "Walking on a Grid Graph." Indeed, students may discover that the number of letters in the diagram on "Pumpkin Paths" is the same as the number of vertices in the grid on "Walking on a Grid Graph" and that the number of line segments in "Pumpkin Paths" is the same as the number of edges in "Walking on a Grid Graph."

They might note that for each vertex in "Walking on a Grid Graph," they can proceed in one of two directions, east or north, and for each letter in "Pumpkin Paths," they can proceed in one of two ways, down left or down right. A student might notice that the preceding statement is not quite true for "Walking on a Grid Graph," because for some vertices—those along the top and those along the right—there is only one way to proceed. But another student might then observe that the same thing happens in "Pumpkin Paths"—from letters on the sides in the bottom half of "Pumpkin Paths," they can proceed in only one direction. Students might even notice that if they turn "Pumpkin Paths" so that the *P* at the top is at the bottom left, they have a slanted version of "Walking on a Grid Graph."

If the students make all these observations—or even most of them—they will probably realize that the number of paths that they can follow to spell *PUMPKIN* is twenty—the same number as for the paths from vertex *A* to vertex *P*. This realization will allow them to solve the problem quite easily.

However, if students need another hint, ask them to consider the number of ways in which they can arrive at each letter on the chart starting from the topmost letter, *P*. The numbers in figure 6.22 indicate the number of ways of going from this letter to every other letter to spell *PUMPKIN*. For example, they can arrive at the third *P* from the left in the middle row from either the second *M* or the third *M* in the preceding row, so the number of ways of arriving at the third *P* in the middle row must be equal to the number of ways of arriving at the second *M* in the preceding row plus the number of ways of arriving at the third *M* in the preceding row. The rule for each entry is therefore

NOW = UP LEFT + UP RIGHT.

In other words, each entry is the sum of the number above it to the left and the number above it to the right. The numbers in figure 6.22 are the same as the numbers in figure 6.20, and the number of paths for spelling *PUMPKIN* is twenty.

The activity sheet "Pascal's Triangle" gives students another opportunity to explore an interesting number pattern. The sheet shows a large triangle composed of hexagons. In each of the rightmost and leftmost hexagons is the number 1. The instruction on the sheet gives the rule for entering numbers in the other hexagons: The number in each hexagon is the sum of the numbers in the two hexagons above it to the left and to the right.

Give each student a copy of the activity sheet and read the instruction aloud. The students should notice that only one hexagon in the triangle has numbers in two hexagons directly above it—the topmost empty hexagon, with the numbers 1 and 1 above it. The students should add the two 1s and enter the sum, 2, in that hexagon. They can then fill in the next row. The empty hexagon at the left will have 1 and 2 above it, so they can fill it with 3. The empty hexagon at the right will have 2 and 1 above it, so they can again enter 3. In the next row, in the first empty hexagon at the left, they will enter 1 + 3, or 4. In filling in the other two numbers in that row, they will enter a 6 and a 4 as they work from left to right. They should continue, obtaining the result shown in figure 6.23. Point out that the triangle can continue forever by adding rows of hexagons at the bottom.

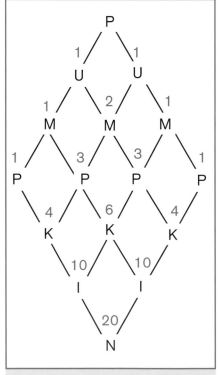

Fig. **6.22.**

Twenty paths spell *PUMPKIN*.

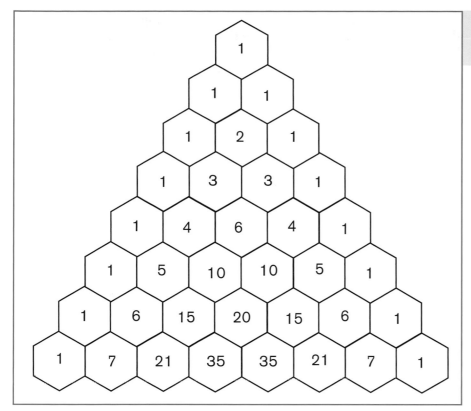

Fig. **6.23.**

The first seven rows of Pascal's triangle

Your students may have already noticed that all the numbers in figure 6.20 (the number of routes from *A* to *P*) and in figure 6.22 (the number of paths to spell *PUMPKIN*) appear in figure 6.23. An important difference, however, is that, just as in sequences discussed in earlier activities, the numbers in this triangle can continue forever. In fact, the numbers in this triangle are very important in a lot of mathematical situations, so the triangle has a special name—*Pascal's triangle.*

The French mathematician Blaise Pascal, who lived from 1623 to 1662, is credited as the first mathematician to study the triangle and discuss its properties. However, mathematicians had known of the triangle for centuries. In China, the mathematician Jia Xian partially described it in the eleventh century, and the Chinese mathematicians Yang Hui and Chu Shih-Chieh described it in the thirteenth and fourteenth centuries, respectively. The Islamic mathematician al-Karaji and the famous Persian poet Omar Khayyam—a noted mathematician and astronomer—also knew of the triangle in the eleventh century. Four centuries later, in the fifteenth century, another Islamic mathematician, al-Kashi, discussed it. In Iran today, the triangle is sometimes called *Khayyam's triangle,* and in China, it is sometimes called *Jia's triangle* or *Yang Hui's triangle,* since Yang's work, although it built on Jia's earlier discoveries, was evidently more widely known.

Have students select crayons, markers, or colored pencils in two colors, and explain that they are going to color Pascal's triangle—at least the part of it that they have calculated. Have them use one color for all the hexagons that contain even numbers and the other color for all the hexagons that contain odd numbers.

When the students have finished coloring, ask them if a "picture" has emerged (see fig. 6.24). Do they see Sierpinski's triangle in the result? Have each student draw lines on his or her work to define the three smaller triangles that make up this Sierpinski's triangle. Ask, "Do you suppose that Pascal's triangle is somehow connected with Sierpinski's triangle?"

Part of the explanation for the similarity is that when a row consists of all odd numbers, the numbers in the upside-down triangle below those numbers are all even, so the students color them the same color. For example, one row of Pascal's triangle contains the numbers 1, 3, 3, 1. The numbers below these are all even, and they begin a large upside-down triangle of even numbers:

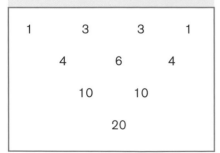

Fig. **6.24.**

The coloring of Pascal's triangle suggests Sierpinski's triangle.

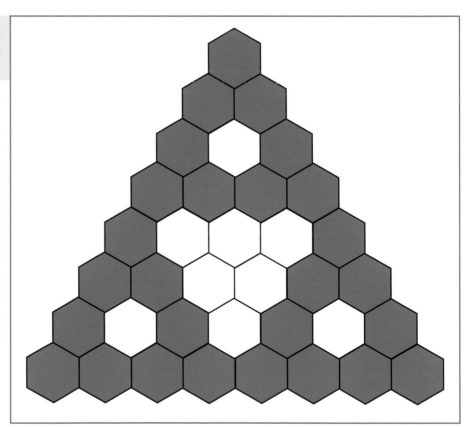

Fig. **6.25.**

When a row consists of all odd numbers, the numbers in the upside-down triangle below those numbers are all even.

The Mathematics in the Investigation

This investigation has examined two types of sequences—those obtained by repeatedly adding a fixed number and those obtained by repeatedly multiplying by a fixed number. It has also introduced NOW-NEXT terminology for describing such sequences recursively. Students have compared these two types of sequences and observed that doubling sequences grow very rapidly—their examination of the legend of the reward claimed by the inventor of the game of chess underscored this conclusion.

In completing the activities in the investigation, students have examined patterns in sequences whose terms consist of different numbers of unit squares or triangles. They have generated successive stages of

Sierpinski's triangle and entries in Pascal's triangle by using recursive procedures. In the process, they have examined various concepts involving whole numbers, including multiples of 3 (and how to tell whether a number is a multiple of 3), congruences (every number is a multiple of 3, one more than a multiple of 3, or two more than a multiple of 3), powers of 2, and square numbers. In coloring Pascal's triangle, they have investigated even and odd numbers.

The discussion of the investigation has not provided explicit descriptions for the sequences that the students have generated and studied. Although in some ways describing sequences explicitly is easier than describing them recursively, those descriptions require a familiarity with algebra and algebraic notation—in particular, a familiarity with the notion of a variable—which students in grades 3–5 do not yet have. For example, a recursive description of the sequence 5, 7, 9, 11, 13, … is accessible to students in grades 3–5. They can both understand and produce the description, "Start at 5 and apply the rule PREVIOUS + 2 = NOW." By contrast, an explicit description of the same sequence—the equation $f(n) = 2n + 3$ or the equation $a_n = 2n + 3$—is beyond their comprehension. The first of these equations uses functional notation, the second uses subscript notation, and both assume familiarity with variables and their use. Explicit descriptions for sequences are more appropriate for students in middle school and high school.

NAVIGATING *through* DISCRETE MATHEMATICS

Looking Back and Looking Ahead

This book has described how teachers can incorporate discrete mathematics into the curriculum in prekindergarten through grade 5. Concrete and informal development in these early years can lay a solid foundation for further study of discrete mathematics in grades 6–12. Students today need to understand and be able to apply discrete mathematics topics such as combinatorics, vertex-edge graphs, and iteration and recursion so that they can be competitive as adults in a fast-changing, technology-rich, information-dense world.

Discrete mathematics topics are engaging, contemporary, and useful. They should routinely be part of classroom learning. As recommended in *Principles and Standards for School Mathematics*, "discrete mathematics should be an integral part of the school mathematics curriculum" (NCTM 2000, p. 31).We hope that this book will help teachers implement this recommendation and bring the power of discrete mathematics to all students in all grades.

NAVIGATING *through* DISCRETE MATHEMATICS

Appendix

Blackline Masters and Solutions

Buttons for the Bucket

Bucket of Buttons

To make the 72 buttons for each bucket, copy this template onto four sheets of poster board or card stock in different colors—blue, red, yellow, and green. Cut out the buttons, and place them in a bucket or another suitable container.

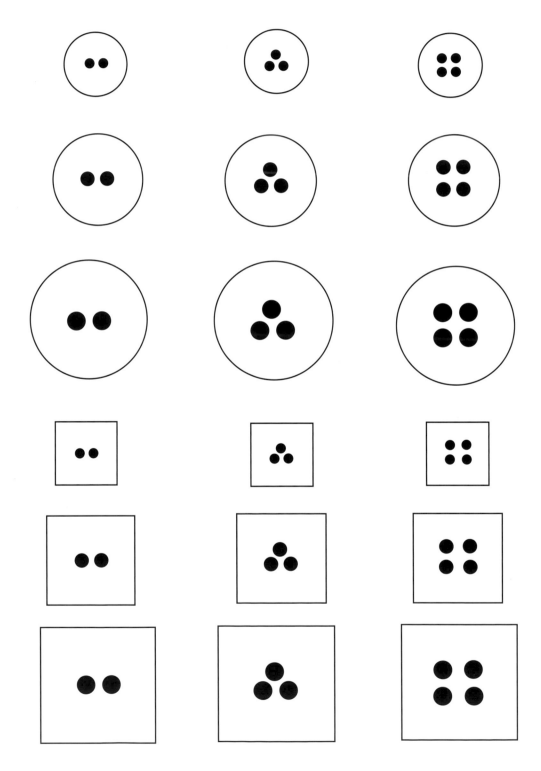

Bucket of Round Blue Buttons

Name _____

Bucket of Buttons—Preliminary Activity 2

Color the buttons at the bottom of the page blue, and cut them out.

1. Sort the buttons by number of holes. How many groups of buttons do you have? _____

2. How many buttons are in each group? _____ How many buttons are there altogether? _____

3. Sort the buttons by size. How many buttons are small? _____ How many buttons are medium-sized? _____ How many buttons are large? _____ How many buttons do you have altogether? _____

4. How many small buttons have four holes? _____

5. Sort the buttons by color. How many buttons are blue? _____

6. Imagine that you have nine more buttons just like your blue buttons, except they are red instead of blue. Draw all nine red buttons, and then draw a picture of *all* the medium-sized buttons—red or blue.

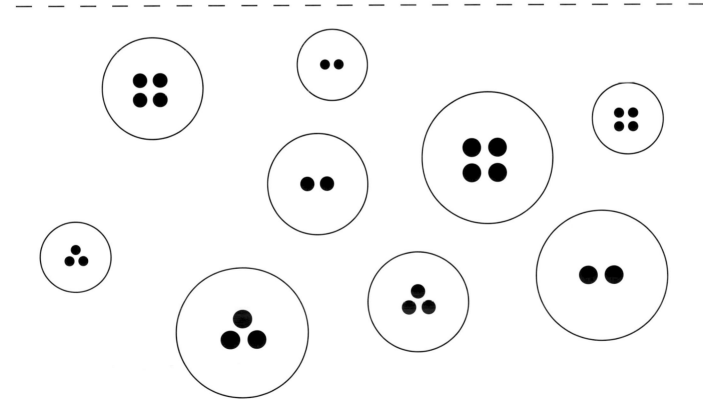

More Buttons in the Bucket

Name _____

Bucket of Buttons–Preliminary Activity 3

The bottom of this page shows four rows of buttons. Each row has six buttons (three circular and three square). Color the buttons in each row with a single color, making all the buttons in the first row blue, all the buttons in the second row red, all the buttons in the third row yellow, and all the buttons in the fourth row green. Cut out the buttons and put them in your bucket.

1. Sort the buttons by color. How many red buttons do you have? _____ How many buttons are blue? _____ How many are yellow? _____ How many are green? _____ How many buttons do you have altogether? _____ How many are red or yellow? _____ How many are blue or yellow? _____ How many buttons are not red? _____

2. Sort the buttons by shape. How many square buttons do you have? _____ How many round buttons do you have? _____ How many do you have altogether? _____ How many buttons are not square? _____

3. Sort the buttons by the number of holes. How many buttons do you have with two holes? _____ How many have three holes? _____ How many have four holes? _____ How many buttons do you have altogether? _____ How many buttons have two or three holes? _____ How many buttons do not have three holes? _____

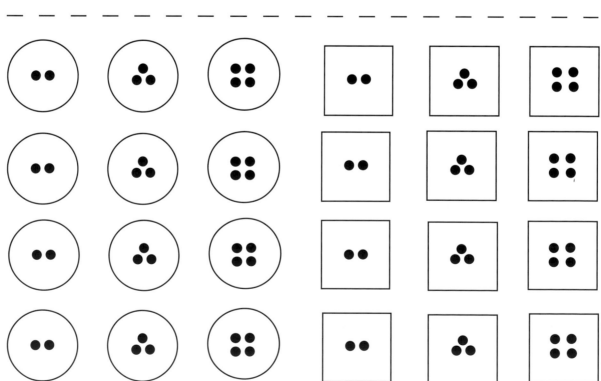

Navigating through Discrete Mathematics in Pre-K–Grade 5

Handful of Buttons

Name _____

Bucket of Buttons—Activity 4

Take a handful of buttons from the bucket. Place each button in the correct space in the Venn diagram.

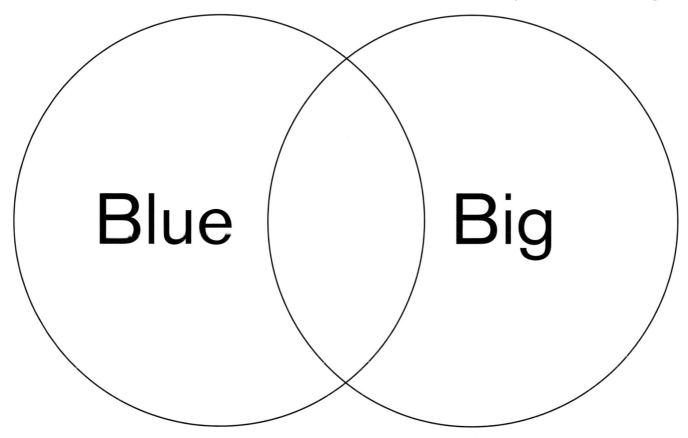

1. How many buttons in your handful are blue? _____

2. How many buttons in your handful are big? _____

3. How many buttons in your handful are blue and big? _____

4. How many buttons in your handful are blue but not big? _____

5. How many buttons in your handful are big but not blue? _____

6. How many buttons in your handful are not blue and not big? _____

7. How many buttons in your handful are blue or big? _____

8. How many buttons in your handful are big or blue, but not both? _____

Shirt Buttons

Name _____

Bucket of Buttons—Activity 5

Work with a partner to color the buttons below blue and cut them out. Use the blue buttons to make as many different shirts as possible by placing them on top of the shirts on the pages titled "Crazy Shirts."

Navigating through Discrete Mathematics in Pre-K–Grade 5

Crazy Shirts

Name _____

Bucket of Buttons—Activity 5

Outfits at Bindu Bear's Boutique

Name _____

Bindu Bear's Boutique—Activity 1

How many different outfits can you show on the bear mannequins?

Navigating through Discrete Mathematics in Pre-K–Grade 5

Outfits for the First Week

Name _____

Bindu Bear's Boutique—Activity 1

Use crayons and a pencil to complete the chart.

	Dotted Pants	Striped Pants
Green Shirt		
Purple Shirt		
Yellow Shirt		

Bear Cutouts

Name _____

Bindu Bear's Boutique—Activity 2

Cut along the dashed lines.

Navigating through Discrete Mathematics in Pre-K–Grade 5

Shoe Cutouts

Name _____

Bindu Bear's Boutique—Activity 2

Cut along the dashed lines.

Graphics for Five Sites

SCHOOL

Navigating through Discrete Mathematics in Pre-K–Grade 5

How to Place the Traffic Lights on Your Graph

Names _____

From Here to There—Activity 3

School

_____

_____

_____   _____

- -

Instructions to the Teacher

1. Make a copy of this page.
2. On the copy, fill in the blanks to label the vertices with the sites that you have chosen for the activity.
3. Draw in traffic lights (🚦) where you want students to place them on their graphs (see fig. 3.8 and the accompanying discussion).
4. Cut these instructions from the bottom of the copy.
5. Make one copy to insert into each plastic bag with the traffic lights that you construct for the activity.

Navigating through Discrete Mathematics in Pre-K–Grade 5

Paths from School to _____

Name _____

From Here to There–Activity 3

List below all paths from the school to the play site, and give the number of traffic lights along each path.

Path	Number of Traffic Lights

How many paths did you find? _____

What is the best path from the school to this play site? _____

How many traffic lights does it have? _____

Circuits That Visit All the Play Sites

Name _____

From Here to There—Activity 4

List below all the circuits that begin at the school, visit each of the other four sites, and return to the school. Give the number of traffic lights along each circuit.

Circuit	Number of Traffic Lights

How many circuits did you find? _____

Which of these circuits involve the fewest traffic lights? _____

Which is the best circuit, and why? _____

Coloring Maps–South America

Name _____

Graphs for the Discrete Explorer–Activity 1

How many colors do you need for this map?

Countries
1. Argentina
2. Bolivia
3. Brazil
4. Chile
5. Colombia
6. Ecuador
7. French Guiana
8. Guyana
9. Paraguay
10. Peru
11. Suriname
12. Uruguay
13. Venezuela

Coloring Maps—States West of the Mississippi River

Name _____

Graphs for the Discrete Explorer—Activity 1

How many colors do you need for this map?

States West of the Mississippi River

1.	Arizona	12.	Nebraska
2.	Arkansas	13.	Nevada
3.	California	14.	New Mexico
4.	Colorado	15.	North Dakota
5.	Idaho	16.	Oklahoma
6.	Iowa	17.	Oregon
7.	Kansas	18.	South Dakota
8.	Louisiana	19.	Texas
9.	Minnesota	20.	Utah
10.	Missouri	21.	Washington
11.	Montana	22.	Wyoming

Navigating through Discrete Mathematics in Pre-K–Grade 5

Coloring Maps–Africa

Name _____

Graphs for the Discrete Explorer–Activity 1

How many colors do you need for this map?

The Western United States

Graphs for the Discrete Explorer—Activity 2

Step 1: Draw a vertex in each state.

Navigating through Discrete Mathematics in Pre-K–Grade 5

Twenty-Two Vertices

Graphs for the Discrete Explorer—Activity 2

Step 2: Connect two vertices with an edge if they share a common border.

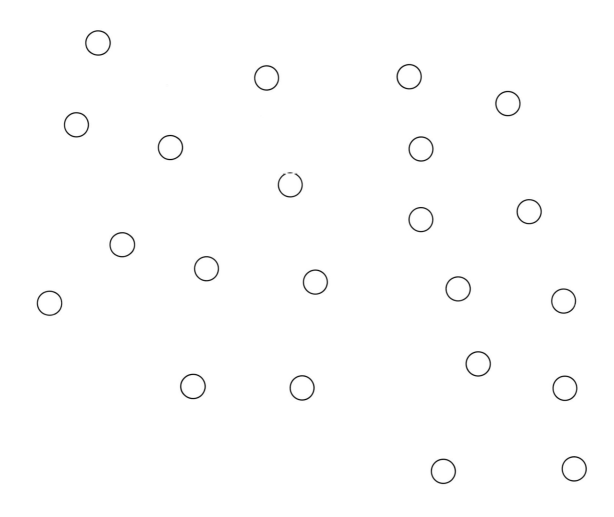

Vertex-Edge Graph of the Western United States

Graphs for the Discrete Explorer—Activity 2

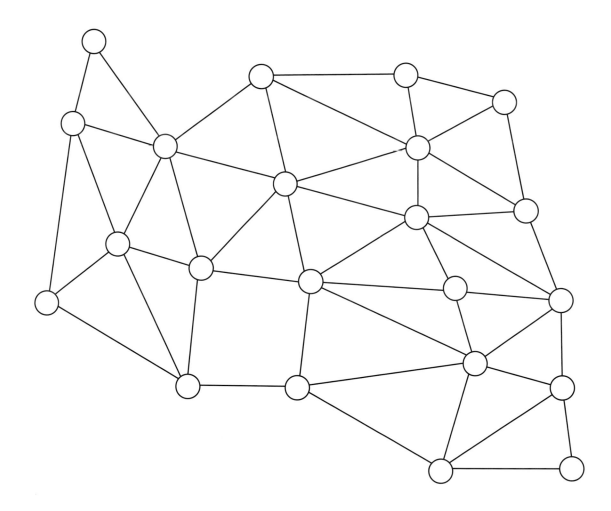

Vertex Coloring–Cycles

Name _____

Graphs for the Discrete Explorer–Activity 2

Fill in the chart, and then answer the questions.

Graph	How Many Vertices?	How Many Edges?	Minimum Number of Colors Needed
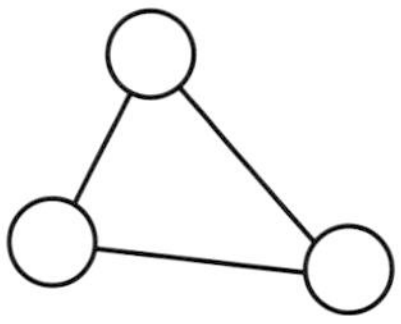	3	3	
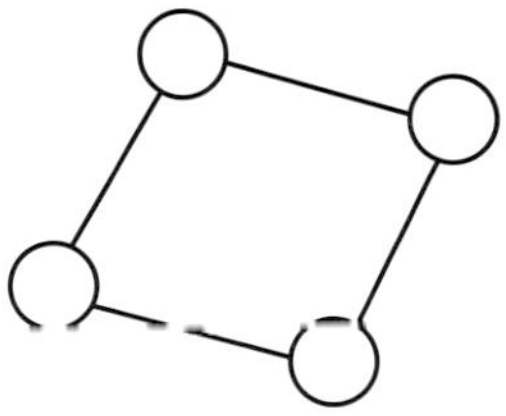			
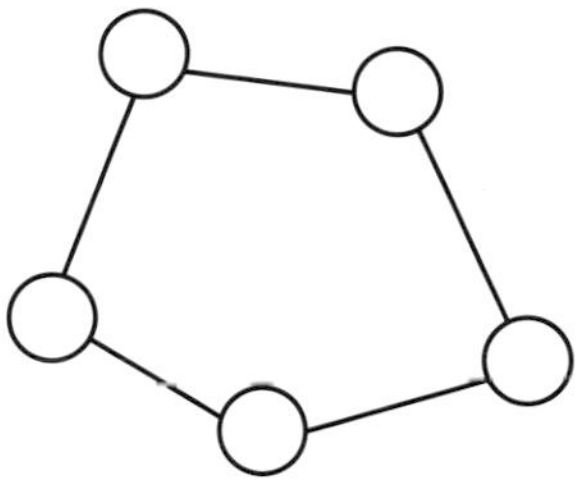			
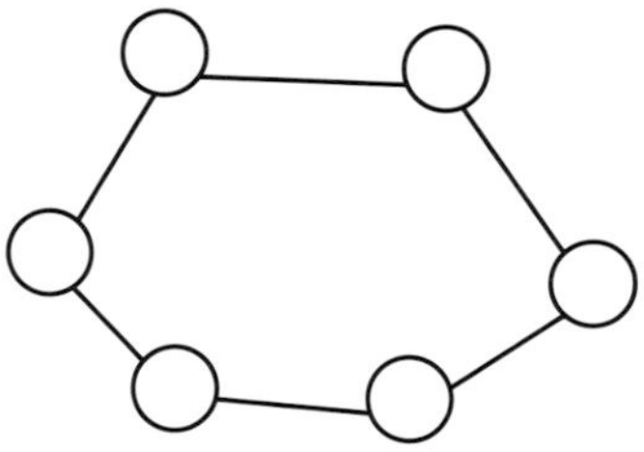			
Draw the next graph in this pattern here.			

1. How many colors do you need to color a cycle with 10 vertices? _____

2. How many colors do you need to color a cycle with 35 vertices? _____

3. Can you write a rule that describes how to find the smallest number of colors needed for any cycle?

Vertex Coloring—Wheels

Name _____

Graphs for the Discrete Explorer—Activity 2

Fill in the chart, and then answer the questions.

Examples of Cycles	Examples of Wheels	Minimum Number of Colors—Cycles	Minimum Number of Colors—Wheels

1. Compare the graphs in each of the four examples. Describe what is the same and what is different about the two graphs in each pair. _____

_____

_____

2. *a.* How many colors do you need to color a wheel if 50 vertices surround the hub? _____

   b. How many colors do you need if 35 vertices surround the hub? _____

3. Write a rule that describes how to find the minimum number of colors needed to color any wheel.

Navigating through Discrete Mathematics in Pre-K–Grade 5

Vertex Coloring–Guess and Check

Name _____

Graphs for the Discrete Explorer–Activity 2

1. Make a conjecture: What is the minimum number of colors that you need to color a copy of the graph below? _____ Why?

2. Use vertex coloring to color the graph. The extra copies give you opportunities to start over if necessary. Circle your final answer.

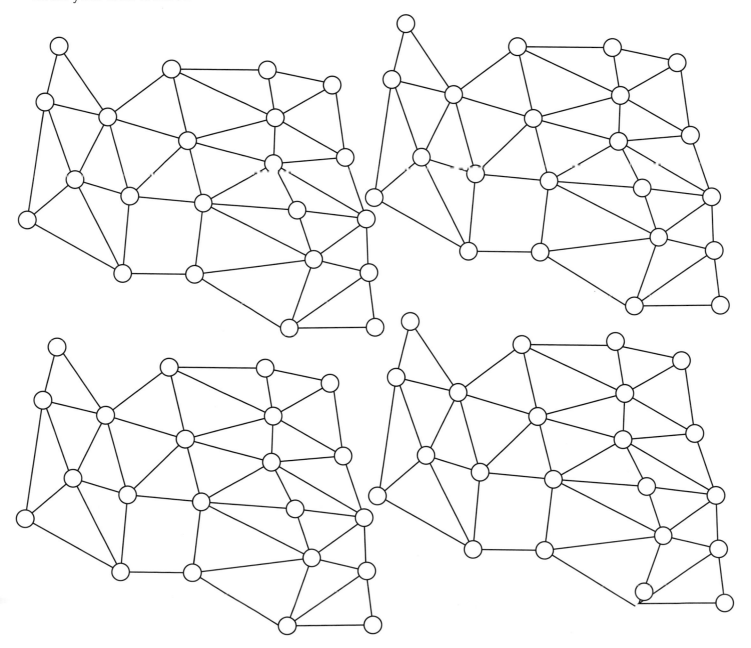

3. What is the minimum number of colors that you need to color this graph? _____

Additional Practice with Vertex Coloring

Name _____

Graphs for the Discrete Explorer–Activity 2

Color the vertices in each graph with the minimum number of colors.

1.

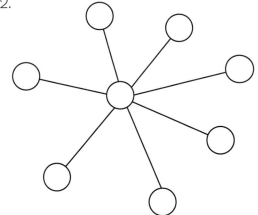

Minimum number of colors: _____

4.

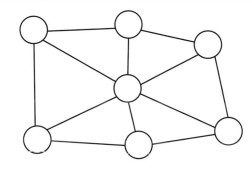

Minimum number of colors: _____

2.

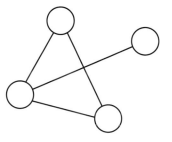

Minimum number of colors: _____

5.

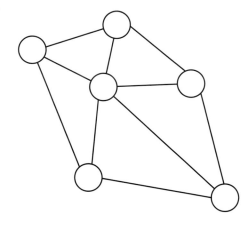

Minimum number of colors: _____

3.

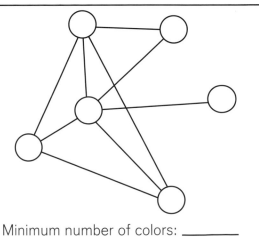

Minimum number of colors: _____

6.

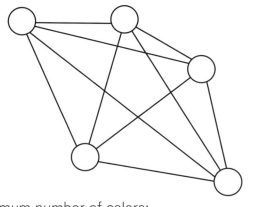

Minimum number of colors: _____

Navigating through Discrete Mathematics in Pre-K–Grade 5

Charlie the Contractor's Problem—Part 1

Name _____

Graphs for the Discrete Explorer—Activity 3

Charlie is a careful contractor who has a small construction business with six workers—Nathan, Ryan, Zachary, Hope, Mary, and Elizabeth. At the beginning of each workday, Charlie assigns his workers to crews. To make the best use of his workers' talents, Charlie assigns any two who have the same skill to different crews. He follows these rules:

- Elizabeth, Nathan, and Hope are all electricians, so they have to be on different crews.

- Mary, Nathan, and Ryan are all carpenters, so they have to be on different crews.

- Mary and Zachary are both masons, so they have to be on different crews.

- Elizabeth, Ryan, and Hope are all plumbers, so they have to be on different crews.

1. Help Charlie assign his six workers to crews so that no crew has two workers with the same skill. Call the crews "crew 1," "crew 2," and so on, and list them in the box below.

2. What is the smallest number of crews that Charlie can create and still be sure that no crew has two employees with the same skills?_____

3. How do you know that you have found the minimum number of crews?

Charlie the Contractor's Problem—Part 2

Name _____

Graphs for the Discrete Explorer—Activity 3

To use a vertex-edge graph to solve the problem:

Step 1:   Decide what the vertices, edges, and colors will represent.

Step 2:   Create a vertex-edge graph that models the situation.

Step 3:   Use the minimum number of colors to color the vertices of the graph.

Step 4:   Write a few sentences that tell how your solution resolves the conflicts and how you know that you have found the minimum number of possible solutions.

Step 1:

The vertices represent

_____

The edges represent

_____

The colors represent

_____

Step 2 and Step 3:

Step 4:

What is the minimum number of crews that Charlie can create and still be sure that no crew has two employees with the same skill? _____

Which employees should you assign to crew 1?

Which employees should you assign to crew 2?

Which employees should you assign to crew 3?

Which employees should you assign to any additional crews?

How do you know that you have found the minimum number of crews?

Using a Tree Diagram to Assign Charlie's Workers to Crews

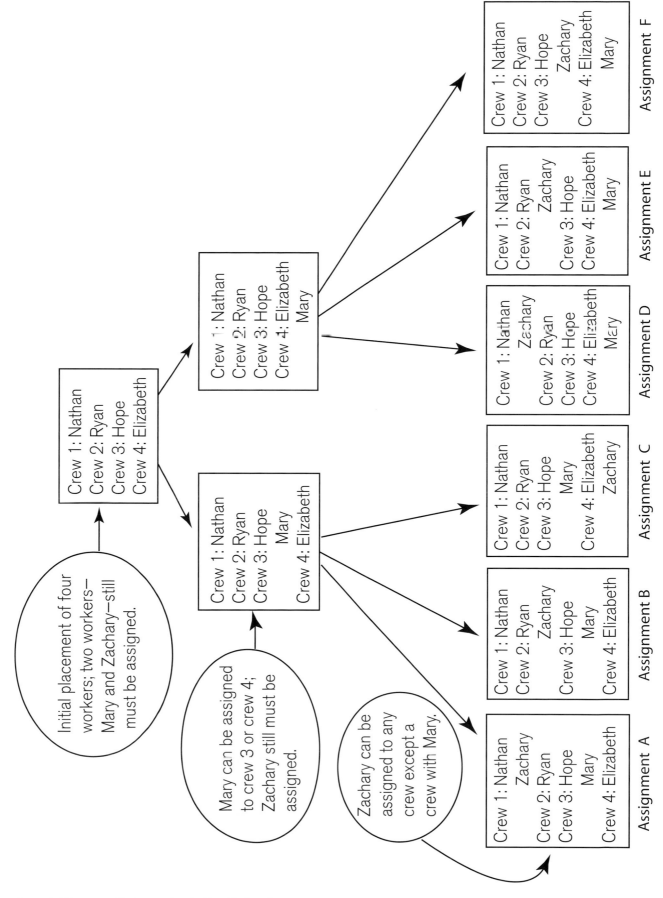

Initial placement of four workers; two workers—Mary and Zachary—still must be assigned.

Crew 1: Nathan
Crew 2: Ryan
Crew 3: Hope
Crew 4: Elizabeth

Mary can be assigned to crew 3 or crew 4; Zachary still must be assigned.

Zachary can be assigned to any crew except a crew with Mary.

Crew 1: Nathan
Crew 2: Ryan
Crew 3: Hope
Crew 4: Elizabeth
        Mary

Crew 1: Nathan
Crew 2: Ryan
Crew 3: Hope
        Mary
Crew 4: Elizabeth

Crew 1: Nathan
        Zachary
Crew 2: Ryan
Crew 3: Hope
        Mary
Crew 4: Elizabeth

Assignment A

Crew 1: Nathan
Crew 2: Ryan
        Zachary
Crew 3: Hope
        Mary
Crew 4: Elizabeth

Assignment B

Crew 1: Nathan
Crew 2: Ryan
Crew 3: Hope
Crew 4: Elizabeth
        Zachary

Assignment C

Crew 1: Nathan
        Zachary
Crew 2: Ryan
Crew 3: Hope
Crew 4: Elizabeth
        Mary

Assignment D

Crew 1: Nathan
Crew 2: Ryan
        Zachary
Crew 3: Hope
Crew 4: Elizabeth
        Mary

Assignment E

Crew 1: Nathan
Crew 2: Ryan
Crew 3: Hope
        Zachary
Crew 4: Elizabeth
        Mary

Assignment F

Advertising for a Garage Sale– Part 1

Name _____

Graphs for the Discrete Explorer–Activity 4

Suppose that your family is having a garage sale, and your job is to place an advertising poster at each intersection of streets in your neighborhood. The vertex-edge graph below represents your neighborhood. The line segments represent streets, the vertices represent intersections, and vertex *H* represents the location of your house.

To complete your task as quickly as possible, you want to choose a route that visits each intersection—a vertex on the graph—exactly once. Can you find a route that begins at your home (vertex *H*), visits each vertex exactly once, and then returns to your home? If so, in the spaces below the graph, list the vertices in the order in which you visit them, beginning and ending with *H*.

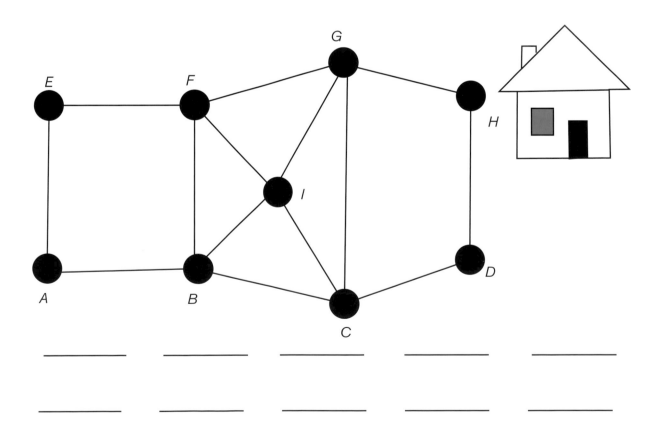

___ ___ ___ ___ ___ ___

___ ___ ___ ___ ___ ___

Navigating through Discrete Mathematics in Pre-K–Grade 5

Advertising for a Garage Sale– Part 2

Name _____

Graphs for the Discrete Explorer–Activity 4

Suppose that a developer has added new streets—*FK, KL*, and *LG*—to your neighborhood since the time of your family's first yard sale. Now your family is planning another sale, and you need to put up posters at the intersections again. Use the new graph of your neighborhood shown below to look for a route that begins at your home (*H*), visits each intersection—a vertex on the graph—exactly once, and then returns to your home. If you can find such a route, use the spaces below the graph to list the vertices in the order in which you visit them, beginning and ending with *H*.

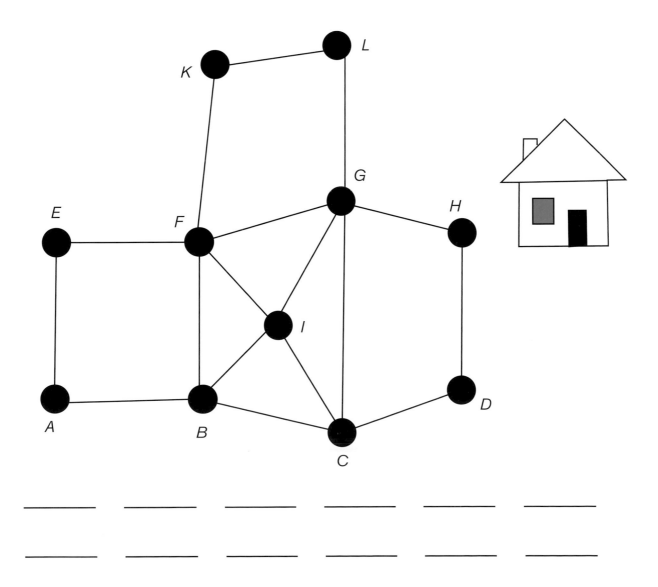

___ ___ ___ ___ ___ ___

___ ___ ___ ___ ___ ___

Advertising for a Garage Sale– Part 3

Name _____

Graphs for the Discrete Explorer–Activity 4

Suppose that since your family's second yard sale, a developer has added more new streets—*BM, MN,* and *NC*—to your neighborhood, this time on the other side. The graph below represents the neighborhood with the new streets and intersections. Your family is now planning a third sale, and once again you must place posters at the intersections in the neighborhood. Can you find a route that begins at your home (vertex *H*), visits each intersection—a vertex in the graph—exactly once, and then returns to your home? If so, in the spaces below the graph, list the vertices in the order in which you visit them, beginning and ending at *H*.

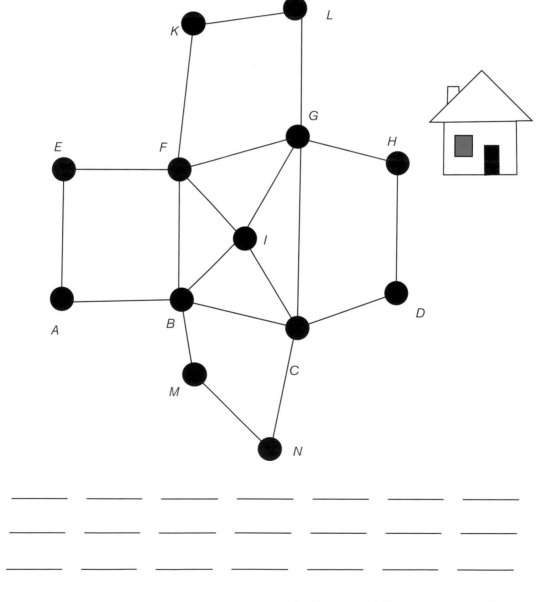

___ ___ ___ ___ ___ ___ ___ ___ ___

___ ___ ___ ___ ___ ___ ___ ___

___ ___ ___ ___ ___ ___ ___

Streets in the Neighborhood

Graphs for the Discrete Explorer—Activity 5

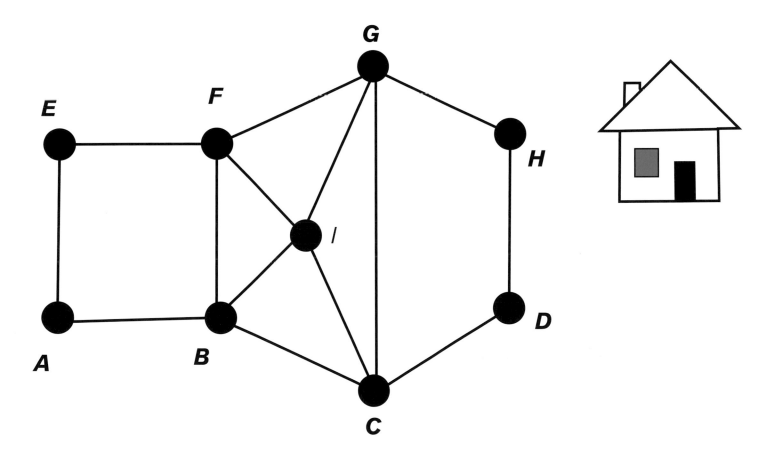

Efficient Newspaper Routes– Part 1

Name _____

Graphs for the Discrete Explorer—Activity 5

Suppose that every day after school you go home, get on your bike, and deliver the evening paper to houses on every street in your neighborhood. You have become very skillful at throwing the papers onto the steps of the houses on both sides of the street. The graph below represents the streets and intersections in your neighborhood, and your house is at the street corner labeled *H.*

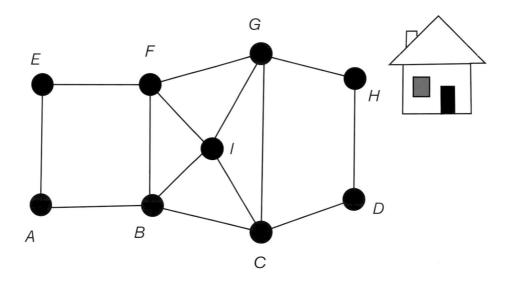

Can you find an efficient paper route that starts and ends at your house (*H*) and travels along every street in the neighborhood just once? Use the two practice maps below to consider routes.

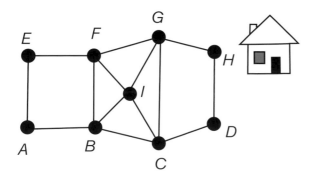

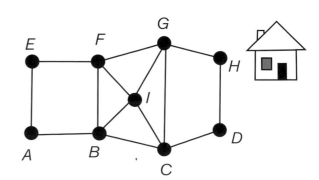

Navigating through Discrete Mathematics in Pre-K–Grade 5

Efficient Newspaper Routes– Part 2

Name _____

Graphs for the Discrete Explorer–Activity 5

Suppose that a developer has added new streets—*FK, KL,* and *LG*—to the neighborhood, and you must now deliver the evening paper to houses on those streets as well as to houses on all the old streets. Can you find an efficient paper route that starts and ends at your house (at the street corner labeled *H*) and travels along every street in the neighborhood just once?

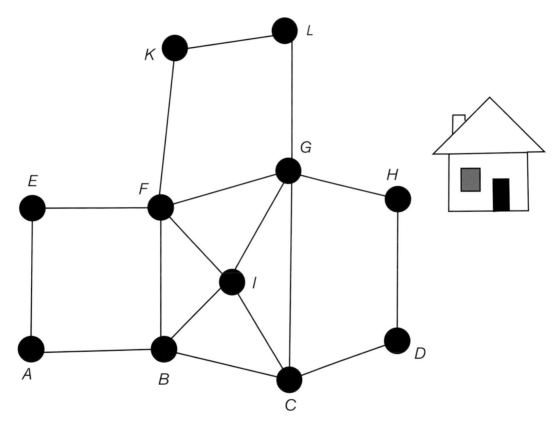

Use the following two practice maps below to help you consider routes.

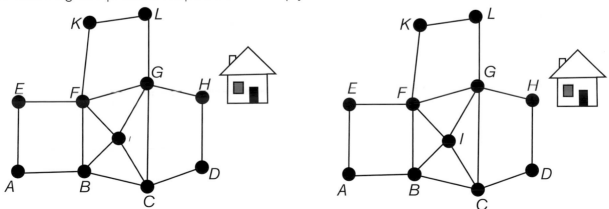

Visiting Vertices or Traveling Edges?—Part 1

Name _____

Graphs for the Discrete Explorer—Activity 5

Consider the vertex-edge graph below:

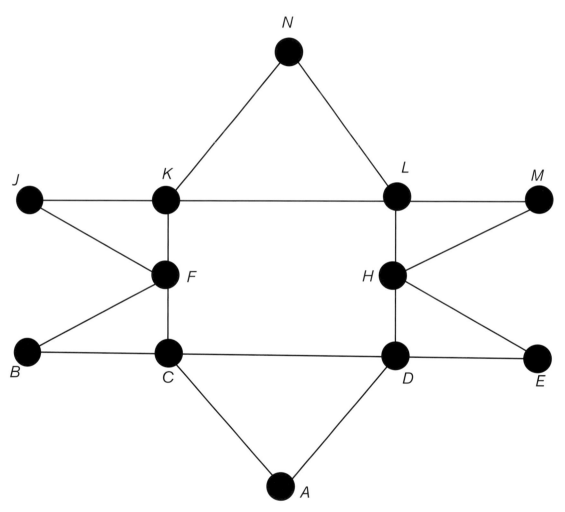

1. Does the graph have a Hamilton circuit? _____

2. If the graph does not have a Hamilton circuit, what is the minimum number of vertices that a path must repeat to include every vertex and return to its starting point? _____

3. Does the graph have an Euler circuit? _____

4. If the graph does not have an Euler circuit, what is the minimum number of edges that a path must repeat to include every edge and return to its starting point? _____

Navigating through Discrete Mathematics in Pre-K–Grade 5

Visiting Vertices or Traveling Edges?—Part 2

Name _____

Graphs for the Discrete Explorer—Activity 5

Consider the vertex-edge graph below:

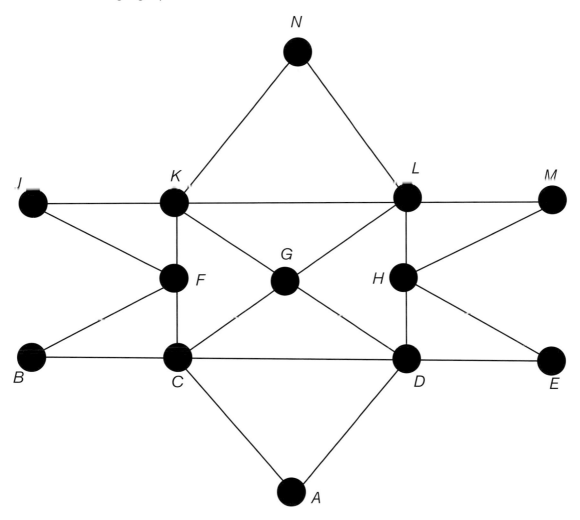

1. Does the graph have a Hamilton circuit? _____

2. If the graph does not have a Hamilton circuit, what is the minimum number of vertices that a path must repeat to include every vertex and return to its starting point? _____

3. Does the graph have an Euler circuit? _____

4. If the graph does not have an Euler circuit, what is the minimum number of edges that a path must repeat to include every edge and return to its starting point? _____

Lion

Navigating through Discrete Mathematics in Pre-K–Grade 5

Bird

Frog

Navigating through Discrete Mathematics in Pre-K–Grade 5

Donkey

Cards for "Guess My Pattern"

Picture after Picture—Activities 1 and 2

Repeating Patterns in Number Sequences

Name _____

Picture after Picture—Activity 1

1. Think about the sequence below:

| 1 | 4 | 3 | 2 | 1 | 4 | 3 | 2 | 1 | 4 | 3 | 2 | ...

a. What pattern repeats to make this sequence?

[ ]

b. What is the next term in the sequence? [ ]

2. Think about the sequence below:

| 1 | 4 | 1 | 1 | 4 | 1 | 1 | 4 | 1 | 1 | 4 | 1 | ...

a. What pattern repeats to make this sequence?

[ ]

b. What is the next term in the sequence? [ ]

3. Think about the sequence below:

| 3 | 1 | 1 | 1 | 3 | 3 | 1 | 1 | 1 | 3 | 3 | 1 | 1 | 1 | 3 | ...

a. What pattern repeats to make this sequence?

[ ]

b. What is the next term in the sequence? [ ]

Guess How I Continue–Part 1

Name _____

Picture after Picture–Activity 2

1. The first nine terms of a sequence appear below:

How might the sequence continue?

2. Describe in words the pattern that you see.

Navigating through Discrete Mathematics in Pre-K–Grade 5

Guess How I Continue—Part 2

Name _____

Picture after Picture—Activity 2

1. The first nine terms of a sequence appear below:

   How might the sequence continue?

2. Describe in words the pattern that you see.

Guess How I Continue–Part 3

Name _____

Picture after Picture–Activity 2

1. The first twelve terms of a sequence appear below:

   How might the sequence continue?

2. Describe in words the pattern that you see.

Guess How I Continue–Part 4

Name _____

Picture after Picture–Activity 2

1. The first twelve terms of a sequence appear below:

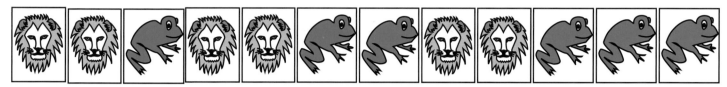

   How might the sequence continue?

2. Describe in words the pattern that you see.

Guess How I Continue—Part 5

Name _____

Picture after Picture—Activity 2

1. The first twelve terms of a sequence appear below:

    How might the sequence continue?

2. Describe in words the pattern that you see.

Navigating through Discrete Mathematics in Pre-K–Grade 5

Guess How I Continue—Part 6

Name _____

Picture after Picture—Activity 2

1. The first twelve terms of a sequence appear below:

   How might the sequence continue?

   ┌───┐
   │   │
   │   │
   │   │
   │   │
   │   │
   └───┘

2. Describe in words the pattern that you see.

What Sequence Starts with ...?
Part 1

Picture after Picture—Activity 3

1. Suppose that a sequence starts with the five terms below:

   What might the next term in the sequence be?

2. Describe in words the pattern that you see.

3. According to your pattern, what are the next ten terms in the sequence?

   _____ _____ _____ _____ _____

   _____ _____ _____ _____ _____

What Sequence Starts with …?
Part 2

Picture after Picture—Activity 3

1. Suppose that a sequence starts with the five terms below:

   What might the next term in the sequence be?

2. Describe in words the pattern that you see.

3. Working with the pattern that you see, use your game cards to show the first twenty terms of the sequence. List your twenty terms below, using the letters *F* for frog, *L* for lion, and *B* for bird.

What Sequence Starts with ...?
Part 3

Picture after Picture—Activity 3

1. Suppose that a sequence starts with the four terms below:

   What might the next term in the sequence be?

2. Describe in words the pattern that you see, and list the next twenty terms, using the letters *F* for frog, *L* for lion, and *B* for bird.

3. Suppose that a different sequence starts with the same four terms:

   What might the next term in the sequence be?

4. Describe in words the pattern that you see, and list the next twenty terms, using the letters *F* for frog, *L* for lion, and *B* for bird.

Navigating through Discrete Mathematics in Pre-K–Grade 5

What Is the Missing Term?—Part 1

Name _____

Picture after Picture–Activity 3

The sequence below has a missing term:

1. Explain why the missing term could be a lion.

2. Explain why the missing term could be a frog.

What Is the Missing Term?–Part 2

Name _____

Picture after Picture–Activity 3

Find a term that you could use to fill in the blank in each sequence.:

Find a different way of filling each blank, and describe the sequences that you created.

1.

2.

3.

4.

Navigating through Discrete Mathematics in Pre-K–Grade 5

Creating Number Sequences

Name _____

Exploring Sequences Step by Step—Activity 1

1. Use the rule NOW + 3 = NEXT

Example:

Rule:	NOW + 3 = NEXT
Place to begin:	Initial value = 2
Sequence:	2, 5, 8, 11, 14, 17, 20, 23, 26, 29, 32, 35, 38, 41, 44, …
---

    a. What sequence do you get if you start with 1? List the first fifteen terms.

    b. What sequence do you get if your initial value is 0? List the first fifteen terms.

    c. What is the eighteenth term in the sequence in part (*b*)? _____

2. Look at the terms in each of the three sequences—the one in the example and the two that you generated in step 1.

    a. Does one of the sequences include the number 26? _____
       If so, which sequence? _____

    b. Does either of the other sequences include the term 26? _____
       If so, which sequence? _____

    c. Does one of the sequences include the number 33? _____
       If so, which sequence? _____

    d. Does either of the other sequences include the term 33? _____
       If so, which sequence? _____

    e. Explain how you know that the number 57 will appear in one of the three sequences.

    f. Which of the three sequences has 100 as a term? _____
       Explain your answer.

    g. Does every whole number appear in just one of these sequences? _____
       How can you explain your answer or show that it is correct? Discuss this question with a partner before writing your ideas.

Other Number Sequences

Name _____

Exploring Sequences Step by Step—Activity 1

1. What sequence do you get if you start with 1 and use the rule NOW + 1 = NEXT?

2. What sequence do you get if your initial term is 0 and you use the rule NOW + 2 = NEXT?

3. What sequence do you get if your first term is 1 and you use the rule NOW + 2 = NEXT?

4. Use the words NOW and PREVIOUS to write a rule and give a start value to generate each sequence below:

    a. 1, 2, 3, 4, 5, 6, 7, 8, 9, 10, 11, …

    Rule:

    Start Value:

    b. 0, 2, 4, 6, 8, 10, 12, 14, 16, …

    Rule:

    Initial term:

    c. 1, 3, 5, 7, 9, 11, 13, 15, 17, …

    Rule:

    First term:

8 × 8 Grid

Exploring Sequences Step by Step—Activity 2

Grids—Part 1

Name _____

Exploring Sequences Step by Step—Activity 2

Complete each part of this activity by yourself, and then check your results with a partner.

1. Cut out the grid on the outside lines. How many grids do you have? _____ Also write your answer in the numbered space at the bottom of the page.

2. Fold the grid in half along one of the lines, and then cut on the line. How many pieces of the grid do you have now? _____ Enter your answer in the numbered space at the bottom of the page, and pile the pieces of the grid in a stack.

3. Cut the pieces in the stack in half, one by one, along one of the grid lines. How many pieces of the grid do you have now? _____ Enter your answer in the numbered space at the bottom of the page, and again pile the pieces of the grid in a stack.

4. Again cut the pieces in the stack in half, one by one, along one of the grid lines. How many pieces of the grid do you have now? _____ Enter your answer in the numbered space at the bottom of the page, and again pile the pieces of the grid in a stack.

5. Again cut the pieces in the stack in half, one by one, along one of the grid lines. How many pieces of the grid do you have now? _____ Enter your answer in the numbered space at the bottom of the page, and again pile the pieces of the grid in a stack.

6. Again cut the pieces in the stack in half, one by one, along one of the grid lines. How many pieces of the grid do you have now? _____ Enter your answer in the numbered space at the bottom of the page, and again pile the pieces of the grid in a stack.

Write the answer to each of the preceding questions in the following spaces.

_____ , _____ , _____ , _____ , _____ , _____ , ...

   1.   2.   3.   4.   5.   6.

Grids–Part 2

Name _____

Exploring Sequences Step by Step–Activity 2

1. Consider the sequence 1, 2, 4, 8, 16, 32, …. Write a general rule to describe the pattern that you see in this sequence of numbers.

2. Use your rule to find the next three terms of the sequence.

   1, 2, 4, 8, 16, 32, _____, _____, _____, …

3. Use your calculator to find the six terms that follow the three terms that you found in step 2.

   1, 2, 4, 8, 16, 32, _____, _____, _____, _____, _____, _____, _____, _____, _____, …

4. Compare the following three sequences:

i.	1, 3, 5, 7, 9, 11, 13, 15, …	Iteration rule: PREVIOUS + 2 = NEXT
ii.	1, 101, 201, 301, 401, 501, …	Iteration rule: PREVIOUS + 100 = NEXT
iii.	1, 2, 4, 8, 16, 32, 64, …	Iteration rule: PREVIOUS × 2 = NEXT

   a. Predict which sequence grows slowest, and explain why it grows slowest.

   b. Predict which sequence grows fastest, and explain why it grows fastest.

   c. Use your calculator to find the fifteenth term in each of these sequences.

   In sequence (i)_____   In sequence (ii) _____   In sequence (iii) _____

   d. Find the sixteenth term in each sequence.

   In sequence (i)_____   In sequence (ii) _____   In sequence (iii) _____

   e. Which sequence actually grows slowest? _____

   f. Which sequence actually grows fastest? _____

Sequences of Shapes and Numbers

Name _____

Exploring Sequences Step by Step—Activity 3

1. The following are the first five terms in a sequence of geometric shapes.

a. Draw the next three terms in the sequence.

_____ , _____ , _____

b. Write the number of squares in each of the first eight terms of the sequence.

_____ , _____ , _____ , _____ , _____ , _____ , _____ , _____ , ⋯

c. How many squares are in the twelfth term of the sequence? _____

2. The following are the first four terms in a different sequence of geometric shapes.

a. Draw the next three terms in the sequence.

_____ , _____ , _____

b. Write the number of squares in each of the first seven terms of the sequence.

_____ , _____ , _____ , _____ , _____ , _____ , _____ , ⋯

c. How many squares are in the twelfth term of the sequence? _____

Navigating through Discrete Mathematics in Pre-K–Grade 5

More Practice with Sequences

Name _____

Exploring Sequences Step by Step—Activity 3

1. Consider the first four terms in the sequence of shapes below.

☐ , ☐☐☐ , ☐☐☐☐☐ , ☐☐☐☐☐☐☐ , ...

    a. Draw the next three terms in the sequence.

    _____ , _____ , _____ , ...

    b. Write the number of squares in each of the first seven terms of the sequence.

    _____ , _____ , _____ , _____ , _____ , _____ , _____ , ...

    c. How many squares are in the twelfth term of the sequence? _____

    d. Write a NOW-NEXT rule to describe the sequence of numbers.

    What is the initial term? _____

    e. Write a NOW-NEXT rule to describe the sequence of shapes.

    What is the initial term? _____

2. *a.* Use some arrangement of squares to make up your own sequence of shapes. On another sheet of paper, draw the first seven terms of your sequence.

    b. Trade papers with a partner and find a number sequence that shows how many squares are in each of the first seven terms of your partner's sequence of shapes. Write a NOW-NEXT rule on your partner's paper to describe your partner's number sequence.

    c. Trade papers again with your partner, receiving your own paper again. Review your partner's work on your sequence. Does the rule that your partner wrote describe the sequence that you created?

    d. Check with your partner on your work. Does the rule that you wrote describe the sequence that your partner created?

A Sequence of Square Shapes

Name _____

Exploring Sequences Step by Step—Activity 3

The following are the first three terms in another sequence of shapes.

1. Draw the next three terms in the sequence.

_____ , _____ , _____ , ···

2. Write the number of small squares in each of the first six terms of the sequence of shapes.

_____ , _____ , _____ , _____ , _____ , _____ , ···

3. How many small squares are in the tenth term of the sequence? _____

4. *a.* Write the first six terms of this sequence by using row-by-column (row × column) notation.

_____ , _____ , _____ , _____ , _____ , _____ , ···

b. Write the first six terms of this sequence by using square notation; that is, write each term as (some number)^2.

_____ , _____ , _____ , _____ , _____ , _____ , ···

Squares on Squares

Squares and Backward Ls–Part 1

Name _____

Exploring Sequences Step by Step–Activity 3

Consider the sequence of shapes:

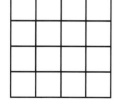, , 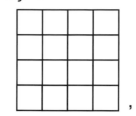, 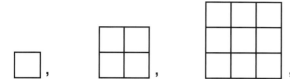, 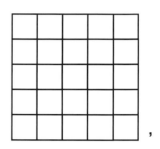, ...

Using steps 1 and 2 below as models, complete steps 3–9 to show that in the sequence—

Each new square shape	is	the previous square shape	plus	a backward L shape.	An equation says this in numbers.
1.	is	☐	plus		$4 = 1 + 3$
2.	is		plus		$9 = 4 + 5$
3.	is		plus		$16 =$
4. 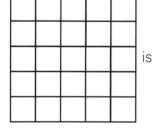	is		plus		

5. The 6 × 6 square   is   the _____ square   plus

6. The 7 × 7 square   is   the _____ square   plus

7. The 8 × 8 square   is   the _____ square   plus

8. The 9 × 9 square   is   the _____ square   plus

9. The 10 × 10 square   is   the _____ square   plus

Squares and Backward Ls–Part 2

Name _____

Exploring Sequences Step by Step–Activity 3

Consider the sequence of shapes:

 , 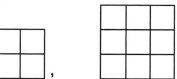 , 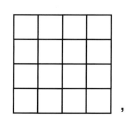 , 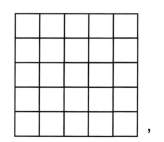 , 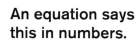 , ...

Using steps 1 and 2 below as models, complete steps 3–9 to indicate that in the sequence—

Each new square shape	**is**	**a 1 × 1 square shape plus some number of backward L shapes.**	**An equation says this in numbers.**
1.	is		$4 = 1 + 3$
2.	is		$9 = 1 + 3 + 5$
3.	is		$16 =$
4.	is		$25 =$
5.	is		$36 =$
6. The 7 × 7 square	is		$49 =$
7. The 8 × 8 square	is		$64 =$
8. The 9 × 9 square	is		$81 =$
9. The 10 × 10 square	is		$100 =$

Fourth Term of a Sequence of Triangular Shapes

Exploring Sequences Step by Step—Activity 4

How Many Paths from *A* to *I*

Name _____

Exploring Sequences Step by Step—Activity 5

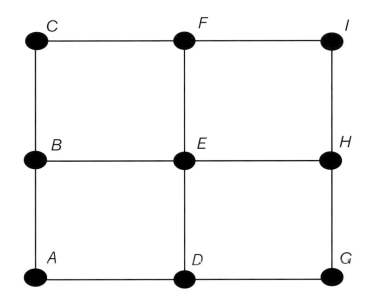

Use the small grids below to show as many paths as you can find from *A* to *I* in the grid graph above.

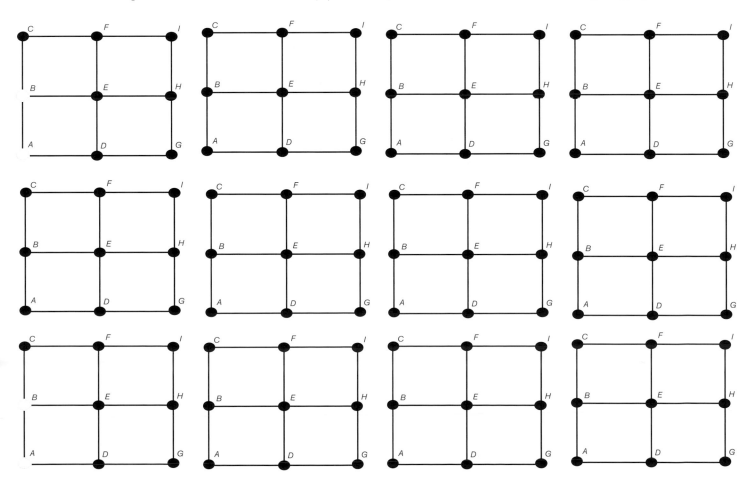

Walking on a Grid Graph

Name _____

Exploring Sequences Step by Step—Activity 5

Imagine that the grid graph below represents your neighborhood:

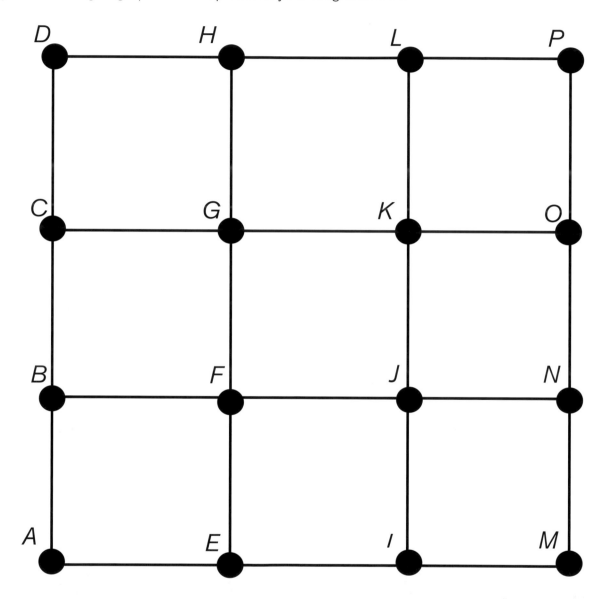

1. On a separate sheet of paper, create a tree diagram that shows all the paths from your house (vertex *A*) to your friend's house (vertex *P*) if you can walk only north or east.

2. Use your tree diagram to create an alphabetical list of all paths.

3. How many different paths did you find?

Navigating through Discrete Mathematics in Pre-K–Grade 5

From *A* to *P* on a Grid Graph

Exploring Sequences Step by Step—Activity 5

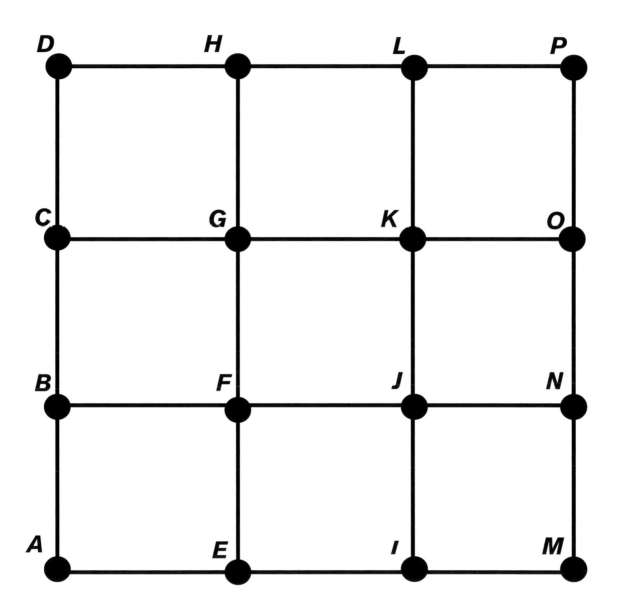

Pumpkin Paths

Name _____

Exploring Sequences Step by Step—Activity 5

How many ways can you spell *PUMPKIN* in the diagram if each letter has to be in the row just below the previous letter to the left or to the right?

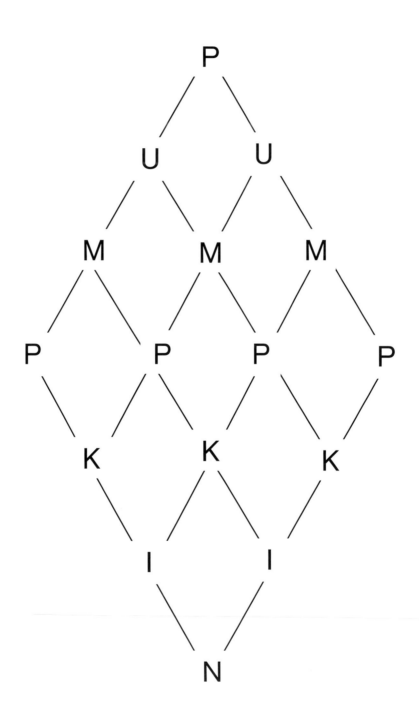

Navigating through Discrete Mathematics in Pre-K–Grade 5

Pascal's Triangle

Name _____

Exploring Sequences Step by Step—Activity 5

In each empty hexagon, write a number that is the sum of the numbers in the hexagons above it to the left and to the right.

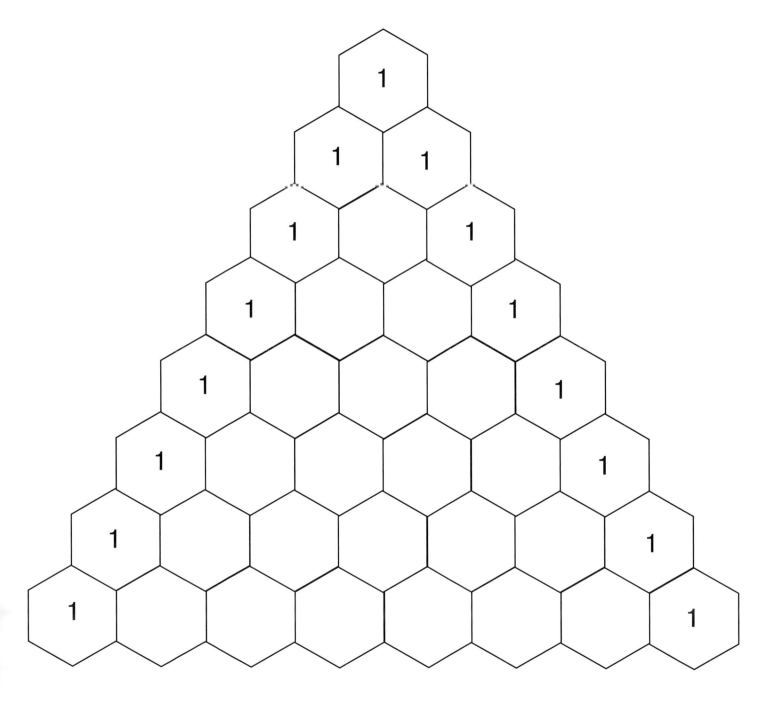

Solutions for the Blackline Masters

Solutions for "Bucket of Round Blue Buttons"

Bucket of Buttons—Preliminary Activity 2

1. The students will have three groups of buttons.
2. Each group has three buttons, and the total number of buttons is nine.
3. Three buttons are small, three are medium-sized, and three are large. The total number of buttons is nine.
4. One small button has four holes.
5. All nine buttons are blue.
6. The students will have six medium-sized buttons—two with four holes (one blue, one red), two with three holes (one blue, one red), and two with two holes (one blue, one red).

Solutions for "More Buttons in the Bucket"

Bucket of Buttons—Preliminary Activity 3

1. Students have six red buttons, six blue buttons, six yellow buttons, and six green buttons. They have twenty-four buttons altogether. Twelve buttons are red or yellow, twelve buttons are blue or yellow, and eighteen buttons are not red.
2. Twelve buttons are square, and twelve buttons are round. The students have twenty-four buttons altogether. Twelve buttons are not square.
3. Eight buttons have two holes, eight buttons have three holes, and eight have four holes. The students have twenty-four buttons altogether. Sixteen buttons have two or three holes, and sixteen buttons do not have three holes.

Solutions for "Handful of Buttons"

Bucket of Buttons—Activity 4

Students' answers to questions 1–8 will vary depending on each child's handful of buttons.

Solutions for "Crazy Shirts"

Bucket of Buttons—Activity 5

The arrangements of buttons below show the eight possibilities:

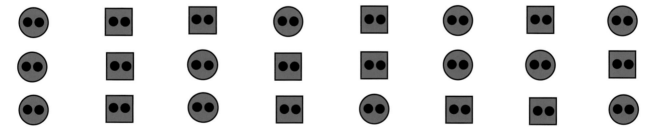

Solutions for "Outfits at Bindu Bear's Boutique"

Bindu Bear's Boutique—Activity 1

The students should color outfits on six bear mannequins:

- One should have a purple shirt with dotted pants.
- One should have a purple shirt with striped pants.
- One should have a yellow shirt with dotted pants.
- One should have a yellow shirt with striped pants.
- One should have a green shirt with dotted pants.
- One should have a green shirt with striped pants.

Solutions for "Outfits for First Week"

Bindu Bear's Boutique–Activity 1

The completed chart is shown:

	Dotted Pants	Striped Pants
Green Shirt		
Purple Shirt		
Yellow Shirt		

Solutions for "Paths from School to _____"

From Here to There–Activity 3

The solutions below are samples for the graph with the vertices labeled and the traffic lights placed as in figure 3.8 (S = school, P = playground, R = roller-skating rink, T = tire park, W = water park).

Paths from School to Playground

Path	Number of Traffic Lights
S to P	7
S to W to P	6
S to W to T to P	9
S to W to R to T to P	13
S to R to W to P	14
S to R to T to P	15
S to R to W to T to P	17
S to R to T to W to P	14

Eight paths from the school to the playground do not repeat any vertices. The best path is from the school to the water park to the playground. That path has six traffic lights.

Paths from School to Water Park

Path	Number of Traffic Lights
S to W	4
S to R to W	12
S to P to W	9
S to R to T to W	12
S to P to T to W	12
S to P to T to R to W	16
S to R to T to P to W	17

Seven paths from the school to the water park do not repeat any vertices. The best path is from the school directly to the water park. It includes four traffic lights.

Navigating through Discrete Mathematics in Pre-K–Grade 5

Paths from School to <u>Roller-Skating Rink</u>

Path	Number of Traffic Lights
S to R	9
S to W to R	7
S to W to T to R	7
S to P to W to R	12
S to P to T to R	13
S to W to P to T to R	12
S to P to T to W to R	15
S to P to W to T to R	12

Eight paths from the school to the roller-skating rink do not repeat any vertices. There are two best paths—one goes from the school to the water park to the roller-skating rink, and the other goes from the school to the water park to the tire park to the roller-skating rink. Each has seven traffic lights.

Paths from School to <u>Tire Park</u>

Path	Number of Traffic Lights
S to W to T	5
S to W to R to T	9
S to W to P to T	10
S to R to T	11
S to P to T	11
S to P to W to T	10
S to P to W to R to T	14
S to P to W to R to T	14
S to R to W to T	13
S to R to W to P to T	18

Nine paths from the school to the tire park do not repeat any vertices. The best path is from the school to the water park to the tire park. It has five traffic lights.

Solutions for "Circuits That Visit All the Play Sites"

From Here to There—Activity 4

The solutions below are samples for the graph with the vertices labeled and the traffic lights placed as in figure 3.8 (S = school, P = playground, R = roller-skating rink, T = tire park, W = water park).

Circuit	Number of Traffic Lights
S to P to W to T to R to S	21
S to P to T to W to R to S	24
S to P to T to R to W to S	20
S to W to P to T to R to S	21
S to W to R to T to P to S	20
S to R to W to T to P to S	24
S to R to T to P to W to S	21
S to R to T to W to P to S	21

Eight circuits start and end at the school, visit all the play sites, and do not repeat any vertices. Two circuits have the fewest traffic lights (20); one goes from S to P to T to R to W to S, and the other visits the play sites in the reverse order—S to W to R to T to P to S. Because these two circuits are essentially the same, neither is better than the other.

Solutions for "Coloring Maps–
South America"

Graphs for the Discrete Explorer–Activity 1

The students will discover that they need four colors for the map of South America. The text (see p. 82) discusses why four colors are necessary. One coloring appears at the right..

Solutions for "Coloring Maps–
States West of the Mississippi River"

Graphs for the Discrete Explorer–Activity 1

The students will discover that they need four colors for the map of the western states (see the discussion on p. 83). One coloring of the map appears at the left.

Solutions for "Coloring Maps–
Africa"

Graphs for the Discrete Explorer–Activity 1

The students will discover that they need four colors for the map of the Africa (see the discussion on p. 84). One coloring of the map appears at the right.

Navigating through Discrete Mathematics in Pre-K–Grade 5

Solutions for "Vertex Coloring–Cycles"

Graphs for the Discrete Explorer–Activity 2

The completed chart appears below.

Graph	How Many Vertices?	How many Edges?	Minimum Number of Colors Needed
(triangle)	3	3	3
(square)	4	4	2
(pentagon)	5	5	3
(hexagon)	6	6	2
(heptagon)	7	7	3

1. Two colors are necessary to color a cycle with 10 vertices.

2. Three colors are necessary to color a cycle with 35 vertices.

3. Students' statements will vary but should express the idea that if a cycle has an even number of vertices, it can be colored with two colors; if a cycle has an odd number of vertices, it can be colored with three colors but not with just two colors.

Solutions for "Vertex Coloring–Wheels"

Graphs for the Discrete Explorer–Activity 2

The completed chart appears below.

Examples of Cycles	Examples of Wheels	Minimum Number of Colors—Cycles	Minimum Number of Colors—Wheels
(triangle)	(wheel on triangle)	3	4
(square)	(wheel on square)	2	3
(pentagon)	(wheel on pentagon)	3	4
(hexagon)	(wheel on hexagon)	2	3

1. In every pair of graphs, both graphs have cycles. Removing the hub and spokes from the second graph, which is a wheel, leaves a cycle that is the same as the corresponding cycle in the first graph. In each pair, the wheel contains one more vertex (the hub) than the cycle, as well as spokes, whose number is equal to the number of vertices in the corresponding cycle.

2. *a.* If 50 vertices surround the hub, three colors are necessary to color the wheel.

   b. If 35 vertices surround the hub, four colors are necessary to color the wheel.

3. Students' statements will vary but should express the idea that three colors are necessary to color a wheel if an even number of vertices surround the hub, but four colors are necessary if an odd number of vertices surround the hub—three colors are insufficient in this case.

Solutions for "Vertex Coloring– Guess and Check"

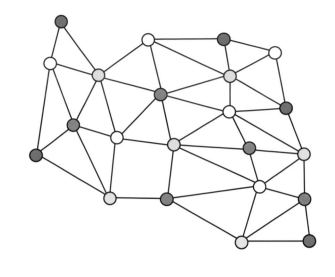

Graphs for the Discrete Explorer–Activity 2

1. Students' conjectures will vary.
2. A coloring appears at the right.
3. The minimum number of colors is four.

Solutions for "Additional Practice with Vertex Coloring"

Graphs for the Discrete Explorer–Activity 2

1. The minimum number of colors is three.
2. The minimum number of colors is two.
3. The minimum number of colors is four.
4. The minimum number of colors is three.
5. The minimum number of colors is four.
6. The minimum number of colors is five.

Solutions for "Charlie the Contractor's Problem–Part 1"

Graphs for the Discrete Explorer–Activity 2

The students' answers to the questions on this activity sheet will vary. The goal of this activity is for students to begin to discuss how to solve such questions.

Solutions for "Charlie the Contractor's Problem–Part 2"

Graphs for the Discrete Explorer–Activity 2

Step 1: Each vertex represents one of Charlie's workers; each edge represents two workers who are "in conflict," or, in this situation, have the same skill; and the colors represent the different crews to which Charlie may assign the workers.

Step 2: A vertex-edge graph appears at the right. The text describes how to construct the graph (see pp. 92–93).

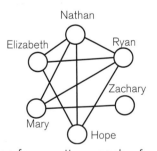

Step 3: A coloring of the vertex-edge graph appears at the right.

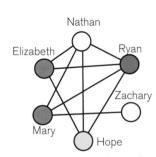

Step 4: Because the graph includes four vertices each of which is adjacent to the others, the minimum number of colors needed for a coloring is four. Therefore, Charlie must make at least four crews. The following table shows six possible assignments of Charlie's workers to four crews.

	Assignment A	Assignment B	Assignment C	Assignment D	Assignment E	Assignment F
Crew 1	Nathan Zachary	Nathan	Nathan	Nathan Zachary	Nathan	Nathan
Crew 2	Ryan	Ryan Zachary	Ryan	Ryan	Ryan Zachary	Ryan
Crew 3	Hope Mary	Hope Mary	Hope Mary	Hope	Hope	Hope Zachary
Crew 4	Elizabeth	Elizabeth	Elizabeth Zachary	Elizabeth Mary	Elizabeth Mary	Elizabeth Mary

Solutions for "Advertising for a Garage Sale–Part 1"

Graphs for the Discrete Explorer–Activity 4

The students' routes will vary. The bold edges at the right show one possible solution.

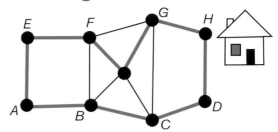

Solutions for "Advertising for a Garage Sale–Part 2"

Graphs for the Discrete Explorer–Activity 4

The students' routes will vary. The bold edges at the right show a solution.

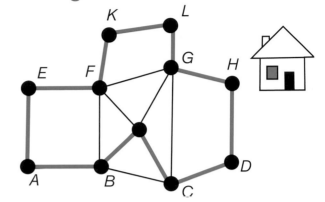

Solutions for "Advertising for a Garage Sale–Part 3"

Graphs for the Discrete Explorer–Activity 4

With the additional streets on the other side of the neighborhood, no route is possible that begins at *H*, visits each other vertex exactly once, and returns to *H*.

Solutions for "Efficient Newspaper Routes–Part 1"

Graphs for the Discrete Explorer–Activity 5

Taken in order, the numbers at the right show a route that begins at *H*, travels along every edge in the graph exactly once, and returns to *H*. Other solutions are possible.

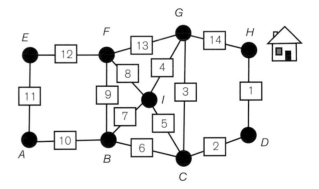

Solutions for "Efficient Newspaper Routes–Part 2"

Graphs for the Discrete Explorer–Activity 5

No route begins and ends at *H* and travels along every edge just once.

Solutions for "Visiting Vertices or Traveling Edges?–Part 1"

Graphs for the Discrete Explorer–Activity 5

1–4. The graph has a Hamilton circuit and an Euler circuit.

Solutions for "Visiting Vertices or Traveling Edges?–Part 2"

Graphs for the Discrete Explorer–Activity 5

1–4. The graph does not have a Hamilton circuit; the minimum number of vertices that a path must repeat to include every vertex and return to its starting point is one. The graph does not have an Euler circuit, either; the minimum number of edges that a path must repeat to include every edge and return to its starting point is two.

Solutions for "Repeating Patterns in Number Sequences"

Picture after Picture–Activity 1

1. *a.* The following pattern repeats to make the sequence:

   b. The next term in the sequence is $\boxed{1}$.

2. *a.* The following pattern repeats to make the sequence:

   $\boxed{1}$ $\boxed{4}$ $\boxed{1}$

   b. The next term in the sequence is $\boxed{1}$.

3. *a.* The following pattern repeats to make the sequence:

   $\boxed{3}$ $\boxed{1}$ $\boxed{1}$ $\boxed{1}$ $\boxed{3}$.

   b. The next term in the sequence is $\boxed{3}$.

Solutions for "Guess How I Continue–Part 1"

Picture after Picture–Activity 2

1. The sequence might continue with one lion followed by four donkeys:

2. The pattern is one lion followed by some number of donkeys, with the number of donkeys increasing by one in each consecutive group.

Solutions for "Guess How I Continue–Part 2"

Picture after Picture–Activity 2

1. The sequence might continue with four birds followed by one frog:

2. The pattern is some number of birds followed by one frog, with the number of birds increasing by one in each consecutive group.

Solutions for "Guess How I Continue–Part 3"

Picture after Picture–Activity 2

1. The sequence might continue with four frogs followed by two lions:

2. The pattern is some number of frogs followed by two lions, with the number of frogs increasing by one in each consecutive group.

Solutions for "Guess How I Continue–Part 4"

Picture after Picture–Activity 2

1. The sequence might continue with two lions followed by four frogs:

Navigating through Discrete Mathematics in Pre-K–Grade 5

2. The pattern is two lions followed by some number of frogs, with the number of frogs increasing by one in each consecutive group.

Solutions for "Guess How I Continue–Part 5"

Picture after Picture–Activity 2

1. The sequence might continue with one frog followed by seven birds:

2. The pattern is one frog followed by some number of birds, with the number of birds increasing by two in each consecutive group.

Solutions for "Guess How I Continue–Part 6"

Picture after Picture–Activity 2

1. The sequence might continue with four frogs followed by four donkeys:

2. The pattern is some number of frogs followed by some number of donkeys, with the numbers of each increasing by one in each consecutive group.

Solutions for "What Sequence Starts with …?–Part 1"

Picture after Picture–Activity 3

1–3. Students might determine the next term in at least three different ways.

a. They might correctly say that the next term is ⬚ if they describe the pattern as a growing pattern consisting of one frog followed by some number of lions, with the number of lions increasing by one in each consecutive group. The next ten terms in the sequence would be the following:

b. They might correctly say that the next term is ⬚ if they describe the pattern as repeating and identify the repeating group as frog-lion-frog-lion-lion. The next ten terms in the sequence would be the following:

c. They might correctly say that the next term is  if they describe the pattern as a growing pattern consisting of one frog followed by some number of lions, with the number of lions increasing by two in each consecutive group. The next ten terms in the sequence would be the following:

Solutions for "What Sequence Starts with …?–Part 2"

Picture after Picture–Activity 3

1–3. Students' answers will vary. The next term in the sequence might be in a number of sequences that have growing or repeating patterns. The discussion (p. 121–22) in the text lists some possible patterns. The list is reproduced below, with the first twenty terms of the sequence created by each pattern:

- It can have a repeating pattern in which frog-lion-frog-lion-bird repeats. The first twenty terms follow for the sequence with this five-card repeating pattern:

F, L, F, L, B, F, L, F, L, B, F, L, F, L, B, F, L, F, L, B

- It can have a growing pattern in which a bird is a marker between groups of increasing numbers of pairs of frogs and lions. Two sequences with growing patterns of this form are described on page 122. In the first such sequence, the first group of increasing numbers of pairs of frogs and lions consists of two pairs, the second group consists of three pairs, and so on. The first twenty terms in the sequence follow:

F, L, F, L, B, F, L, F, L, F, L, B, F, L, F, L, F, L, F, L

In the second such sequence, the first group has two pairs, the second group has four pairs, the third group has six pairs, and so on. The first twenty terms in the sequence follow:

F, L, F, L, B, F, L, F, L, F, L, F, L, B, F, L, F, L, F, L

- It can have a growing pattern in which frog-lion-frog-lion is a marker between increasing numbers of birds. The first twenty terms follow for such a sequence:

F, L, F, L, B, F, L, F, L, B, B, F, L, F, L, B, B, B, F, L

- It can have a growing pattern in which frog-lion is a marker between increasing numbers of birds, with zero birds occurring after the first marker. The first twenty terms follow for such a sequence:

F, L, F, L, B, F, L, B, B, F, L, B, B, B, F, L, B, B, B, B

Solutions for "What Sequence Starts with …?–Part 3"

Picture after Picture–Activity 3

Students' answers will vary for all parts of this activity sheet. The list below identifies six different sequences and the first twenty terms in each; other sequences are possible:

- Possible sequence 1: A sequence with a three-card repeating pattern, *L-F-B*. The first twenty terms of the sequence follow:

L, F, B, L, F, B, L, F, B, L, F, B, L, F, B, L, F, B, L, F

- Possible sequence 2: A sequence with a four-card repeating pattern, *L-F-B-L*. The first twenty terms of the sequence follow:

  L, F, B, L, L, F, B, L, L, F, B, L, L, F, B, L, L, F, B, L

- Possible sequence 3: A sequence with a growing pattern in which frog-bird is a marker following an increasing number of lions. The first twenty terms of the sequence follow:

  L, F, B, L, L, F, B, L, L, L, F, B, L, L, L, L, F, B, L, L

- Possible sequence 4: A sequence with a growing pattern in which frog-bird is a marker following an increasing odd number of lions. The first twenty terms of the sequence follow:

  L, F, B, L, L, L, F, B, L, L, L, L, L, F, B, L, L, L, L, L

- Possible sequence 5: A sequence with a growing pattern in which lion appears as a front marker and bird appears as a back marker with an increasing number of frogs between the markers. The first twenty terms of the sequence follow:

  L, F, B, L, F, F, B, L, F, F, F, B, L, F, F, F, F, B, L, F

- Possible sequence 6: A sequence whose pattern is a mixture of repeating and growing—in the first group, one each of lion, frog, and bird; in the second group, two each of lion, frog, and bird; in the third group, three each of lion, frog, and bird; and so on. The first twenty terms of the sequence follow:

  L, F, B, L, L, F, F, B, B, L, L, L, F, F, F, B, B, B, L, L

Solutions for "What Is the Missing Term?—Part 1"

Picture after Picture—Activity 3

1. The missing term could be a lion because the sequence could have a growing pattern that consists of one frog followed by some number of lions, with the number of lions in each consecutive group increasing by one.

2. The missing term could be a frog because the sequence could have a five-card repeating pattern: frog-lion-frog-lion-lion.

Solutions for "What Is the Missing Term?—Part 2"

Picture after Picture—Activity 3

Students' answers will vary. Some possibilities follow; many others exist.

1. The missing term could be  if the sequence has a three-card repeating pattern. Or the missing

term could be  , , or if the sequence has a six-card repeating pattern.

2. The missing term could be if the sequence has a repeating pattern of three lions followed by three frogs.

Or the missing term could be if the sequence has a growing pattern in which (*a*) two lions follow a growing number of frogs, with two more frogs in each consecutive group, or (*b*) both the number of frogs in each

group and the number of lions in each group increase by two. Or the missing term could be if the
sequence has a six-card repeating pattern.

3. The missing term could be if the sequence has a five-card repeating pattern. The missing term could also

be if the sequence has a growing pattern in which one donkey precedes a growing number of lions and
birds, with two more lions and birds in each consecutive group (the sequence might continue with one donkey, followed by four lions, followed by four birds, and so on).

4. The missing term could be any animal if the sequence has a six-card repeating pattern, or the missing term could be

if the sequence has a growing pattern in which the numbers of birds and donkeys in equal-sized groups
increase by one in each consecutive pair of equal-sized groups; the sequence that begins with three birds and three
donkeys could thus continue with four birds followed by four donkeys, and then five birds followed by five donkeys,
and so on.

Solutions for "Creating Number Sequences"

Exploring Sequences Step by Step—Activity 1

1. *a.* The rule NOW + 3 = NEXT and a starting value of 1 give the sequence 1, 4, 7, 10, 13, 16, 19, 22, 25, 28, 31, 34, 37, 40, 43, ….

   b. The rule NOW + 3 = NEXT and an initial value of 0 give the sequence 0, 3, 6, 9, 12, 15, 18, 21, 24, 27, 30, 33, 36, 39, 42, ….

   c. The eighteenth term in the sequence in part (*b*) is 51.

2. *a.* Yes; the sequence that starts with 2 includes the number 26.

   b. Neither of the other sequences includes the term 26.

   c. Yes; the sequence that starts with 0 includes the number 33.

   d. Neither of the other sequences includes the term 33.

   e. The term 57 is in the sequence that starts with 0. The students should note that that sequence contains all numbers that are multiples of 3, and 57 equals 3×19, so it is in that sequence.

   f. The term 100 is in the sequence that starts with 1. The students should note that that sequence contains all numbers that are 1 more than a multiple of 3, and 100 is 1 more than 99, or 3×33, so 100 is in that sequence.

   g. Yes; every whole number appears in just one of the three sequences. To see why this is so, students can arrange the three sequences so that the terms appear in columns, as discussed in the text (see p. 134):

   2, 5, 8, 11, 14, 17, 20, 23, 26, 29, 32, 35, 38, 41, 44, …

   1, 4, 7, 10, 13, 16, 19, 22, 25, 28, 31, 34, 37, 40, 43, …

   0, 3, 6, 9, 12, 15, 18, 21, 24, 27, 30, 33, 36, 39, 42, …

Alternatively, students can say that every whole number appears in exactly one of the three sequences because each number that is a multiple of 3, like 57, is in the sequence that starts with 0, each number that is one more than a multiple of 3, like 100, is in the sequence that starts with 1, and each number that is two more than a multiple of 3, like 74, is in the sequence that starts with 2. All the whole numbers are thus accounted for and appear in exactly one of the sequences. Fifth graders who have learned division may also say that dividing a number by 3 gives a remainder of 0, 1, or 2, and the number will be in the sequence that begins with its remainder.

Solutions for "Other Number Sequences"

Exploring Sequences Step by Step—Activity 1

1. If your rule is NOW + 1 = NEXT and you start with 1, the sequence that you obtain is 1, 2, 3, 4, 5, 6, … (all counting numbers).

2. If your rule is NOW + 2 = NEXT and your initial value is 0, the sequence is 0, 2, 4, 6, 8, 10, … (all even numbers).

3. If your rule is NOW + 2 = NEXT and your first term is 1, the sequence is 1, 3, 5, 7, 9, 11, … (all odd numbers).

4. *a.* The rule is PREVIOUS + 1 = NOW, and the start value is 1.

   b. The rule is PREVIOUS + 2 = NOW, and the initial term is 0.

   c. The rule is PREVIOUS + 2 = NOW, and the first term is 1.

Solutions for "Grids—Part 1"

Exploring Sequences Step by Step—Activity 2

1. Students should have one 8 × 8 square grid.

2. Students should have two pieces of the grid, each of size 4 × 8 (or 8 × 4).

3. Students should have four pieces of the grid, each of size 4 × 4.

4. Students should have eight pieces of the grid, each of size 2 × 4 (or 4 × 2).

5. Students should have sixteen pieces of the grid, each of size 2 × 2.

6. Students should have thirty-two pieces of the grid, each of size 1 × 2 (or 2 × 1).

   The sequence that the students should have created is 1, 2, 4, 8, 16, 32, ….

Solutions for "Grids—Part 2"

Exploring Sequences Step by Step—Activity 2

1. Students' answers will vary. Four possible general rules are NOW × 2 = NEXT, NOW + NOW = NEXT, PREVIOUS + PREVIOUS = NOW, and PREVIOUS × 2 = NOW.

2. The next three terms of the sequence are 64, 128, 256.

3. The next six terms are 512, 1024, 2048, 4096, 8192, and 16384.

4. *a.* Students' answers will vary.

   b. Students' answers will vary.

   c. The fifteenth term is 29 in sequence (i), 1401 in sequence (ii), and 16,384 in sequence (iii).

   d. The sixteenth term is 3l in sequence (i) 1501 in sequence (ii), and 32,768 in sequence (iii).

   e. Sequence (iii) grows fastest.

   f. Sequence (i) grows slowest.

Solutions for "Sequences of Shapes and Numbers"

Exploring Sequences Step by Step—Activity 3

1. *a.* The next three terms in the sequence appear below:

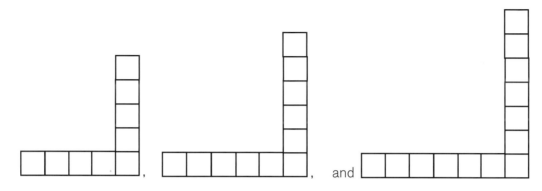

   b. The number of squares in each of the first eight terms of the sequence is 1, 2, 3, 4, 5, 6, 7, and 8, respectively.

   c. Twelve squares are in the twelfth term of the sequence.

2. *a.* The next three terms in the sequence appear below:

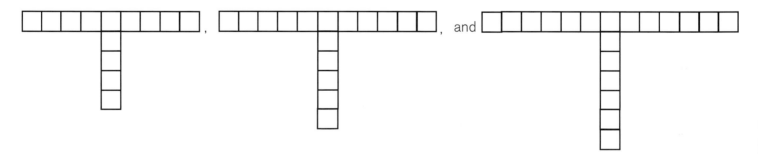

   b. The number of squares in each of the first seven terms of this sequence is 1, 3, 5, 7, 9, 11, and 13, respectively.

   c. Twenty-three squares are in the twelfth term of this sequence.

Solutions for "More Practice with Sequences"

Exploring Sequences Step by Step—Activity 3

1. *a.* The next three terms in the sequence appear below:

   b. The number of squares in each of the first seven terms of this sequence is 1, 4, 7, 10, 13, 16, and 19, respectively.

   c. The twelfth term of this sequence has thirty-four squares.

   d. The sequence of numbers is given by the rule NOW + 3 = NEXT, with initial term 1.

   e. The sequence of shapes is given by the rule NEXT = NOW + 3 squares placed at each end of the T, with initial term ▢.

2. Students' answers will vary.

Solutions for "A Sequence of Square Shapes"

Exploring Sequences Step by Step—Activity 3

1. The next three terms in the sequence appear below:

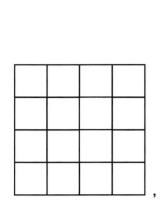 , 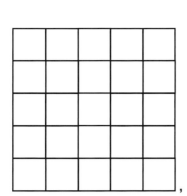 , and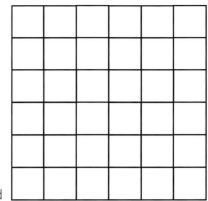

2. The number of small squares in each of the first six terms of the sequence is 1, 4, 9, 16, 25, and 36, respectively.

3. The number of small squares in the tenth term of the sequence is 100.

4. *a.* $1 \times 1, 2 \times 2, 3 \times 3, 4 \times 4, 5 \times 5, 6 \times 6, \ldots$

 b. $1^2, 2^2, 3^2, 4^2, 5^2, 6^2,$

Solutions for "Squares and Backward Ls—Part 1"

Exploring Number Sequences Step by Step—Activity 3

3. 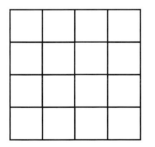 is 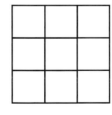 plus 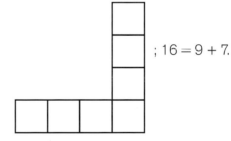 ; $16 = 9 + 7$.

4. 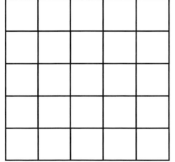 is 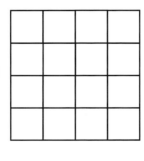 plus 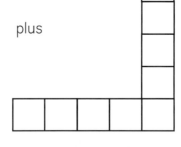 ; $25 = 16 + 9$.

5. The 6×6 square is the 5×5 square plus a backward L of height 6 (11 small squares); $36 = 25 + 11$.

6. The 7×7 square is the 6×6 square plus a backward L of height 7 (13 small squares); $49 = 36 + 13$.

7. The 8×8 square is the 7×7 square plus a backward L of height 8 (15 small squares); $64 = 49 + 15$.

8. The 9×9 square is the 8×8 square plus a backward L of height 9 (17 small squares); $81 = 64 + 17$.

9. The 10×10 square is the 9×9 square plus a backward L of height 10 (19 small squares); $100 = 81 + 19$.

Solutions for "Squares and Backward Ls – Part 2"

Exploring Number Sequences Step by Step–Activity 3

3. Students should represent the 4 × 4 square as a 1 × 1 square and three backward Ls, as shown, and write the equation 16 = 1 + 3 + 5 + 7.

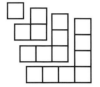

4. Students should represent the 5 × 5 square as a 1 × 1 square and four backward Ls, as shown, and write the equation 25 = 1 + 3 + 5 + 7 + 9.

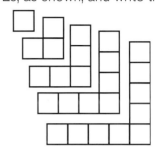

5. Students should represent the 6 × 6 square as a 1 × 1 square and five backward Ls, as shown, and write the equation 36 = 1 + 3 + 5 + 7 + 9 + 11.

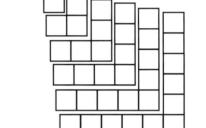

6. The 7 × 7 square is a 1 × 1 square plus six backward Ls;
   49 = 1 + 3 + 5 + 7 + 9 + 11 + 13.

7. The 8 × 8 square is a 1 × 1 square plus seven backward Ls;
   64 = 1 + 3 + 5 + 7 + 9 + 11 + 13 + 15.

8. The 9 × 9 square is a 1 ×1 square plus eight backward Ls;
   81 = 1 + 3 + 5 + 7 + 9 + 11 + 13 + 15 + 17.

9. The 10 × 10 square is a 1 × 1 square plus nine backward Ls;
   100 = 1 + 3 + 5 + 7 + 9 + 11 + 13 + 15 + 17 + 19.

Solutions for "How Many Paths from *A* to *I*?"

Exploring Number Sequences Step by Step–Activity 5

The number of paths from *A* to *I* is six:

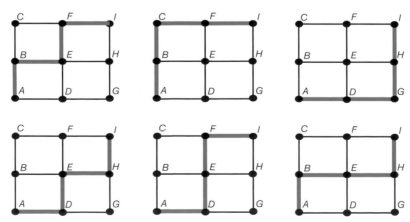

Navigating through Discrete Mathematics in Pre-K–Grade 5

Solutions for "Walking on a Grid Graph"

Exploring Number Sequences Step by Step—Activity 5

1. The following tree diagram shows all the paths from vertex *A* to vertex *P*.

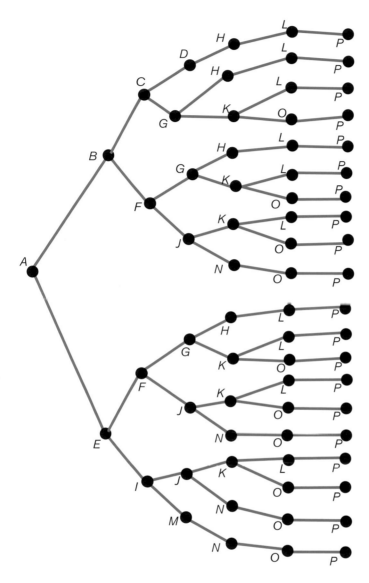

2. An alphabetical list of all paths follows:

- *A-B-C-D-H-L-P*
- *A-B-C-G-H-L-P*
- *A-B-C-G-K-L-P*
- *A-B-C-G-K-O-P*
- *A-B-F-G-H-L-P*
- *A-B-F-G-K-L-P*
- *A-B-F-G-K-O-P*
- *A-B-F-J-K-L-P*
- *A-B-F-J-K-O-P*
- *A-B-F-J-N-O-P*

- *A-E-F-G-H-L-P*
- *A-E-F-G-K-L-P*
- *A-E-F-G-K-O-P*
- *A-E-F-J-K-L-P*
- *A-E-F-J-K-O-P*
- *A-E-F-J-N-O-P*
- *A-E-I-J-K-L-P*
- *A-E-I-J-K-O-P*
- *A-E-I-J-N-O-P*
- *A-E-I-M-N-O-P*

3. The number of different paths from *A* to *P* is twenty.

Solutions for "Pumpkin Paths"

Exploring Number Sequences Step by Step—Activity 5

The number of paths is twenty.

Solutions for "Pascal's Triangle"

Exploring Number Sequences Step by Step—Activity 5

The completed diagram appears below.

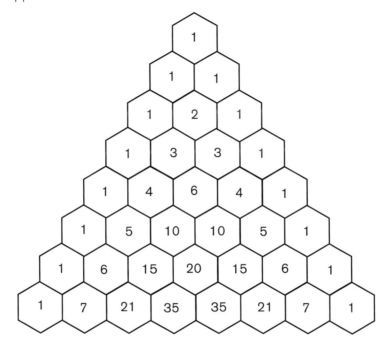

Navigating through Discrete Mathematics in Pre-K–Grade 5

References

Alper, Lynne, Daniel M. Fendel, Sherry Frasier, and Diane Resek. *Interactive Mathematics Program.* Emeryville, Calif.: Key Curriculum Press, 2003.

Consortium for Mathematics and Its Applications (COMAP). *Mathematics: Modeling Our World.* New York: W. H. Freeman & Co., 1999.

———. *For All Practical Purposes.* 7th ed. New York: W. H. Freeman & Co., 2006.

Crisler, Nancy, and Gary Froelich. *Discrete Mathematics through Applications.* 3rd ed. New York: W. H. Freeman & Co., 2006.

DeBellis, Valerie A. "Discrete Mathematics in K–2 Classrooms." In *Discrete Mathematics in the Schools,* edited by Joseph G. Rosenstein, Deborah S. Franzblau, and Fred S. Roberts, pp. 187–201, Vol. 36, DIMACS Series in Discrete Mathematics and Theoretical Computer Science. Providence, R.I.: The American Mathematical Society; Reston, Va.: National Council of Teachers of Mathematics, 1997.

DeBellis, Valerie A., and Joseph G. Rosenstein. *Making Math Engaging: Discrete Mathematics for K–8 Teachers.* Greenville, N.C.: Javelando Publications, 2005.

Greenes, Carole, Mary Cavanagh, Linda Dacey, Carol Findell, and Marian Small. *Navigating through Algebra in Prekindergarten through Grade 2. Principles and Standards for School Mathematics* Navigations Series. Reston, Va.: National Council of Teachers of Mathematics, 2001.

Hamberg, Charles L. "Graphs, Colors, and Chromatic Numbers." *NCTM Student Math Notes.* January 1998.

Hart, Eric W. "Discrete Mathematical Modeling in the Secondary Curriculum: Rationale and Examples from the Core-Plus Mathematics Project." In *Discrete Mathematics in the Schools,* edited by Joseph G. Rosenstein, Deborah S. Franzblau, and Fred S. Roberts, pp. 265–80. Vol. 36, DIMACS Series in Discrete Mathematics and Theoretical Computer Science. Providence, R.I.: The American Mathematical Society; Reston, Va.: National Council of Teachers of Mathematics, 1997.

———. "Algorithmic Problem Solving in Discrete Mathematics." In *Teaching and Learning Algorithms in School Mathematics,* 1998 Yearbook of the National Council of Teachers of Mathematics (NCTM), edited by Lorna J. Morrow and Margaret J. Kenney, pp. 251–67. Reston, Va.: NCTM, 1998.

Hart, Eric W., Margaret J. Kenney, Valerie A. DeBellis, and Joseph G. Rosenstein. *Navigating through Discrete Mathematics in Grades 6–12. Principles and Standards for School Mathematics* Navigations Series. Reston, Va.: National Council of Teachers of Mathematics, 2008.

Hirsch, Christian R., James T. Fey, Eric W. Hart, Harold L. Schoen, and Ann E. Watkins, with Beth Ritsema, Rebecca Walker, Sabrina Keller, Robin Marcus, Arthur F. Coxford, and Gail Burrill. *Core-Plus Mathematics.* 2nd ed. Columbus, Ohio: Glencoe McGraw-Hill, 2008.

Kenney, Margaret J., ed. *Discrete Mathematics across the Curriculum, K–12.* 1991 Yearbook of the National Council of Teachers of Mathematics (NCTM). Reston, Va.: NCTM, 1991.

Kring, Bill. "Squares on the Geoboard." *NCTM Student Math Notes.* November 1999.

Kritzer, Karen L., and Claudia M. Pagliaro. "Math according to Mooch." *Teaching Children Mathematics* 9 (May 2003): 503–12.

Mathematical Association of America (MAA). *Report of the Committee on Discrete Mathematics in the First Two Years.* Washington, D.C.: MAA, 1986.

Maurer, Stephen B. "What Is Discrete Mathematics? The Many Answers." In *Discrete Mathematics in the Schools*, edited by Joseph G. Rosenstein, Deborah S. Franzblau, and Fred S. Roberts, pp. 121–32. Vol. 36, DIMACS Series in Discrete Mathematics and Theoretical Computer Science. Providence, R.I.: The American Mathematical Society; Reston, Va.: National Council of Teachers of Mathematics, 1997.

McGivney-Burelle, Jean M. "Connecting the Dots: Network Problems That Foster Mathematical Reasoning." *Teaching Children Mathematics* 11 (January 2005): 272–77.

National Council of Teachers of Mathematics (NCTM). *Curriculum and Evaluation Standards for School Mathematics*. Reston, Va.: NCTM, 1989.

———. *Discrete Mathematics and the Secondary Mathematics Curriculum*. Reston, Va.: NCTM, 1990.

———. *Principles and Standards for School Mathematics*. Reston, Va.: NCTM, 2000.

———. *Curriculum Focal Points for Prekindergarten through Grade 8 Mathematics: A Quest for Coherence*. Reston, Va.: NCTM, 2006.

Numeroff, Laura. *If You Give a Mouse a Cookie*. New York: Harper Collins Publishers, 1985.

———. *If You Give a Moose a Muffin*. New York: Harper Collins Publishers, 1991.

———. *If You Give a Pig a Pancake*. New York: Harper Collins Publishers, 1998.

———. *If You Take a Mouse to the Movies*. New York: Harper Collins Publishers, 2000.

———. *If You Take a Mouse to School*. New York: Harper Collins Publishers, 2002.

Pittman, Helena C. *A Grain of Rice*. New York: Random House Children's Books, 1995.

Rosenstein, Joseph G. "Discrete Mathematics in 21st Century Education: An Opportunity to Retreat from the Rush to Calculus." In *Foundations for the Future in Mathematics Education*, edited by Richard A. Lesh, Eric Hamilton, and James J. Kaput, pp. 214–24. Hillsdale, N.J.: Lawrence Erlbaum Associates, 2007.

Rosenstein, Joseph G., Deborah S. Franzblau, and Fred S. Roberts, eds. *Discrete Mathematics in the Schools*, Vol. 36, DIMACS Series in Discrete Mathematics and Theoretical Computer Science. Providence, R.I.: The American Mathematical Society; Reston, Va.: National Council of Teachers of Mathematics, 1997.

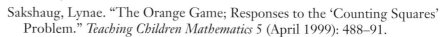

Sakshaug, Lynae. "The Orange Game; Responses to the 'Counting Squares' Problem." *Teaching Children Mathematics* 5 (April 1999): 488–91.

Souhrada, Terry. "Do It Again, Sam." *NCTM Student Math Notes*. May 2002.

Systemic Initiative for Montana Mathematics and Science (SIMMS). *SIMMS Integrated Mathematics: A Modeling Approach Using Technology*. Dubuque, Iowa: Kendall/Hunt Publishing Co., 2006.

Tannenbaum, Peter. *Excursions in Modern Mathematics*. 6th ed. Upper Saddle River, N.J.: Pearson Prentice Hall, 2007.

Ziemba, Elizabeth J., and Jo Hoffman. "Sorting and Patterning in Kindergarten: From Activities to Assessment." *Teaching Children Mathematics* 12 (January 2006): 236–41.